The App Millionaire:
How to Make
"Sleep Money" with a
Micro-Business

By Greg Shealey

No part of this publication may be reproduced, stored in a retrieval system, or transmitted in any form or by any means, electronic, mechanical, photocopying, recording, scanning, or otherwise, except as permitted under Section 107 or 108 of the 1976 United States Copyright Act, without the prior written permission of the author.

Although the author and publisher have made every effort to ensure that the information in this book was correct at press time, the author and publisher make no representations or warranties with respect to the accuracy or completeness of the contents of this book and do not assume and hereby disclaim any liability to any party for any loss, damage, or disruption caused by errors or omissions, whether such errors or omissions result from negligence, accident, or any other cause.

Copyright © 2013 by Greg Shealey. All rights reserved.

Published by Greg Shealey.

For more information, visit www.TheAppMillionaire.com.

To Zoe & Zai.
Daddy Loves You!

Table of Contents

A Word of Caution..viii

PART I
JUST SOME GUY

The Background 3

Chapter 1	Building a Business from a Business 11
Chapter 2	The App Millionaire 29
Chapter 3	Sleep Money 47
Chapter 4	What is a Micro-Business?..53
Chapter 5	Micro-Business "No-No's" 73
Chapter 6	Business Failure, Business Success 77
Chapter 7	Base Hits and Other Realistic Expectations 99

PART II
THE CAVALRY

Chapter 8	Master vs. Mastermind 107
Chapter 9	Getting Started In Business – How to Build a Micro-Business...115
Chapter 10	Outsourcing 151

Chapter 11   How to Build an App Business.................................. 165

Chapter 12   App Your Business 177

Chapter 13   Marketing 185

Chapter 14   Loans vs. Credit Cards..207

PART III
MOVE IT FORWARD

Chapter 15   Move It Forward... 219

Chapter 16   The Lazy Businessman... 231

Chapter 17   Passion and Fear 239

Chapter 18   Bet on You 263

Chapter 19   Paying It Forward... 277

Notes:.. A

A Word of Caution

This is a book about business, ideas and life.

Let me warn you: what I say in this book will not appeal to everyone. In fact, some of the concepts in this book may be rather off-putting to some or, at the very least, contrary to popular opinion. Others you will have encountered before - only said a bit differently. It is not my intent to be controversial or offensive to anyone; I am just sharing my experience. I know that there are many people out there who are eager to have a breakthrough in life – to get beyond the point of feeling stuck and unfulfilled. My intention, therefore, is to speak to those of you have an entrepreneurial spirit and are ready to make something happen. I am talking about those who are open-minded and who recognize that there are many ways to accomplish a goal. If you are hungry for a new way of being and doing, and if you're ready to explore different ideas and opportunities, let this work serve as a resource for you. If you want to go from where you are to being a successful business owner, let me share with you what I know.[1]

- Greg

---

[1] Note that in regards to gender identity (i.e., the terms "he" and "she" and similar gender-related terms), the male gender is used for the sole sake of convenience. None of what is said in this book is meant to be construed to apply to only one of the sexes.

PART I
JUST SOME GUY

"I am only the average man but, by George, I work harder at it than the average man."

- Theodore Roosevelt, 26th President of the United States

The Background

*L*et me tell you how it all started...
I was raised in Pittsburgh, Pennsylvania. I was the sixth of eight children, and we lived in a neighborhood called Homewood. Homewood is a very blue-collar, working class community. My father was a foreman at a local construction company around the time that I was born. Due to a job loss, he was forced to go into business for himself, as there were very few opportunities available for those with his experience and skill level.

My father believed that because he was an experienced and talented foreman, he knew everything there was to know about the construction business. He created his first construction company, Evans Construction, and forged ahead. While he ran his own business, he also engaged in remodeling and renovation side projects in our neighborhood. As I quickly learned, being an outstanding foreman and a successful businessman are two very separate things. They require different sets of skill, know-how and ways of thinking. Unfortunately for my father, he knew very little about the business side of the construction industry, which would create enormous difficulties for him professionally, and for our family, on a personal level.

It took little time for Evans Construction to run into considerable trouble. My father was very capable when it came to physical labor and managing the allocation of supplies for a particular project while working for an established company. However, when he was tasked with the entire set of activities which encompass the running of a successful construction business, from marketing and advertising, to negotiating contracts and purchase orders, he failed miserably. My father simply could not manage the day-to-day operations of his business, and had no concept of how to implement efficient business systems into his company. As a result, he made a series of poor business decisions when it came to the projects he accepted, and that led to crushing debt loads and a progressively eroding reputation. Due to his mounting business mishaps, my father had no choice but to rename the company. Daven Construction was born. This, however, made little difference, as people knew that he was the owner, and the reputation of the old company very quickly attached itself to the new one. The business trend also did not change, as the same mistakes were repeated.

The problems which plagued both of my father's construction companies came to bear on our home life. The purpose of owning and running a business is to generate income in such a manner that permits both the company to profit, and improves the owner and employees' standard of living. Neither was accomplished. Due to the many difficulties my father was having, we, his children, were frequently pressed into service, helping him out with all sorts of tasks so as to help him save labor costs. As a result, I got to witness his business mismanagement on quite the up-close and personal level, seeing how he was making mistakes at every possible turn. While I would scramble to help him correct the errors, it simply seemed like the moment one problem had been ironed out, another three instantaneously appeared. Of course, as setbacks plagued his companies and kept him (and us) occupied, he neglected his home life and duties.

Because of the construction company problems, money was always in short supply in our house. With such a large family – there were ten mouths to feed in total - this problem really hit hard. My father would try to compensate by offering to do contract home renovation work for friends and neighbors. Unfortunately, due to the issues he was facing with his company, he would often neglect such projects, causing them to remain incomplete for months or even years. Friendships ended as he made those close to him wait until he, eventually, got around to finalizing their project. This hurt our family's reputation and, as I mentioned, either strained or broke friendships and relationships which had once been strong.

It is due to these experiences with the family business that I vowed I would never go into business for myself. I, instead, knew, at that time, that I needed to go to college in order to eventually find a profession that would hopefully guarantee me stable employment. In order to get into college, I needed to focus on my grades a little more. My grades in high school weren't what you might consider exemplary, so I enrolled in a local community college in order to improve my academic record.

At the junior college, I majored in business. At the end of that program, I was granted admission to a four-year university in Atlanta, Georgia. While I was there, I gave my future some thought and changed my major to one which I believed would provide me with better employment possibilities: education. I did this because I saw that at the time, educators were in demand, rarely laid off, and enjoyed the entire summer off. I believed that I had it all planned out but my older and wiser sister, Lorraine, who knew me very well, told me that she was convinced I would be unfulfilled as an educator. Though I thought she was wrong, she, ultimately, turned out to be one hundred percent correct. When I became an educator, I felt I was very different from the rest of the teachers in terms of my style, philosophy and motivations. That later led to a career change.

As a teacher, I educated students using a unique approach - one steeped more in practical wisdom than in theoretical information found in a textbook. I called it Mr. Shealey's Alternative Learning Theory, which is based on the following premise: "Ask a lot of questions," "Listen," and "Don't forget." I taught all of my students those fundamental lessons. I wanted them to know that much knowledge in life can be gained by simply seeking it, retaining it, and applying it. In my classroom, everyone was encouraged to question everything – even what I told them.

While I truly enjoyed teaching and watching the success of my students as they moved forward in their educations and in life, in general, I found myself unfulfilled. I wanted to experience growth and achievement as well. Despite the fact that I had personally witnessed and experienced so many problems with my father's business, and despite vowing to never enter that realm, entrepreneurship called to me. Deep down inside of me, I knew that was the direction in which I wanted to head. I thought to myself, "Perhaps business success skips a generation," With that, my life and career took a dramatic turn.

I knew that I wanted to be in business, but I didn't know in what capacity. I hadn't seriously sat down to iron out a business plan or to even ponder what kind of business I would run. At first, I thought I would just find something to supplement my teacher's salary – something that I could do part-time, which would scratch the itch and teach me a few things. I wasn't looking to launch anything big or time-consuming. I wanted something that would be easy to manage, would require low start-up funds, could function with minimal management, and would give me little headache. I, certainly, didn't want to be involved in anything that would cause me to put my lifestyle at risk like my father had done to our family, but I knew I definitely had to do something.

While the family construction company had turned me off to business ownership, I had learned several extremely valuable life lessons from my father. First, never leave a job unfinished. Second, "the proof is in the pudding," which is a saying that means the best way to truly judge something is to experience it yourself – if something has been done once, it can be done again, only better. With these in mind, I developed the habits and practices which would lead to business success.

My earliest lessons in business management were vivid and memorable examples of the very worst business practices. I watched someone who was an expert in a particular line of work fail miserably at running a business, despite trying extremely hard to succeed. This begs the question: "Are entrepreneurs born or made?" My answer to that is "Both." I've learned through the operations of my business endeavors, that running a profitable business requires you to have a certain set of skills, none of which are really all that hard to cultivate. It was Bill Gates who said the key to running a successful business is to bring in more money than you spend. He could not have been more correct. The skill set needed to effectively run a business can be learned and mastered. Skills like budgeting, inventory tracking, competitive pricing, projecting sales and having a sense for which products will sell and which ones will not, can be learned as you grow your business. But along with those skills, you do need to have certain personal disciplines that will help you to establish a vision. After all, the primary function of your business is to generate income.

When I thought, retrospectively, to the time when I was helping my father with his business, I began to very clearly see the basics of the business model that I wanted to own and run. It was part-time and small, easy to manage, required low start-up funds, and wouldn't put my lifestyle at risk. That specific business wouldn't immediately reveal itself to me: it took some years and vocational evolution to arrive at that "A-ha" moment, but the seed had been planted.

My first business was called BioFit and Wellness. It was an online company that made supplemental workout programs for people with busy schedules. At BioFit and Wellness, we created CD's and DVD's that walked people through several short workouts that lasted approximately 10 minutes long.

These short workouts were intended to be supplemental workouts for the office when a person couldn't get to the gym but wanted to do something without getting too sweaty. We made gorgeous videos in a studio with great editing and sound.

In addition, I was the fitness expert for Discovery Health. I wrote numerous fitness and health related articles for discoveryhealth.com. These fitness articles were very popular with their online viewers, so I had lots of exposure. All the articles ended by saying that I was the president and founder of BioFit and, and they linked directly to my site.

In one month it was reported that one of my articles had over 300,000 hits! If I could convert just 1% of those hits, that would be 3,000 sales! I could live with that. Perfect set up, right? Of course. Wrong. The business was a flop. People didn't buy. I had to move on to something else.

* * *

Though BioFit and Wellness was a certified business disaster, I did not give up on my goals of being an entrepreneur. Because the City of Atlanta was in a state of rapid growth, there were plenty of other business opportunities. Atlanta was quickly morphing from a provincial southern city steeped in southern tradition and history into an international business hub with sensational diversity. The housing market was experiencing an unparalleled boom, and entering it as a side business was quite the safe choice for anyone with even the slightest amount of entrepreneurial know-how. I eagerly jumped in with two feet and began my career as a real estate investor.

There's something about being in Atlanta, or any bustling market for that matter, that can cause you to seriously change the way you think. In my case, the more success I experienced, the easier it was for me to devise and implement habits and practices that led to my further success. I learned to think big living in Atlanta, and that shift in my thinking is the single most important element that moved me from being an employee to being an employer.

In almost no time, earnings from my part-time hustle grew to the point where they were outpacing my teacher's salary. Less than two years later, I did what I thought I would perhaps never do: I was operating my own general contracting company. It's sometimes very ironic how life unfolds: I went from being an educator, to being an investor and finally to owning a general contracting company, something that had, for many years, seemed repulsive to me. Much like my early years working with my father in his construction business, it was very much a love-hate relationship.

As my construction business began to grow and evolve, I started to notice inefficiencies in the way the businesses within the construction industry operated, particularly among the smaller general contractors. This included my own business. There were plenty of productivity tools on the market to help business owners like me organize their operations, from calendar management software to estimating programs designed specifically for construction contractors. There was no shortage of desktop tools in this field. The problem was that I didn't work in an office. I, certainly, did not work from a desktop.

I, just some guy from Pittsburgh, had an idea.

Chapter 1

Building a Business from a Business

"No matter what, expect the unexpected. And whenever possible BE the unexpected."

- Lynda Barry, Cartoonist and Author

"To expect the unexpected, shows a thoroughly modern intellect."

- Oscar Wilde, Writer and Poet

Sometimes you begin a journey, not realizing what your destination will be. Life can be funny that way. You may set out thinking you know exactly where you're headed, only to find out that there was more in store than you originally planned. Something. Totally. Different.

What started off as a side project for me to earn some extra money soon became a thriving business. The more my construction business grew, the busier I became. I had never in my life been stretched so thin. Being a small business owner, I was, in some way, responsible for every aspect of the business. Every aspect! I had to focus on getting the contracts, managing the projects, managing the employees working on the projects, and ensuring that the "back end" bookkeeping and operational responsibilities were properly handled. On some days, I would spend so much time in the car, going to and from meetings and construction sites, that I would have a whole days' worth of half-eaten meals in my car. Other times, when I met someone who asked me what I did for a living, I would jokingly say, "rip and run." I felt like that's what I spent my days doing – ripping and running from site to site, back to the office, and back out into the field. I had so much to do and very little time in which to do all of it. I was exhausted.

Like many business owners, I sought opportunities to become more efficient in my work. I had to. I bought expensive desktop software to streamline my operations and be more organized. I was looking for any process to get more done in less time. I knew I needed a workable system because, at the rate my business was growing, I wouldn't be able to manage for much longer without a reliable system. Given the amount of money I spent on desktop software, I figured it had to be something that could help me.

The best thing about software systems is that they can make your life much easier. The worst thing about software systems is that you actually have to learn how to use them. Sometimes, the time it takes to learn the product renders the product cost ineffective. I learned that quickly, as I tried various systems to help me streamline my business. I tried a general project management program that wasn't specific to the construction field. I also tried construction-specific software that ended up operating more like a brainteaser than like a productivity tool. There were programs that were work-able, however, they weren't really work-*ing* for me and what I needed to do. It just took too much time! I always found myself reverting back to what made me the most comfortable - doing the work by hand. I'd jot down notes on random sheets of paper, with the intent of incorporating the information into my jazzy software system. But... it just didn't seem to work out that way. It just wasn't quite right for what I needed to do to become more efficient.

Given that so much of my business was done outside of the office, the time I spent manipulating data and reports in my software application was time taken away from the work that had to be done in the field. Of course, I could have hired more people to help me. But...remember, I was running a small business operation. Was it a good time to incur the expense of an additional salary? When I performed a cost benefit analysis on hiring an additional person at that time, my conclusion was that I needed to find a way for me to be more efficient in handling all of those matters for which I was directly responsible. Yet, let me be honest, I absolutely hated this part of the business. Totally hated it! I wanted to be out in the field. I wanted to shake hands and kiss babies, so to speak, while increasing the exposure of the company's brand. I had no desire to be in my office formatting bids and sorting through reports. For my business to continue to work, I could not be tucked away in my office. There had to be a better way.

* * *

Because the construction business is one that requires mostly field-based work, being in my office for much of the day was not efficient for me. I spent most of my work hours on someone's work site or moving around from site to site. There were often times that my workday felt disjointed. While out in the field, I gathered information like measurements and project plans, but I didn't actually process that data until I was in my office. I carried a laptop with me, but moving around construction sites with it proved to be cumbersome. Plus, using it to capture data while on-site was often challenging because I would usually have to find a location at which to set up the computer so that I could work and use my software system. If the sun was out that day, finding an appropriate location was even more difficult because I needed to be in a spot where I would be able to view the screen. Either way, I felt as though I had to physically separate myself from my work environment in order to process the data I gathered on-site and in order to stay organized in my business operations. What I really needed was a tool that would allow me to utilize and process the information I acquired on-site, without me having to be away from the site in order to do it. I needed a simple way to, for example, take down estimates for bids on projects, put them into a bid proposal format and quickly issue the bid to the prospective client without having to leave the site and submit the proposal to the prospective client later that day or the next day.

One day, I found myself sitting in my living room watching a CNBC program on cable TV that discussed the rise of mobile apps. By this time, smartphones and similar handheld devices were increasing in popularity. The program highlighted how the "Average Joe" developer was earning a substantial living by designing mobile applications for handheld devices. The show focused on how these developers designed mobile apps to help solve basic problems. They highlighted apps that could, for example, generate expense reports instantly from restaurant and car rental receipts. That's when I said to myself, "I need to develop an app for *my* business," since I was, obviously, having problems being organized. I needed to get more productive and efficient. I also needed to be able to do it on-site. Suddenly, I had what Oprah Winfrey calls an "A-ha moment." Why hadn't I thought of this before?! Every one of my team members already had a smartphone of some sort. We were using the Palm Treo (which is probably considered a dinosaur at this point) to send schedules to our field construction crews. We also used it to instantly share notes about problems we were having throughout the day. Sometimes it would be a note about the unavailability of a certain material or about an issue with access pertaining to a particular site. It could be anything. Whatever the case, using the Treo as a tool, we were able to get the relevant notice out to certain members of the team simultaneously.

Other members of my team had different, but similar devices. Since everyone on the team was already familiar with the smartphone, it only made sense that I find a way to use that device as an effective tool for my business. We needed a program that could be done by phone. With that, my field managers and I would likely close more sales on the basis of at least two factors: (1) my potential customers would be impressed with the highly technological nature of my business and (2) my team could produce more contracts... faster. Deal terms could be captured on the spot. I decided to design a productivity app to address my business needs.

There was only one real problem: I didn't have the first clue as to how to develop an app. Not only was I not the "Average Joe" developer highlighted in the CNBC program that had inspired me; I wasn't a developer at all! All I knew was that having an app for my business made a whole lot of sense.

* * *

The emergence of apps presented tremendous opportunities – both on the user and developer sides. From the user perspective, no longer was there a need for full-blown desktop software in order to accomplish certain tasks. Even further, no longer did a user even need a computer – laptop or otherwise. With the availability of mobile apps, many basic functions could be performed by this small, handheld device. So a person without a computer could still do a variety of things. By purchasing specific apps, at a relatively low price (i.e., most from 99 cents to $5.99), someone could identify and pay for just those functions for which they had the greatest need – without having to spend hundreds or thousands on an actual computer.

From the developer perspective, apps made being in the technology business a more level playing field. Even guys like me, who had no experience developing apps, could create apps, at reasonable prices. Mobile apps, by virtue of being so simplified, made it possible for someone who was not technical, but who could think logically, able to create a product for use on these technical platforms. Computer software programs, on the other hand, tended to require more money, more time, more personnel and more overall involvement.

According to the CNBC program that introduced me to the app development world, these mobile applications were revolutionizing the means by which people communicate, play and process data. I wanted to be a part of it. While I was extremely motivated to become an app developer, that didn't change the fact that I knew very little about apps and the app development business. I had plenty to learn. Up to that point, I had just been an average user of apps. I didn't put too much thought into how they worked or where they came from, so long as they functioned properly on my phone. I had no need to garner much more information than that. I used the calculator, the calendar, and played some games, here and there. If I was going to get into this business, however, I was going to treat it like any other endeavor. I would do my research and learn what I needed to know to make it work. I'm not the type who researches and analyzes to the point of paralysis, but I wanted to get a solid understanding of the industry and how it evolved.

Some Background

If you're reading this book, you're probably, at least, vaguely familiar a mobile application. A mobile app is designed to be a small-scale version of a full-scale software application. By definition (i.e., the word "mobile") the mobile app operates on a handheld device. Even though it is a form of software, it is made to function differently than the more robust version of the software would function on a computer. Decades ago, in the 1980s, the common platform for mobile apps was the handheld computer. Back then, single-function handheld personal digital assistants (PDAs) looked more like lettered calculators and were equipped with alarms, calendars, organizers and a few other bells (no whistles). Over time, the concept of pocket computers evolved and matured. Handheld PDAs picked up features like "notebook" and the touch screen, which worked with a small, plastic pen called a stylus.

With the increased popularity of smartphones came an increased demand for tools that would make these devices even more useful. As is the case with most new technologies, apps began as simple-functioning productivity tools, like calendars and "to-do" lists. Over time, however, they evolved into highly interactive programs that allowed one to do everything from watch television to create 3D panoramic images of their neighborhood. These apps – these tools that could be used on the go for increased productivity or for sheer entertainment – were changing how people operated their business and personal lives. They gave people flexibility and freedom that they didn't previously have. No longer were people slaves to their paper notebooks, desktops, or laptops. They had information at their fingertips and they could take that information with them wherever they went. Naturally, this easy access to information affected the dynamics of business and personal transactions.

This was one of the messages conveyed in the CNBC story – things were changing, and they were changing quickly. Just as the computer software industry had its boom, so would the mobile app industry. Those who could capitalize on this impending market opportunity had the chance to make themselves rich.

The Game Changer

The debut of Apple's iPhone in 2007 laid the foundation of a mobile app industry explosion. The iPhone was designed to revolutionize the mobile phone like the iPod had revolutionized the music industry in the six years prior. In introducing the iPhone, Steve Jobs, then CEO of Apple, Inc., said the new iPhone was created to be "way smarter" than any other smartphone before it and "super easy to use." Where previous smartphones had included features that could make usage rather confusing, the iPhone was designed with an intuitive user interface. All iPhones came with Apple's iOS operating system, which allowed the iPhone to easily communicate with all Mac computers.

When it was introduced, most were in awe of the iPhone. I, certainly, was. The screen had a sleek and completely smooth surface, with only one home button at the bottom of the screen. It was thinner than any other smartphone on the market at the time. There was no physical keyboard like the other smartphones and it didn't have a permanent keypad. Features could be accessed through the phone's innovative multi-touch technology which allowed users to navigate menus using one or more fingers, not a stylus. Because there was no keyboard at the bottom as compared to the Palm Treo phones that my team and I used, the iPhone's screen was much larger than most phones at the time – 3.5 inches – and perfect for touch screen technology.

The iPhone was amazing! Just plain amazing! Even for a person who was not interested in technology or who had no interest in a smartphone, this particular smartphone was intriguing. Even based on its look, alone, people wanted to see it, feel it and play with it. It was a topic of conversation. It was all over the news – not just technology news. This cool new gadget, which cost upwards of $600, was something so unique that even those who had no interest in obtaining one, still wanted to be exposed to it. They wanted to see how it would allow a user to swipe photos across the screen and shrink and enlarge images. They wanted to see how a phone could actually go into landscape orientation automatically, simply by turning the phone to the side. It was cool! I say all this to make one main point: the iPhone was not just a new product; it was the start of a revolution.

It's entry into the market absolutely transformed the cell phone industry and led to the explosive growth of the app development market space. When Apple launched the App Store for iPhone in 2008, both app developers and iPhone users had one platform through which they could connect. The App Store was true to its name; it was a store that sold (or gave away) mobile applications – and lots of them. Apps could be showcased to iPhone users in a single location. An iPhone user could easily purchase an app, through a series of clicks. The app would then be downloaded to their phone for immediate use. Prior to the store's launch, developers really had no reliable means of effectively reaching iPhone users, except by creating marketing campaigns and depending on app reviews and word of mouth to encourage purchases from their own websites. Apple's App Store itself is an app that was installed on all iPhones. The App Store is the number one marketplace for buying and selling new applications. As of this writing, there are over 700,000 mobile applications available for download from the App Store including free apps, paid apps and subscription services.

As I mentioned before, I was familiar with the smartphone and used them in my business, however, the Palm Treo was no iPhone. Nothing was even close to the iPhone. With the introduction of this phone, what Apple did was raise the bar for not only smartphones, but for the tools that are used on these phones. Suddenly, the existing smartphones on the market seemed shabby in comparison. The iPhone quickly became the gold standard of smartphones. As such, developing for this phone became a focus for shrewd developers.

I wanted to be one of those shrewd developers. Even though I was just starting out, it made no sense for me to aim low. It was clear that Apple had set the standard, so I wanted to be a part of what they were doing. Why not? That was the storyline of the CNBC program. Someone was creating these tools and methods for increasing the efficiency of these smartphones and folks were making good money doing it. Because these apps were so much smaller than their full-size computer-based counterparts, they were easier to design, develop and bring to market. In fact, because of the truncated nature of mobile apps, a developer would be at a disadvantage if they were unable to simplify the product enough for use on a smartphone. This offered opportunities for the "Average Joe" who could develop a simple, but functional and useful program. I didn't see why I couldn't be one of those guys who could do that.

Listen, I don't play around when it comes to my money. I had to seriously evaluate whether it made sense for me to dedicate time, money and effort to this idea of mine, given that I knew nothing about how to go about developing the product. I spent a significant amount of time determining how much the idea I was contemplating could potentially save me in terms of work hours and, in turn, dollars. I concluded that, with an effective application, our daily operations stood to increase in efficiency by at least 40%. I considered the time I and members of my team spent driving between client sites and our office, as well as the time spent dealing with computer-based technical and software issues. I then balanced that against what I stood to gain in terms of time, money and effort to get the app complete and in workable form. I thought about what would be involved in learning how to get it done from start to finish, especially given the fact that I was starting from zero, so to speak. When I weighed each of these factors, it seemed clear to me that finding a way to create this tool would be well worth the money, time and effort I would spend. Furthermore, if I found the tool to be helpful, it was possible that others would find it to be helpful, too. If it was a tool that could pay for itself through sales, it made sense to give the idea a shot.

The application would essentially act as an abbreviated version of the desktop programs I had been using. It would include the aspects of the programs we used the most - only those functions that were needed out in the field. I wanted to create an app designed specifically for the construction industry that was easy to use, efficient, and suitable for field use so that no one on my team would have to duplicate work or lose time and clients driving back and forth across town to type up documents. I wanted the ability to use a smartphone to access an application that would create invoices, estimates and materials lists to be completed on-site and sent by email.

The first thing I did in order to design the app was to sit down and contemplate what the app would look like. I determined what images would be on different screens. Next, I tried to figure out how it would function on a phone and what it would need to include to save time and increase productivity. I made lists of features and came up with a handful of ideas. I even sketched pictures of what I thought the program would look like on my phone – invoices, estimates, job pricing tools, materials lists. The sketch included prompts and menus with scribbles of the functions that would be accessed through each menu. Based on my experience implementing desktop software, I knew I had to make the program simple enough so that it could be learned and applied very quickly – with virtually no real learning curve. After all, a mobile app was not supposed to be as involved as a desktop app. It was supposed to be very user-friendly and so logical that it will not require a detailed explanation.

Once I had a solid idea of what I wanted the app to do and how I wanted it to function, I had to map out the entire functionality of the app and how it would generate data. I created a flow chart of sorts that demonstrated a path from data input to data output. By the time I was finished with my initial drawings, charts, and graphs, I knew exactly how the app was supposed to function. If you pressed X button on Y screen, Z would happen. If you pressed A button on B screen, C would happen. I knew it inside and out. Since it was a simple program, it didn't take me too long to figure that out.

I then set out to find an app designer who could do the work I needed done. I went into the app business with no previous experience in anything tech-related, but I did understand how to successfully manage a project and successfully run a business. The principles are universal; it's only the execution that changes. It was apparent that I needed to build a team to help me. They were the ones with all of the technical knowledge. Knowing that Apple was the pre-eminent platform was not enough. Getting my app developed and on this platform was the challenge. Apple has high standards. When I researched the requirements an app had to meet in order to be placed in the App Store, I was overwhelmed. There was no way that I would be able to assimilate all of the rules and requirements that Apple insisted upon. It was just too much. Plus, I didn't even understand what most of it meant; I didn't speak "techanese." The one great thing about this realization was that it gave me clarity. I was clear that, even if I had wanted to learn how to make the apps myself (which I didn't), it was simply not an option. I would have to hire the help – someone with the knowledge and technical skill – or else I wouldn't be able to do it. Knowing, for sure, that was the route I would have to take, I was relieved that my concern would simply be who I would get to help me.

Embracing the idea of outsourcing, I found a fantastic pool of global talent, at reasonable prices, by using online human resource platforms. I had to sift through a slew of web designers who claimed that they could help me create exactly the app I needed to my exact specifications. Anyone who didn't have experience developing an app for Apple did not have a chance. I had one goal in mind at this point, and I wasn't going to let anyone's lack of experience (except my own) get in the way of me achieving it. We will talk about this process extensively later in the book, in the Outsourcing chapter.

To begin the development process, I mapped out the steps, scheduled milestone dates and made sure my app developers were able to reach me when they needed me. When it was all said and done, my new tech company, (that I later named iQuick Tools) was on the verge of launching my first productivity app. Everything my construction team needed to deliver quality work on the spot was available right from their smart phones, no desktop computer necessary. What was most amazing to me was that I created something that – even though it would benefit my team – could also benefit others around the globe. Sure, there were other platforms being used, but the Apple App Store was the panacea. It offered exposure unlike any of the other platforms, which could catapult our brand into the hands and homes of millions of people around the world. Just being associated with the Apple brand had immense benefits for my business. Anywhere that the Apple App Store reached, I would be there as well, with my own productivity tool. My small idea had grown into one with global reach. I was so excited. I was in the app development business.

* * *

A year after Apple released the iPhone, Google followed with the release of the Android in September of 2008. The Android platform was designed for both smartphones and tablets. Like Apple, Android users have access to a variety of applications that extend the functionality of their mobile devices through the Play Store (originally, the Android Market). Android Play Store is Google's online marketplace for apps, music, books and other media designed for Androids. Unlike the App Store, Android's Play Store offers mainly free apps and offers developers more access to Android users by having more lenient requirements when deciding which apps to include in the Android Play Store. This can be a good thing if you're a new developer because you can get a chance to create your app and get it uploaded to the marketplace without much fuss.

After Apple, Android was the next platform for iQuick Tools. The Android platform competed directly with Apple's iPhone. Like Apple, the Android platform offered superb smartphone functionality, but also provided the synergistic benefits of being compatible with Google and its web-based applications. By this time, I had already put together a family of apps on iPhone; transitioning to include Android made perfect sense. Thankfully, it was not too difficult. The Google platform's challenge was not getting onto the platform; it was successfully competing on the platform. Unlike Apple, Google had far fewer barriers to entry. There were all kinds of apps – from the very good to the extremely bad – on Android simply because their app requirements were less stringent. Many of the Apps on Android were offered at no cost, so, naturally, anyone porting apps from iPhone had to consider whether or not to modify their business model. I was no different. With the barriers to entry being so much lower on Android, the competition there was much steeper. There were just more apps available from which people could choose. Now, the quality of some of these apps left much to be desired, but that did not change the fact that consumers could select any number of these competitive apps from among the bunch.

It took approximately 4 months from the day I watched that CNBC special to get my first app uploaded and ready for sale in the Apple App Store. Over the next 3 years, I developed 32 apps through iQuick Tools. As I write this book, 10 more apps are going through various stages of the development process. I am continuing to move forward and push ideas into the marketplace. Some of the apps I developed were done in under 2 months and a few have hit the market within 4 weeks of conception. You'll learn the details of how that happened as you journey with me through this book.

* * *

The precursor to iQuick Tools was my full-scale construction business, NPI. My experience with NPI sparked the idea to build one app that would help me be more efficient in that business. One app turned into another, then into several others. At this point, I believe that NPI benefits from the work of iQuick Tools as well, because when people learn more about how iQuick Tools began, they are also exposed to the story of NPI. So, not only did I develop a micro-business via iQuick Tools; I also strengthened my existing traditional business. Other small businesses have grown in this manner.

App development has emerged as a promising new opportunity for those who are committed to making it work. iQuick Tools has evolved into a profitable, streamlined enterprise - a very small, portable, flexible and profitable operation. Because my name is associated with several apps on both the Apple and Android platforms, I am often contacted by larger companies wanting me to develop apps for their businesses. What they don't realize is that my company is a home-based business that is operated solely by me. No one develops apps for iQuick Tools except for me, with the help of my online team. I have no permanent staff – only the contractors I hire for each individual project. This is a company that I, literally, run from my home office, kitchen table or a local coffee shop (depending on my mood for that day).

It is so flexible and small an operation that I am still the active principal running the business, while running my other businesses as well. My construction company is still profitable and continues to grow every year. My other micro-businesses remain in operation as well (you'll learn more about those later, too). iQuick Tools is a supplement to the other projects I am working on, and still manages to grow, despite my divided attention. That's what makes micro-business such a viable option. They are low maintenance and, when operated properly, they will not be a "time-suck" like a large, more involved business enterprise. The proof is in the pudding.

I'm not special. I like to think of myself as just "some guy." Just like the "some guy" who created Instagram, and just like the "some guy" who created Facebook or any other successful enterprise with which you are familiar. I don't say this to suggest that the people who have created successful companies, products and apps don't possess certain qualities that have contributed to their success. I say this only to make the point that we are not extraordinary. I am not extraordinary. They are not extraordinary. Were you to utilize the same concepts and employ a similar line of thinking as myself and others in business, you could produce the very same, if not better, results.

Most app businesses are just like mine - micro-businesses that are small, profitable, portable operations run by a small group of individuals, if not one person. Often, these are businesses that launched using very little start-up capital and very few resources - human or otherwise. I say this from personal experience. If you do not yet see the value and opportunity in these kinds of small businesses, allow me to engage you in the discourse that I'm offering in this book. Do not believe that app businesses always consist of teams of developers and tech experts. You'd be surprised by how many of these apps are developed by *some guy* who just decided to create an app for one reason or another. Trust me! I've done it! I'm that guy! At the age of 12, Thomas Suarez was a self-taught app developer with two published apps on the market. If he can do it, you should not be intimidated.

One of the many benefits of starting an app development business is that the market is not dominated by big business. That's not to say that the playing field is level, but it's getting pretty close. App markets are goldmines and a little guy, untested and unproven, can find himself earning thousands of dollars in residual income without having to invest a large amount of startup capital. Now, there are some industries that are dominated by big business. For some businesses, the barriers to entry are exceptionally high and to the extent that one lacks substantial resources, he will not be able to enter that field and have any reasonable chance for success. Think: pharmaceuticals. Think: a gaming establishment. The good thing for me and you is that the mobile app industry is not one of those mammoth industries that cannot be easily penetrated by the average person. It's quite the contrary. I'm not saying it's easy. What I'm saying is that it's much more doable than you may think and that you should not delude yourself into thinking that you could not succeed in a business of this sort or that a business of this sort is not worth your while. To think that a small or micro-business cannot be a seriously profitable enterprise is an imprudent mindset to take. These kinds of businesses present great opportunities to earn substantial income.

Here's the paradox: by thinking of business in small - i.e., micro – terms: you open yourself up to big - very big - opportunities. If you think small, you're less likely to feel overwhelmed or paralyzed in the idea-generation phase. This means that you might be more inclined to actually make some progress - to actually do something, instead of continuing to just think about it. If you think what I'm saying is kinda... ridiculous... consider the story of Instagram.

Instagram is a photo-sharing app that allows users to quickly apply filters to pictures taken by mobile phone. Before partnering up, Instagram co-founders Kevin Systrom and Mike Krieger worked in a series of tech companies and startups. In early 2010, Systrom developed a check-in app called Bourbon for whiskey enthusiasts to check-in at different local establishments, much like what Foursquare offers. Instead of checking in, he found that users were posting images of not just their whiskey, but various aspects of their daily lives. It was around this time that Mike Krieger joined him and the two began to study how photo apps were being used socially.

The two came up with an idea and tested it for several months, tweaking the design and the user experience. They created something that was as fun and easy to use, with fantastic filter features. The app also provided a strong social element, enabling users to make the filtered photos public within just three clicks. In the fall of 2010, Instagram was launched and within 24 hours, the app had 25,000 users. The timing could not have been more perfect. When the new iPhone 4, with its much-improved camera, came to market just 3 months thereafter, Instagram had a million users with absolutely no marketing. Even though the app was only available on the iPhone platform, the number of users grew to 27 million.

Instagram launched on Android in March 2012 and acquired a million new users the first day of its release. The level of social engagement that was available on Instagram posed a direct threat to Facebook. In 18 months, Instagram had gone from launch to 30 million users. Even with 30 million users, they still only had 13 staff members! In April of 2012, Facebook acquired Instagram for $1 billion. When Instagram was purchased by Facebook, the company still had only 13 employees. Thirteen! If that doesn't show how something that started small can turn into something huge quickly, I don't know what does.

Let this book lead you down the path to a new way of thinking. As you take this journey with me, forget about big business; at least for the time being. Consider the value of thinking and creating on a smaller level those things which have the potential to be big. But do not get married to the idea of big success, as if anything less than large-scale is not good enough. Not everyone will produce an Instagram or a Craigslist. What you can produce, however, is a business and business model that works for you and what you want to accomplish. Though you may not end up selling it to Facebook one day for a billion dollars, you may just create something that still affords you the life you desire. It may give you extra time to pursue your interests. It may give you enough income to replace the income you earn from your 9 to 5 or, it may catapult you into that ubiquitous category known as "the 1%." Who knows?

The point is this: you never know what can happen. When I started investing in real estate, I had no idea that I would end up becoming a general contractor. When I started my general contracting business, I had no idea that I would become an app developer or an App Millionaire. I started out not knowing the first thing about developing apps. But... it worked. And still does.

Although I run a successful general contracting company, I have come to realize that I was onto something with my initial thoughts to start and maintain something small and manageable. Even though my contracting business was successful from the start, knowing what I know now, my first foray into entrepreneurship would have been with a micro-business, which was my original inclination. I would have become an App Millionaire much sooner and with fewer hard knocks along the way.

Chapter 2

The App Millionaire

"If you are lucky enough to find a way of life you love, you have to find the courage to live it."

- John Irving, Author, *A Prayer for Owen Meany*

App Millionaire: One who develops a profitable business system - a micro-business system - that, with minimal continued management, will produce income sufficient to support his lifestyle.

Who or what is an App Millionaire? To make it easy to understand let me just tell you a story about a guy who went from being a 9 to 5 employee to an App Millionaire. Meet Justin. While working for the City as a Lab Technician, he started mowing lawns on the weekends to earn extra money. As his clients increased, but the number of hours in the day did not, Justin hired some neighborhood teenagers to help him mow the lawns he could not manage. While continuing to work his day job, Justin operated his expanding business, using his young helpers to mow while he was at work. As the business, and Justin's income, grew, he was soon in the position to quit his 9 to 5 and work on his business full-time.

Over time, Justin's service reputation grew, along with his business. He hired more help and, within two years, was earning over $150,000 annually in gross revenues – not an extraordinary income, once expenses and taxes were accounted for, but, definitely one on which he could support his family. Justin had a reputation for having a remarkably professional team, whose competence matched their superb quality of customer service. The more requests for advice that Justin received, the more he realized that, apparently, there was a lack of lawn care information that was reader-friendly and well-organized. So he had an idea to develop a website that would serve to educate people, as well as, possibly, serve as a platform from which he could sell organic lawn care products such as newly developed low water usage grass seeds and organic fertilizers.

With the help of one of the neighborhood teenagers who worked with him, Justin developed a great-looking website for his business, which included both information on his company's services, and also general lawn care tips. Occasionally, Justin would receive organic lawn care-related questions through his website related to providing lawn care, to which he would happily respond.

The website included a section in which he sold the organic fertilizer and grass seed products. With just a little online marketing suddenly, he went from running a local lawn care business, to running a global lawn care information service and store. He was selling lawn care products to people from all over the country! His niche market was earth-friendly lawn care products. What made the situation even better for Justin was that he no longer relied on his lawn care service business as his sole means of income. Soon, his online lawn care business with little overhead out-produced his lawn care service. So, during the slow lawn care seasons, he still generated income because he was no longer servicing just his city and surrounding areas. He had potential clients all over the world.

You're probably wondering why I would include a story about a guy who successfully built a website about organic lawn care products in a book called *The App Millionaire*. Here's the simple answer: an App Millionaire doesn't, necessarily, have to create his income through mobile or desktop apps. More to come on this later.

But First, What is an App?

The term "app" is short for "application." It is a form of software mainly designed and built to perform functions on a mobile OS (operating system) platform. The two most common forms of mobile platforms are the smartphone (e.g., iPhone, Android phone) and the tablet (e.g., iPad, Kindle Fire, Galaxy, Surface, etc). An app is similar to desktop software in that it allows one to perform certain functions, but it is usually not as robust as desktop software because it is designed to be used on the go and for smaller transactions. These apps can range from performing arithmetic calculations to entertaining its user through various games and music playing functions. There are thousands of apps for many different purposes. They are less complicated, as compared to desktop software, and are not laden with a lot of underlying code, so as to prevent them from moving slowly. They come in downloadable form. That is, you download them right to your Smartphone or other mobile device with a few simple taps of your phone screen. No longer is it necessary to use a computer to access your favorite games, websites, blogs and software. It all can be done right through your phone.

As you can probably imagine, the people who design and bring these apps to market are making money from them. Whether downloaded for free or purchased by the consumer, apps can quickly become a strong source of income for the person who designed, developed and made it available to the public. With enough apps or with an app that is extremely popular, one can make a tremendous amount of money – enough to become an App Millionaire.

I mentioned before, however, that an App Millionaire does not have to make his money through mobile or desktop apps. As used in the term "App Millionaire," the word "App" is a metaphor for the working system that one puts in place – the system that, once properly set up, produces the continuous income. Allow me to illustrate: a mobile app is a small software program that provides value for anyone who has a smartphone and has access to the application, right? The app can be a game, productivity tool, business resource, social network, or almost anything you can think of. Once the app is built, it can be utilized the same by individuals locally and around the world. It does not have to be rebuilt for each individual person – no. This one app can be used by multitudes of people, even though it is only one product. Since each of those individuals, presumably, gain value from their use of the app, they are willing to pay for it. The person who made the app gets dollars from each of the people who use the product. Yes, this one product. In essence, the app is a small system – a program - that continues to function over and over again. Just as one would develop a mobile app, there are other systems – business systems - that can be developed to function just like this.

Now, for the purpose of this discussion, the term "Millionaire" represents one who has produced a substantial enough level of financial wherewithal to support his lifestyle without continuing to actively produce income. The question to ask here is, "Could I continue to maintain my lifestyle if I stopped actively working?" For the App Millionaire, the answer is emphatically, "Yes!" This is true, even though the App Millionaire may not yet have a minimum of a million dollars in actual dollars or assets. An App Millionaire is not, always, a millionaire in these terms. He is one who has set up a low overhead working system that, were it to continue to run effectively, would, more than likely, put him to millionaire status. In the meantime, he enjoys the fruits of his labor – not having to trade his hours for dollars or wonder how he will pay for next week's groceries.

Remember, true wealth is quantified in time as well as dollars. The more net income your business earns while considering your total lifestyle expenses, the longer you can maintain the desired standard of living. The simple formula for lifestyle standard of living is: Income - Expenses + Time + Activities = Lifestyle. The more net income you earn along with the type of activities you like to do will determine how long you can sustain a chosen lifestyle. If you are a person who likes to ride horses twice a week, golf 8 times a month and vacation with your family every season, you will certainly need the time and income to maintain this lifestyle. Right? Therefore, the more available time you have, coupled with your net income, will determine if this is your reality or a fantasy. Many people believe that a man with a million-dollar business is most likely a wealthy man, but that's not always accurate. A man with a business that earns a million dollars, but who has no free time, is just a "busyman," not, necessarily, a wealthy businessman. On the other hand, a man who has just one remaining dollar after continuously fulfilling all of his necessities and lifestyle goals is a wealthy man, although he may not be a man of wealth. This is just one of the many reasons why I believe in the micro-business model (we'll talk more about the micro-business model later). When designed correctly, the micro-business owner may increase the possibility of having available time for lifestyle choices.

Why Become and App Millionaire?

An App Millionaire is not just a person with money. He goes about his earning in a nontraditional manner. He does not go about living in a manner that renders him a stressed out, agitated high-earner. He does not go into his job or business and work 70 hours a week. He does not neglect vacations out of fear that, in his absence, his entire empire will be at risk. The App Millionaire, instead, is a person who has both income and lifestyle – a combination of having money as well as the time to enjoy it. There are other benefits that one enjoys when choosing to be an App Millionaire, instead of simply someone with money.

Control Your Own Destiny

In order to control your destiny, you must be able to control the factors that contribute to it - primarily how you spend your time and how you earn your income. With these two factors within purview, it is easiest to feel that your life is in your hands. Because you make decisions regarding your business operations and income, you determine the direction in which these things go. Working for yourself and on the projects you select, instead of working on projects that others select for you, means that you are in the position to chart a course of action that will be most beneficial to you and your family. You will be the boss.

Work for Yourself... Wherever

Being your own boss has numerous benefits – all of which boil down to two attributes: (1) control and (2) freedom – control over what you do and the freedom to go about it in the manner that you see fit.

An App Millionaire is not the typical entrepreneur. Yes, he works for himself, but he has done more than simply create his own job, as in the case of a lawyer or plumber. He has not created a brick and mortar store for which he must constantly deal with typical matters such as inept employees calling in sick, or suppliers who do not ship products on time. He is not wedded to completing his work in any particular place or location –as long as he has access to a means of communication, such as the telephone or internet.

Control Your Lifestyle

When you're in charge of your income and your time, you are well-positioned to create the kind of lifestyle you would like. Remember, Income - Expenses + Time + Activities = Lifestyle. If, for example, you like to sail, with money, you can afford to purchase the equipment and boat you would like, and with time, you can actually get a chance to get out to see and experience the water. In the absence of one, you would have a tough time engaging in your hobby.

Contemplated within my definition of "App Millionaire" above, is the idea that there are two types of App Millionaires: (1) the type that actually builds apps to produce millions and (2) the type that produces millions through other avenues (i.e., micro-businesses). This book will address both. You choose which one you'd like to be.

* * *

You're reading this book for a reason. My hunch is that (a) you're over living the mediocre life you've been living and are looking for a change (Type 1 App Millionaire), (b) you're okay with where you are in terms of your lifestyle and income, but you realize that apps and technology are critical to one making substantial income over the coming years and you want to learn more (Type 2 App Millionaire), or (c) a combination of both. If you are moreso in the (a) category, I commend you for picking up this book and committing to reading the information I'm providing. For you, moving toward becoming an App Millionaire may require a tremendous shift in both how you think and what you do. For those more squarely in the (b) category, becoming an App Millionaire may be less of a shift in thinking and more of a shift in method of doing.

Mr. App Millionaire vs. Joe Schmo

Earlier we met Justin. Now, let's meet Joe Schmo. What differentiates an App Millionaire from a regular Joe Schmo? In one word: Desire! Napoleon Hill, the author of *Think and Grow Rich,* was one of the first to use the term "burning desire" and I find it to be a very important concept. This desire manifests itself as the characteristics of one who, typically, succeeds in creating the lifestyle they want. Desire makes one work harder than others. (Let me tell you: if I had a nickel for every time I heard someone say, "Work smarter, not harder," I would have reached App Millionaire status long ago. The reality is that working harder *is* working smarter.) While it is certainly important that one "work smarter," there is no getting around the hard work requirement. At some point, during some period – whether it is a period of months, years, or decades – you will have to work hard in order to achieve the kind of success characteristic of the App Millionaire. The goal is to keep this hard work phase as short as possible. But know that you will never get around hard work. Never! Every successful entrepreneur I know can point to a particular period in their life during which they busted their tails unlike any other point in time. This is the "blood, sweat and tears" to which we often hear achievers refer. How did he do it? Desire! No one can sustain hard work through any significant length of time without it – that overwhelming drive that makes one stay up late, wake up early, sacrifice and push. Desire trumps fear. Desire makes one take risks. Most importantly, desire makes one find a way.

Finding A Way

Figuring out how to do something is not the App Millionaire's biggest challenge – deciding whether to do it is. Again, it's about whether a system can be designed that will be workable and profitable. If a proper system cannot be designed, it's not something the App Millionaire will endeavor to do. An App Millionaire is an innovator – not someone who just follows the flock, chasing wild ideas.

However, if he can come up with a system that seems workable and profitable, it's just a matter of how to go about getting it done. To an App Millionaire, there's always a way... and he's going to find it! He will go about it in the following ways:

Organized Thinking

You cannot be a complete and utter scatterbrain and think that you will get anything, let alone App Millionaire status, accomplished. To be clear: there is a difference between an innovator, who is able to juggle multiple thoughts and ideas in his head at the same time, with a clear end result in mind, and a scatterbrain, who allows random thoughts to continuously float around in his mind, without any connection to a particular set of actions. Ask yourself (and be honest): am I a scatterbrain or, am I an innovator? If you are a scatterbrain, all hope is not lost. I will give you some concrete steps you can take to organize your thinking and ideas and connect them to particular actions. More on that in the Chapter 10 on how to build a micro-business.

Success in any endeavor requires some level of focus. You do not need to have laser beam focus, but you definitely have to have a handle on what your goals are and what you will need to accomplish them. While multi-tasking can and does work, it is a good idea to have in mind the steps that need to be taken in order to get the goal accomplished.

Assessing Risk

Every project involves some level of risk, furthermore success is never guaranteed. Since a fundamental principle behind the App Millionaire concept is to start small with a micro-business, the biggest area of risk assessment is time and whether it should be used in the proposed endeavor. If so, how much? Starting capital is always a factor (even though the amount is likely to be a relatively low sum), but it is not a primary factor, as it would be for someone pursuing a traditional business. The concern here is how much time and effort will need to be diverted from other projects, in order to make your project profitable.

Utilizing Resources

It is not uncommon for an App Millionaire to run a one person show; however, he quickly learns to become a pro at assembling teams and utilizing resources. Take Justin, for example. Even when working in his lawn care service, before building his website, he started off on his own. Soon, he solicited the help of the teenagers in his neighborhood. When it was time to build his website, having no knowledge of how to do it himself, he, again, solicited the assistance of someone who could help him accomplish his goal. What you will learn about in this book is how to find resources from all around the world by outsourcing for the services needed to build and run your business.

Getting Started

The typical App Millionaire does not stay in the starting block for long. Once he pulls together a reasonable, workable plan, he, immediately gets started on it. This is what separates true entrepreneurs from the masses. While the masses talk about what they want to do, the entrepreneur actually does it. As a good friend of mine says, "In business, there are two kinds of people – people who do and people who don't." There's no in between. There are no others." Once you get started in business, you will quickly become acquainted with others who claim to be in business like you. Be wary of those who do more talking than doing. They may approach you will all kinds of "opportunities" and pie-in-the-sky ideas that will only serve to derail you from your own objectives. Do not allow such individuals to waste your time or dilute your focus.

Please understand this: "The cavalry is not coming." No one is coming to make your goals easier to obtain. You – and only you – are responsible for your success (or lack thereof).

Let's get back to our story about Justin. By expanding his market from just his area to the entire world, Justin increased his income substantially – so much so that the income he earned through his micro-business was more than what he made through his full-service lawn care business. Since the full service lawn care business required much more of his energy and left him spending long hours away from his family, he soon realized that his lifestyle could be much better (i.e., easier) if he were not running the service business. True to form, Justin groomed one of the teenagers who had worked with him in how to run the business. Upon the young man's college graduation, Justin sold it to him. Thereafter, Justin lived solely off of the income from his micro-business. That is when Justin, officially, became an App Millionaire.

I will not say that "anyone" can be an App Millionaire, because that simply isn't true. The kind of person who becomes an App Millionaire is one who believes in and exercises certain critical habits over a period of time, long enough to produce the success they desire.

Note some of Justin's qualities: he was willing to work hard, provided the kind of customer service that kept people coming back, and kept his overhead low enough to produce solid profits. He also did not get complacent in where he was in his business; he recognized opportunity, acted upon it, and down the line, helped someone by selling his business to them. Each of these qualities is important.

To anyone who comes to me and asks for mentorship advice, I say, "I don't believe you will succeed." Period! I don't say this because they appear to lack any particular quality (although they probably do lack certain essential qualities); I say this because the vast majority of people will not commit to performing hard work over the required period of time it takes to become successful. I'm not talking about years, here. For the most part, people cannot perform a task that requires discipline for even a period of a month or two!

Let me make one thing very, very clear, first and foremost: Show me an App Millionaire like Justin... and I will show you a confident person. Why? Because you have to be confident to get certain things done in life. You have to believe in yourself in order to take an idea from being just a set of thoughts, into a living, breathing end product or service. It takes faith in what you're doing in order to, day after day, take the various steps that move you closer to your end goal. If you don't believe in your ability, no one else will. You have to remind yourself – repeatedly and constantly – that you're capable and able to accomplish what you want to accomplish. If you do not fully subscribe to what you want to do, eventually you have to (have to!) get to the point where you are wholeheartedly "sold out" to your plans. Building that confidence can take some time, but it is absolutely critical. You may need to first prove to yourself that you can make some progress. By taking little steps and making small accomplishments, you effectively, are giving yourself a regular series of "atta boys." Those regular doses of positive affirmation are what you may need.

Here's another thing: If you do not have an overwhelming desire to work for yourself and be responsible for your income, time and destiny, you will not become an App Millionaire. To say that you want a different life is not enough. To say that you want to be your own boss is not enough. You must feel that the life you lead now is totally contrary to how it should be. You will have to believe that your situation is so dire that drastic measures may be necessary to change it. You must be of the mindset that you cannot possibly imagine carrying on as you are for the next decade, or even the next five years... or hell, for some of us, even the next few months! You have to say to yourself, "There's got to be a better way," and, therefore, be in the constant process of seeking out how you will better your circumstances and level of overall happiness.

You will first have to commit to changing. You've heard it said many times before: If what you're doing isn't working, you must do something different. Second, you must be willing to do what is necessary to create a different outcome in your life – even if it requires something dramatic. As an example, I had a mentee who was so disgusted with where she was in her career and business life that she started waking up at 4:30 in the morning so that she could work on her own business before heading to her job to further someone else's business. She scaled back on going out and entertainment time and buckled down for a few months in order to get her business off of the ground. Within that period of time, she developed and launched a successful ecommerce website called ThePerfectContract.com, through which she sells business, personal and legal document forms to the internet community. My advice to her was the same advice that I give to others: Move it forward – everyday! Not every other day. Not in your spare time. Every... single... day! Unlike others, who complain, but do nothing, she actually did something! It all started with her commitment to making change in her life and her willingness to do something dramatic to bring that change to fruition.

As I previously stated, you don't have to build mobile apps to be an App Millionaire. You don't have to have a technical background. You don't have to be a techno-geek. However, I would be remiss if I did not include a section that directly addresses how one can build riches through a mobile app business. I will discuss details on how to build apps in a later part of the book; for now, I will cover the important high-level points.

You don't have to know how to build an app in order to develop one. That is the most fundamental thing you must understand about being an App Millionaire. You can become rich by developing systems, even if you don't know how to develop the system yourself. You don't have to know how to build a website in order to have it generate income for you. Nor do you need to know how to build a new model of hiking boot in order to sell 500,000 pairs of them. What you do need to know how to do is develop a profitable system (or make good use of one that already exists). What the product or service is becomes secondary.

Type 1 App Millionaire – Technologically Inclined People

For the person who is technologically inclined, becoming a Type 1 App Millionaire should not be difficult, assuming you're able to come up with an idea and actually follow through with it. Knowing how to code and build a mobile or desktop app means that you do not need to rely on anyone else to get your product developed. With that kind of knowledge and know-how, you can develop something saleable and build it just how you like. Your biggest challenge will be learning about the process for getting an app registered with Apple, Android and other platforms. Neither of these is difficult to do, once you learn what steps need to be taken.

Type 2 App Millionaire – Non-Technical People

Meet the Type 2 App Millionaire: Me! When I endeavored to do my first app, I knew nothing about the process. Nothing at all! I'm not a technology nerd and I know nothing about coding or operating systems. To this day, I know very little about developing (and don't ever want to learn).

What I do know, however, is business. In fact, I love developing businesses and business systems. Even though my background is education, I am an entrepreneur at heart. While I was teaching, I started a health care business (which failed miserably) then a real estate investment company on the side. That led to a general contracting company, which later gave me the idea to design my first app, which is one that is related to construction. Now, I have developed more than 40 apps and counting. That's why I tell you that the thing that differentiates the App Millionaire from a regular Joe Schmo is the desire to succeed – not technical know-how. I know this from personal experience.

The secret to becoming a Type 2 App Millionaire is learning how to successfully manage a project. Yes, project management. We've already established that a Type 2 App Millionaire does not have the technical knowledge to actually build the business system (i.e., the app, website or other tool), so what he does is find the people who do know how to build the system and manage them in the building process. He determines in his mind how he would like the system to operate and how he'd like it to function, then he hires the people who know how to build the system and make it function as he desires. You don't need to have specialized skill. You just need to have access to it.

Now, getting people to do what you want them to do is much easier said than done. Ask any manager – entrepreneur or otherwise. Managing people is a true skill that one must develop in order to be successful in business. Note that I said managing people is the skill – not managing things. There is a big difference. People who are successful at managing things usually have specialized knowledge, which makes them a master of that particular thing. Contrary to popular belief, this may serve as a limitation in what they are able to do because their sphere of impact relates to that portion of the business system on which they work. For example, a person who repairs an automobile motor is a master of that particular "thing" - motors. The person who, on the other hand, can manage 25 people, who each repair different parts of the automobile, is the master of a "system." As odd as this may sound, the person who is the master of a "thing" is a victim of his own specialized knowledge. Henry Ford, who is considered one of the world's greatest innovators, once said, "Specialized knowledge is among the most plentiful, and the cheapest forms of service which may be had! If you doubt this, consult the payroll of any university." Why? Over time, your influence on the system, as whole, is very limited.

* * *

For either type of App Millionaire – Type 1 or Type 2 - one does not need a lot of money to get started. He does not dump tens of thousands of dollars into some elaborate website or app or go and borrow money to get his business started. No. He starts small, using the money he has from his own monthly cash flow. If the business you're contemplating requires a large initial outlay, it is not a micro-business and is not the foundation of an App Millionaire wealth pile.

Another factor that contributes to the success of an App Millionaire is his ability to reinvent without reinventing. In other words, he knows how to multiply his efforts without starting from scratch each time. This creates tremendous time and money savings, which allows him to create exponential revenue growth without repeating initial project outlays.

As I said, I encourage people to just go ahead and get started. Many of you are in the position to do that. There are some of you reading this, however, who are not in the position to get started and may need to seriously evaluate whether pursing the life of an App Millionaire is something that you are in the position to do. If any of the scenarios below apply to you, you probably are not ready to go into entrepreneurship.

You're Flat Broke

You don't need much money to start a micro-business (by definition), but you do need some. If you're going to start a website, for example, and you do not know how to build it yourself, you will need to get someone's assistance to help you build it. That will probably cost, at least, a little bit of money, even if you outsource the process and get a great price. If you do know how to build a website, there will still be costs associated with hosting and marketing the site. Although you can keep these expenses minimal, they are still expenses that need to be paid.

I would suggest that one put aside at least $500 to get started if building a website with no know-how. For those wanting to build an app with no know-how, I would suggest you prepare to spend at least a minimum of $1500. This is on the low end, but, depending on the simplicity of your app, it may get you started.

You're Immobilized by Fear

If, when you look back on recent years, you realize that you have been talking about entrepreneurship, but have yet to really jump out there and actually do something about it, you're scared of something. I'm no psychologist, but I know that there are some fears that typically hold someone back from pursuing their goals. For example, you may be afraid of success, afraid of failure, or afraid that your wife will be upset with you for spending money on a venture. I don't know. Whatever your fear, you can either get over it (perhaps that's easier said than done, but I'm not here to make excuses), or accept the fact that you will work for someone else for the rest of your life and they – not you – will run the show.

You Crumble at the First Sign of Trouble

Let me tell you: you're not in business until the crap hits the fan and you clean up the mess. In other words, you will need to be the motivator and the problem-solver. If you're not fixing something, you're not a businessperson. Trust me: there will always be something to fix or make better. If you're the type of person who cannot function in the absence of smooth sailing, understand that being in business can drive even the best of us to drink.

You "Kinda"' Want to Be an Entrepreneur

I cannot stress this enough: you have to really, really want this in order for it to work. Even though you're starting out small and simple, you're still running a business and, in doing so, you will encounter the challenges that come with being a business owner. Because you will be working for yourself, you will have to constantly push yourself to do what you need to do - day in and day out. If you're working a job full-time, while building your business, this will not be an easy thing to do. Add the stresses of daily life – family obligations, health concerns and mental fatigue, and you'll be asking yourself, "Why am I doing this?" It is on those days that you will need to have an answer. You must know why you are making the sacrifices in terms of time, money and energy in order to build your business. If you don't have a very strong "why," it will be very easy to simply give up. After all, you will not have spent much money, or invested in inventory, so your largest loss will be in time and energy spent. That is why you can't "kinda" want to be your own boss. You must believe that it is critical to your future.

We covered the who and why – who does, can and should become and App Millionaire and why one would even want to go about becoming one. In the next chapter, we will discuss how to do it.

Chapter 3

Sleep Money

*"Days are expensive. When you spend a day you have one less day to spend.
So make sure you spend each one wisely."*

- Jim Rohn, Entrepreneur, Author and Motivational Speaker

Simply stated, "sleep money" is money you earn, even while you're sleeping. It is comprised of revenues that you generate, whether or not you are actively working. It is money that is a byproduct of functioning systems that you have created, which produce income for you on an ongoing basis.

On the surface, it may seem that sleep money is synonymous with the commonly understood term, "passive income." While the two terms are similar in that they both involve dollars earned while not actively working, there are very notable differences between the two.

According to the Internal Revenue Service of the United States (the behemoth government entity that determines how citizens and residents will pay taxes to the government), there are only two forms of passive income – (1) a rental activity or (2) a business in which the taxpayer does not materially participate.[1] Other forms of income that do not involve direct work activity may seem like passive income, like portfolio income, royalties, lottery winnings, and retirement income,

---

1 IRC § 469(c)

but, for tax purposes are not deemed as such.[2] Nevertheless, at least in the United States, layman understanding of the term "passive income" has come to include all of those forms of income mentioned above – from rental activity to retirement income – because none of them are generated by one's continuous, active participation. For the purposes of this discussion, we will go with the layman understanding of the term.

The biggest difference between "sleep money" and "passive income" is that sleep money is produced as a result of your own efforts – from business systems that you have designed. A quick example would be someone's portfolio of mobile and desktop apps. Passive income, on the other hand, comes from a range of investment vehicles, like stocks, bonds, pensions and 401(k) funds. With regard to the latter two items – pensions and 401k funds – one could argue that the income generated from these, comes as a result of one's own work efforts and, as such, should be classified as sleep money. Not so. Sleep money derives from business systems, not funds earned on the basis of prior "hours for dollars" trade situations.

Any scenario in which hours are being traded for dollars cannot be classified as one that yields sleep money because all revenues received are directly based on continuous work efforts. In turn, any passive income that derives from the trade of hours for dollars cannot be deemed sleep money because the money originated from an "hours for dollars" trade scenario. While dividends and other payments from investment vehicles like pensions and 401k plans are, clearly, considered passive income, they cannot be deemed sleep money vehicles because they derive from employment situations in which one worked and received compensation. In other words, you worked for someone, they paid you and they either agreed to put aside funds for you, or you made the choice to put aside funds for yourself (via 401k) and they agreed to, on some level, match your efforts.

Additionally, any system that produces income for you, but is one over

---

2 IRC § 469(e)(1), PLR 8943055, and PLR 8943055

which you have no control, cannot be classified as sleep money. While income from your stock portfolio is certainly income you earn without having to work, it is income over which you have no control. The income does not come as a result of a business idea or system you put in place; it comes as a result of you having invested a certain sum of money in another person's or company's business idea or system. Therefore, you have very little control, if any (depending on the class and amount of your stock ownership), over that business and how it operates. In the vast majority of cases, you have no involvement, whatsoever, in the building of the company. The business was created by others, it is operated by others and your impact on the future of the business is, basically, slim to none. Unless you are a major shareholder, you cannot make a decision that can produce a substantial impact on the company's bottom line, like you could if you were running a company of your own. You are simply an investor who receives a return on your investment at regular intervals. This all assumes, of course, that the company in which you invested is a profitable one, such that you are even afforded a return on your investment.

Let's go back to Justin. When he was operating the lawn care service business, he was trading hours for dollars. Even though each of the hours earned were not hours he worked himself, his business income was contingent upon someone mowing a lawn, trimming a shrub, or blowing some leaves. The moment the service activity ceased, so did Justin's revenue.

With his online lawn care information center and store, however, Justin was "selling" at all times of the day, whether or not he was actively involved. The information he offered on the site provided value to his readers at any moment of the day and could provide this value for various people all at the same time. Once he captured the information and products on the site, the value could be received on a repeated and continuous basis, whether or not he ever added any additional information or products to the site. Once he set-up the system whereby he provided information deemed valuable and useful by the public, and by which he could have products sent directly via drop shipment through a fulfillment company to his client's, Justin had in place a system that produced sleep money. If he never touched the website again, he would continue to receive checks in the form of advertising income, as well as checks from the drop shipper for his portion of the proceeds from product sales.

I do not want to give the impression that earning sleep money is easy. Sometimes it can be but often, it's not. Once one has done the work necessary to put in place the working system (or systems) that will create sleep money, however, the sleep money is definitely easy money. Once again, understand this: putting the system in place is not easy; the system you put in place creates the easy money. The key is remembering that the difficulty, per se, is in the front-end investment of time, energy and good decision-making. Once the initial investment is made, the output is easy. With the micro-business design, which is supposed to require little ongoing maintenance, your sleep money machine should run very smoothly.

For the App Millionaire with a mobile or desktop app business, sleep money can be checked on a daily basis. For me, each morning, after my kids have gone off to school - sometime between breakfast and checking my email - I look to see how much money I earned from my apps sales during the previous 12-24 hours. Since Android provides very real-time updates, I am able to go to the Google Play Store to see just how many of each of my apps I recently sold. I am even able to learn the country in which my purchasers reside. It is a process that, literally, takes minutes. So when I say that sleep money is money you earn while you're sleeping, I'm not exaggerating.

For the App Millionaire who does not run a mobile app business, sleep money can be in a variety of forms – most of which involve a simple check of one's bank balance. The person whose micro-business income comes from the sale of exercise DVDs, for example, might just check their PayPal or Google Checkout balance to see how much money was generated in DVD sales over the prior 24 hours. The same would be true for someone who sells products through a website.

Who wouldn't want to earn money while they sleep? Perhaps the greatest advantage of earning sleep money is that, by systemizing your income, you avail yourself of the most value asset you have... time. Your income is no longer directly linked to the time you spend continuously working on a particular project. By earning income the sleep money way, the one thing to which most people dedicate the majority of their time – earning income – does not eat up the bulk of your time. With this extra time, you can do any number of things – for business or pleasure – while maintaining the lifestyle you desire.

Now let's do the math. Just imagine if you earned $100 to $150 dollars a day from just one micro-business. Sounds just ok, but not enough to change your lifestyle, right? Now try to imagine having 10, 15 or even 20 different micro-businesses that produce the same amount of daily income on average. Doesn't the idea of creating micro-businesses become more attractive? What would your life be like if you didn't spend the majority of your time earning an "hours for dollars" living? Would you have better relationships with your friends and family? Would you feel more energized? Would the stress that has caused some of your current ailments be alleviated? Would you just be... happier?

Chapter 4

What is a Micro-Business?

"Less is more."

- Ludwig Mies van der Rohe, German-American Architect

A "micro-business" is just as it sounds – a very small business. Beyond that limited statement, the definition of a micro-business is as varied as are the types of potential micro-business opportunities that exist. My definition of a micro-business is based upon certain characteristics - primarily, on who operates the business and how they go about doing that. In short, a micro-business is one that is typically characterized by low start-up costs, low barriers to entry (i.e., it doesn't require years of schooling or large capital outlays, which most people do not have), consists of only 1 to 5 employees, and low continued overhead.

The important thing to remember is that just because the word "micro" is in front of it doesn't mean you can forget that the word "business" is there. Even though it's a small business, it needs to be treated like a real business. One of the biggest mistakes a micro-business owner can make is treating their business like a hobby, meaning, working on it only when they are in the mood. All in all, a micro-business is simply a small-scale business. You can make quick decisions with fewer people in the decision making process. You have more flexibility – need to go help out a relative? Often, you can take your micro-business on the road with you. I started my first micro-business, iQuickTools.com, with less than $2,000. When this company got up and running, I recouped the start-up capital I invested in less than one month.

For both a Type 1 and Type 2 App Millionaire, identifying profitable and manageable business systems is critical. One vehicle that is accessible to anyone with desire to be an entrepreneur is a micro-business. It's small, flexible, and can be made profitable very quickly.

Characteristics of a Micro-Business

The characteristics of a micro-business make it appear, at least on the surface... easy. These are the easiest of businesses to start because they are designed to be low maintenance. Getting one started should be low cost, and maintaining the functioning of the business should not require extensive management. When compared to most other business types, a micro-business is one that operates in a manner that is very lean and efficient. No elaborate offices with shiny oak furnishings. No multiple levels of decision-making. A micro-business can make a lot of good products using very little resources – at least, in the beginning, as many micro-businesses start out being micro, but end up growing into much larger entities.

If one finds themselves engulfed in complexity with regard to overhead or human resources, the micro-business is not properly functioning or is designed incorrectly. It should function as a very small to small-sized business. A micro-business does not have a complex organizational structure that involves the participation and decision-making of multiple individuals. It is not, at least in the beginning, a large entity. The goal with a micro-business is not to start something big; the goal is to start *something*. Setting up complex organizational structures, elaborate business plans and cumbersome product offerings serves as a delay tactic. Often, this hinders even those with the best of intentions, leaving them perpetually in the starting blocks. Your goal should be to think of something that is simple, small, flexible and potentially profitable.

Small. Portable. Flexible. Profitable.

As you analyze and research an appropriate micro-business for yourself, remember to keep things simple. Think small. Think portable.

Think flexible. Think profitable. Let me say this again: Think small... Think portable... Think flexible... Think profitable. As author, Tim Ferriss, explains in his bestselling book, *The 4-Hour Workweek*, you're basically looking for a "muse" – a business that you can own, that will be very profitable, but that you will not have to spend much time running. That is exactly what a micro-business offers – more with less.

By virtue of its main characteristics – simple and small – a micro-business design may lull entrepreneurs into bad habits. Because it is a micro-business, in which often, little financial investment was made, sometimes the business is treated carelessly by less seasoned entrepreneurs. Having spent little money on the start-up cost and running it primarily as a one to five person operation, one may handle a micro-business carelessly - as if it is a hobby, and not a real business. That reckless business style can be the cornerstone of business failures. Many beginning entrepreneurs do not have insight to identify the difference in the two.

Let's take a closer look. The difference between a "hobby" and a business, in this context, is that a business is operated for profitability, while a hobby is operated mainly for entertainment or to past idle time. Even though a micro-business can be made profitable quickly, high profits may not, necessarily, come quickly. It takes some time and plenty of diligence to keep a micro-business recognized and working. Some less committed entrepreneurs give up within just a few months or even a few weeks of opening. They don't exert the time or the energy it takes to make the enterprise run properly. This rapid rate of failure is, unfortunately, common among micro-business owners. Unlike a true business, when you take up a hobby, regardless of how serious you take it, you have the opportunity to stop working on it at any time. On the other hand, a true business venture does not offer that same freedom. A business start-up usually takes time to develop and grow. To increase your probability of success, never treat your business endeavors like a hobby. You, as a businessperson, do not have the same freedom to stop working towards your success. To run a successful micro-business, one has to stay away from the pitfalls that usually land a business – big or small - in the red. Bad management, poor planning, failure to control costs, and overall bad decision-making will quickly run a business into the ground.

The Advantages of Owning a Micro-Business

Why do people start their own businesses? It's often the case that traditional small business owners leave their 9 to 5 jobs in search of more freedom. What they find is that they work more hours as a self-employed person than they did as an employee. They traded in their bosses for clients and swapped out a cubicle for a home office or even a brick and mortar business. You'd better believe they spend a significant amount of time laboring in their businesses. The difference between the traditional small business owner and the App Millionaire, however, is the system. It is the system that gives you back your freedom and enables you to take your hands off the day-to-day operations. The system you put in place is what will help you to keep your business running smoothly without you having to micro-manage every aspect of the operations. Your system is what will help you to minimize your overhead and keep expenses in check.

The primary benefit of starting a micro-business is that risk is limited. Micro-businesses are quick-start ventures. The financial barriers and red tape that may have kept you from opening a traditional small business are minimized in the micro-business structure. Micro-businesses require very little money and resources to launch. If it's set-up properly, a micro-business can be profitable for the owner without requiring him or her to invest a lot of time into the business. You can make money around the clock – and earn sleep money.

Micro-businesses offer flexibility. With the proper system in place, the goods and services the business provides can become almost interchangeable. That means you can change the focus of your micro-business and transition into other markets easier than you would be able to in a traditional small business. The transition is not always immediate, but changing course with your micro-business is a far simpler process than with a traditional small business.

Usually Self-Managed

A micro-business, like any other business, is borne out of the mind of an individual. It is not uncommon for it to be a one-person show. If others are employed by the company on a regular basis, these employees are often family members or friends of the business owner. However, an increasing trend is to hire online contract workers on an as-needed basis. The number of employees usually does not exceed about five people.

Quick and Easy Start Up

With an idea and a bit of direction, a micro-business can quickly come into being. Once a person takes their knowledge and know-how and applies it to a project, a micro-business is underway. This start-up approach does not, necessarily, involve the setting up of a corporate entity (although many micro-businesses are set up this way and it is an easy thing to do).

Low Start-Up Cost

As defined, a micro-enterprise does not involve high start up costs. The person who starts a micro-business usually takes money that he already has, or keeps start-up costs so low that the business can be operated with funds out of his monthly cash flow. Any high-end expenses may be borrowed, but the amount of these loans or credit will often be small (more info on loans versus credit cards later). He may even take a cash advance on a credit card in order to get the business started.

Low Overhead

With a micro-business, the idea is to start small and stay lean. Of course, the aim of any for profit business is to keep revenues as high as possible and expenses as low as possible. With a micro-business, however, keeping costs low is critical. Remember, these businesses are, typically, started with very low start-up capital. There are little, if any, funds available to borrow from banks as working capital (aside from the entrepreneur's personal bank account), so there is little room for the micro–business entrepreneur to make errors that will require large cash outputs on behalf of the business.

Usually Home-Based

Don't worry about start-up appearance. Justin's online lawn care business, as well as iQuick Tools, still operates from home. If possible, keep the business functioning from your home to keep the initial start-up costs, as well as continued overhead, low. Working from home also alleviates the time and energy one would spend in locating a proper place for an office or business site. The convenience of working from one's home goes without saying. I always say "it's better to do good than look good." Now, with today's home based micro-businesses, all you need is a good web developer and a live business phone answering service like what you could get through Phone.com or Grasshopper to look professional. It is easier than it ever was before to do both.

Often Internet-Based

As we all know, the internet has made it possible for people to do business from anywhere at any time. It has also provided countless means by which anyone can do business around the world. With there being so many ways to make money on the internet, individuals who do not have the capital and/or time to start a traditional brick and mortar business or service now have a vehicle that can be used to do business without the trappings of a traditional start-up. Most micro-businesses are internet-based companies. What contributes to their success is their global appeal. An online business is not limited to marketing to just a local area. It can have customers all over the world.

With the utility and functionality of today's smartphones, the internet is literally, in the palm of one's hand. Where there is internet access, there is a way to do business. For example, it is not uncommon for me to be at my gym riding a recumbent exercise bike while discussing a project with a developer in India, China, or Indonesia. For me this is now as common as a call home to my mom. Often I'm amazed when others are amazed that I commonly talk or chat with people all over the world. I often think to myself, "You're missing the boat and why aren't you doing this too?"

If you have a well-built website in hand, a good marketing knack, and can find ways to get social recognition without wasting a huge chunk of cash on marketing, you can reach a global audience. People are shopping online, studying online, dating online, and socializing online - literally, living their lives online.

Often Portable

Since the typical micro-business does not have a fancy office location and often relies on the internet in some form, it can be operated from anywhere (well, wherever one has internet access). This means that it is possible for a micro-business entrepreneur to, literally, run his business from anywhere. Yes, anywhere. This can even be some exotic oceanfront location, or your neighborhood coffee shop. Remember the gym? Well, I have closed major development deals at my gym right in between weight-lifting and spin class. I'm sure you can imagine how this kind of flexibility and freedom immensely adds to the quality of one's life. Being able to work from a variety of locations not only makes me more productive, but also makes my work more enjoyable. When I am feeling stifled or unfocused when working in my home office, I can take my kids to the park and work from a park bench while they run around. The change in scenery renews my energy and the time spent in the presence of my children is priceless to both them and to me. The portability of a micro-business makes it a highly favorable business type.

Easily Dissolvable

A micro-business often does not have a complex corporate structure; typically, it has one owner, and has few, if any, employees. Therefore, dissolving or closing the business is usually fairly easy. If the business is not proving profitable, the micro-business entrepreneur is not stuck in a cumbersome or drawn-out liquidation process that involves attorneys and accountants. There is no corporate board that must reach a consensus, and, typically, no complex division of company assets. As easy as the business is to start, it can, similarly, be ended.

Some micro-business entrepreneurs end up having their businesses dissolved by default. They simply stop paying attention to it, or, otherwise, cut if off from its lifeline. For a web-based business that "lifeline" is web hosting. The website cannot be accessed in the absence of a host (e.g., GoDaddy.com, Hostgator, etc). If the hosting fees are not paid, the website will no longer be available. No website... no business. For a different type of micro-business, like an ebook publishing business, one could simply stop publishing and marketing books. Eventually, sales will slow and/or dry up altogether.

Simple Tax Structure

With no employee expenses (unless you want them), no tax issues and no heavy overhead, you'd find micro-business to be a very beneficial endeavor. If you can utilize internet power well, you can get the required attention and earn a good income that gradually increases with time, as you grow more skilled at business development and design. By the time you are a micro-business expert, your income level is one that can make any accountant shrink in envy.

Being Your Own Boss

As mentioned earlier, in a micro-business, you are your own boss. The profit belongs to you, the time is yours and there is no one to order you around. It's a direct interaction with clients and there is no third party to throw their rules and requirements at you. Not only that, but as I said before, often you can work anywhere and at anytime, provided that there are communication facilities available.

Disadvantages of a Micro-Business

Though a micro-business offers the opportunity for wealth development, fun and spontaneity, it also has its share of issues and hardships. It's all too easy to start a micro-business, get a website, get tools for your service, and then say, "Voila! I have a business!" The challenge lies in taking the next step. How are you going to attract customers? What strategies will you use that are cost effective? What is the current market demand and are you providing something that will really make a customer want to sit back and listen to you? If the answers to these questions are a "No" or, "I don't know," you may be in for a rough time.

Remember that although a micro-business is not as complex as other businesses, it does need focus and attention, especially if you want to it grow into something bigger. Also, remember you are the owner-operator of your business; hence, you must make the decisions, take the brunt of all problems and face the consequences. Some people take these duties of their business very lightly and end up with a failed venture. As easy as it may seem, if you don't have the right tools and directives, it is likely that you will not succeed in business. I am quite confident that this book offers the right direction and the right action plan needed for you to succeed.

Once you decide to start a micro-business, I recommend you conduct a thorough market analysis and bring in target customers (who could be friends and family) to give you feedback on the business idea. I have already listed the advantages of having a micro-business. Listed below are some of the common problems people face with micro-businesses.

Chances of Rapid Failure

Because a micro-business owner is often the only operator, he has to manage everything. From marketing to negotiations, buying/selling, from monetary transactions to customer service - it all has to be done by the owner. In the beginning, a lack of focus in any of these areas could lead to an increased possibility of failure. One unsatisfied customer can mean trouble for the entire business. Ineffective marketing strategies will keep you stuck in the starting blocks. So, once you decide to become a micro-business owner, be prepared for a lot of rough sailing.

Customer Acceptance

Another factor for failure is customer acceptance. What are the chances that customers will accept products that come from a new company that has no track record? What is it that you're offering customers that will make them acknowledge you? What is your unique selling proposition? Who is your target audience? Why do they need your product? Why do you think your service is good for them? How will you attract them to your business? These, and many more questions, should be on your top list of market research when you decide to get on with your business idea. If you don't know your target audience like the back of your hand, your business can fall flat.

Difficult to Raise Capital

A micro-business is a low risk, high reward endeavor only if it can maintain a level of success or profit. This is difficult if you don't utilize the right tools to promote your business amongst your target audience. In some lines of business, it can be difficult to generate incremental capital or income. Although you may make a profit, you cannot spend beyond a certain point. If you do not re-invest back into your business it may become difficult to grow. Like I mentioned earlier, a micro-business offers opportunity for acquiring substantial income, but if additional capital is needed to grow your business, getting a traditional business loan may be difficult.

Of course, you can make your micro-business a successful endeavor – if you are determined to get past all of these issues. They are not walls, but rather hindrances that can effectively be handled, provided you have the patience, the wisdom, a thirst for knowledge, and the ability to execute effectively.

Not the Typical Small Business

Considering the characteristics explained above, you must also understand that a micro-business is not the typical, "small business." The micro-business entrepreneur is not the plumber, but, rather, the guy who started the on-call plumbing service. He is not the construction laborer; he is the guy who has set-up an online construction company referral service. He is the designer of a new way of doing business. The table on the page that follows highlights some major differences between a micro-business and more traditional small businesses.

What makes a micro-business attractive is the lifestyle it can support. First of all, like a larger business, it can produce a very high level of revenue, so the income potential of a micro-business entrepreneur is endless. The fact that the business started with little capital does not mean that it cannot (or should not) grow into an enterprise with high volume sales. The reality is...it can! Many of the companies that have grown into household names over recent years were started as micro-businesses. Think: Craigslist. Think: Jibber Jabber.

These characteristics make the micro-business one that provides for tremendous flexibility. Without the trappings of a traditional office, your micro-business will allow you work from anywhere. With a computer and/or Smartphone, your management duties (which should not be extensive) can be covered while you are on vacation. Again, since the internet runs 24 hours, 7 days a week, and all over the world, you can conduct much of your work activities on the days, during the hours, and in the locations of your choice. Since it's your business and you can operate it from, virtually, anywhere, you can work when you are most productive. When you've set up your system, and with these factors in place, you should be producing more in less time.

Types of Micro-Business

There are numerous types of micro-businesses. Figuring out which type to pursue will be an exciting process for you if you choose to go that route. In a later chapter, I'll give you some solid tips on how to identify a micro-business that would be good for you. In the meantime, I will provide you with some examples of popular kinds of micro-businesses that are being successfully operated all around the world.

Mobile App Companies

Of course! This is one of the ways I made my money. Mobile apps have become an effective way for start-up developers to market their skills and know-how, while providing value in exchange for dollars. Additionally, through the contracting of developers, innovative entrepreneurs have found an entrance into the world of app development and marketing. Through a range of different types of apps, developers and entrepreneurs are finding ways to make money through this vehicle. Many of the apps you see on your Apple, Android, Windows, or Blackberry device were built by an individual like you – meaning someone who used their own, limited resources and did not have the budget of a major corporation or venture capitalist. The person who has coding skills can build the app himself. More importantly, as this book will teach you, the person without such technical skills can also build mobile and desktop apps. Yes, I'm talking about the guy sitting next to you on the subway. Just a regular guy. Remember, the business opportunities that technology provides are not reserved for technology buffs. Anyone can find a way to use technology to his or her advantage.

eCommerce Websites

The term "ecommerce" refers to the buying and selling of goods and services via an electronic format, typically the internet. Sites like Amazon.com and Half.com have made online buying and selling a way of life for many of us around the world. The internet has become the world's largest buying/selling hub, where millions of products are sold through online transactions throughout the day. Many people now prefer to buy products online in the comfort of their home and have these products delivered to their doorstep, rather than spend gas driving around the city in order to purchase what they need.

Any website from which products can be purchased and delivered is considered an ecommerce website. These sites range from the simplest of sites - in which there is only one product for sale and the website has only one page – to some of the world's most popular and elaborate sites like eBay.com and Walmart.com. Tens of millions of products are sold on these sites on a daily basis.

Now Amazon.com and eBay are, of course, examples of very, very large ecommerce sites. These large dealers often, however, have affiliate programs that allow an ecommerce newcomer to participate in and profit from the buying and selling process. By being affiliated with a larger dealer, the newcomer has access to that retailer's brand and its line of products, and can then profit by serving as a direct line to the target market.

Online Learning Management Systems

With the rising costs of traditional education and the increased level "busyness" these days, education has evolved. It is not uncommon for someone to have earned a bachelor's or graduate degree through an online program, without ever stepping into a traditional classroom setting. People now utilize video conferencing and other technology platforms to teach and learn new skills.

If you're an "expert" (and, by "expert," I mean only that you know more than the average person would on the subject), you can set up a small online learning system, where people pay a certain fee to take classes from you, earn some type of certificate, and/or have access to the educational materials you've created.

This provides a great opportunity for teachers who want to have their own micro-business or for anyone with specialized knowledge to share information with others who will gladly pay for it – with each party working from the comfort of his own home.

Website eMercials

If TV and radio have commercials, then websites have emercials. Unlike media commercials, which are restricted to just major TV channels, emercials appear throughout the internet. Many of these emercials are made to promote websites, eproducts, ebooks and other products that may or may not be sold in a traditional retail store.

Some emercials, on the other hand, are used to enhance the online presence of products and/or services that can be found off-line. Businesses want to be known and recognized in the online world as much as they are known in the off-line world. From small entrepreneurs to multi-national companies, every business needs to have an online portal if widespread exposure is desired. Having videos to promote products is a good strategy by which one can earn customer satisfaction, as people tend to appreciate visual cues.

As is the case with apps and websites, these emercials are often designed and created by ordinary folks who just want to gain exposure for their product or service. If you have the video and/or digital production, editing, design and directing know-how to create the emercial, you can create the emercial yourself. If you don't, you can always outsource it. (Are you starting to see a theme related to outsourcing, here?) If you don't know how to do video editing, but you have a great speaking voice, you can do your own voice over and have someone else do your editing. Many emercials are done through graphic manipulations and this method is very cost effective (in other words, it's much cheaper to do than you would think). With a little creativity and resourcefulness, you can find a way to make things happen.

Self-Published Books (Including eBooks)

I say this all the time: everyone has at least one book in them. Yes, I'm talking to you, you, and you! Anyone who has lived for any appreciable period of time has had experiences, developed skills, or gained insight into something in which others would likely find some value. Today, becoming a published author takes little more than one's dedication to put the words on paper. So what, you have bad grammar and syntax? Just outsource the editing work to an online editor. So what, you're not able to develop your thoughts into words? You can outsource to a ghostwriter. The days of a would-be author submitting a manuscript to forty publishing houses, only to be rejected by all of them are over. Today, if you have something you want to say, you can just write it, without depending on someone else believing in you or your idea. If you believe in you, you can publish your own book on your own time, using your own money. One stop shop self-publishing companies such a Createspace.com, LuLu.com and Xlibris are very popular companies that help author get their books in all the major book stores. You can do this through a traditional paper book format, or through an electronic format. These days, consumers seek both. For either format, there are several companies out there willing to help you get your publishing business started by helping you expose your writing to the marketplace (e.g., Books-a-Million, Barnes and Noble, Apple's iBooks Store, Amazon, etc.), at a reasonable price. By the way, do you think I wrote and edited this book all by myself? Moving on...

Blogs

Most of us know that the term "blog" is short for "weblog." From this, you have probably gathered, that a blog is some kind of log that one finds on the web. Basically, that's what it is – a log of someone's thoughts, ideas, feelings, travels, happenings, or anything else they'd like to share with the world. Blogs have become so evolved that you may not even realize that some of your favorite websites are really just well-managed blogs – the thoughts and ideas of some individual person who has put these ideas into an organized fashion on the web. Two popular business blog sites are johnchow.com and mattcutts.com. For three examples of popular entertainment-related blogs, see perezhilton,com, and sandrarose.com, bossip.com.

People around the world have set up blogs on any number of subjects, and have become successful in doing so. You may wonder how. They did it by getting so many people interested in their chosen topics that those people come to their blog and spend time actually reading it! Once people land on the blog, there are several ways to convert this traffic into dollars. You can sell merchandise, ask for donations or include ads on the site that produce income for you when someone clicks on them. The better the info you provide on your blog, the better the blog. The better the blog, the more traffic it attracts. Once traffic is increased, the opportunity for income, such as through paid clicks in advertisement is increased as well. For many, operating a blog is an exercise in doing business as a micro-business.

	Micro Business	Traditional Retail Business	Skilled Trade	Professional Services	Multilevel Marketing
Sales Model	Sale of various products and/or information	Sale of products	Sale of services & parts (e.g, plumber, mechanic)	Sale of intellectual services (e.g., lawyer, doctor)	Sale of various products and/or services
Start-Up Funds	Low	Medium to High	Medium to High	Medium to High	Low
Start-Up Process	Quick	Several months to years	Years (training and/or certification	Years (training or certification	Quick
Management	Self and contractors	Employees	Self and/or employees/contractors	Self and/or employees/contractors	Self and, indirectly, "downline"
Market	Globally networked individuals	Local vicinity	Local vicinity and any area to which tradesperson will travel	Local vicinity and any area to which service provider will travel	Those within reach of network (predominantly local)
Human Resources	1 to 5 people (usually 1)	Varies, depending on the store size	Usually 1	1- 10 people, depending on the size of the firm	1, with up to hundreds (or thousands) in "downline" network
Overhead	Low	High	Low to Medium	Low to Medium	Low
Income Model	Sleep money	Sale of products	Sale of trade services, typically on hourly or project basis	Sale of professional services, typically on an hourly or project basis	Sale of products or services. Commissions on the sales of others in "downline" network
Operations	Home-based (may operate wherever Internet is available)	One or more locations	Store front location and significant travel to client sites	Home-based or off-site office	Home-based and significant off-site meetings with network
Tools	Computer Internet	Storefront Cash registers Inventory	Tools for particular service (varies) Computer	Tools for particular service Computer	Educational tools for particular business Sales processing tool

Micro-Business vs. Other Business Types

Low= $0.00 -$3,000   Medium= $3,001 - $15,000   High= $15,001+

I, wholeheartedly, believe in the opportunities that come with starting a micro-business. Some real examples of my micro-businesses are listed below. Most of these businesses were started with less than $1,000 in start-up capital. Some of them were started by one person. But more importantly, none of them were started by someone with technical skills.

Mobile App Companies

iQuick Tools (www.iQuickTools.com)

Online Leaning Management Systems

CTQ Group (www.CTQGroup.com)

eCommerce Websites

The Perfect Contract (www.ThePerfectContract.com)

All About Leases (www.allaboutleases.com)

Website eMercials

Very Simple Ads (www.VerySimpleAds.)

FrugAd (www.FrugAd.com)

Self-Published Books

The App Millionaire (Greg Shealey, Ph.D)

FIT: The Roadmap to a Better Body (Greg Shealey, Ph.D)

Lifestyle Design

Having a successful micro-business is not just about money – it's about lifestyle as well. Imagine having increased productivity that allows you to have more time to spend with your family (when it's your business, you can even work with your children!), more time to spend traveling, and more time to do the things you enjoy doing. To know that you've created something from which you are able to survive and provide for your family is a very rewarding feeling.

People choose to operate these types of businesses for a range of different reasons. For the person who is employed, a micro-business can serve as a means to supplement one's income and build a business, without risking one's primary income source. It represents the opportunity to one day escape corporate America or a wage-earning lifestyle altogether. The micro-business can be developed and built during one's off-work hours, without interfering with that primary income source. That "day job" income can provide the funds needed to get the micro-business off the ground. The business can, then, be operated without the fear and worry that often accompanies joblessness and/or a failing business. Though you may be extremely excited by the prospect of doing your own thing, for some it may be advisable to keep your job while you build your business. With stable income, you will make better long-term choices for the business, not decisions based on fear and the need for immediate revenue. Remember, a micro-business, like any other business, is an experiment – until it works. Do not expect it to immediately yield enough revenue to replace your previous income or support the lifestyle you desire. The goal is to get to the point at which you can count on your business income as your main source of income. Until then, keep your "day job" and do your best to build your business simultaneously.

The person who owns and operates a micro-business is, typically, a person who wants out (or was forced out) of the traditional wage-earning income model, or out of a traditional brick and mortar business. This person seeks a different kind of lifestyle – one with more freedom, flexibility, leisure time and, of course, dollars. It is not uncommon for a recently unemployed person to reinvent himself as a micro-business entrepreneur. For him, the starting of the micro-business may be for the purpose of creating a job for himself, since finding one in the market has not proved possible. His intention may be based solely on the desire to replace the income he once had. Having a business may not be his genuine desire, but he, certainly, likes supporting himself.

For the person who runs a traditional business, a micro-business can offer freedom – freedom from working the business all the time.

Most owners of retail stores (particularly those who operate less than a handful of stores) spend a significant amount of time in the store, finding products and managing staff. I have a couple of friends who own stores and, invariably, they deem their physical presence in the store as critical to the successful functioning of the business. Many storeowners work substantially more hours than any wage-earning employee. Where there is value in having the reward of being one's own boss, there is a major burden associated with feeling like one needs to be in the business all of the time to make sure that it runs properly. A micro-business alleviates that pressure by allowing the business owner flexibility in how and where they choose to work. Additionally, the trouble of managing regular employees is reduced, if not eliminated altogether. As I said before, this does not mean that there is no hard work involved. There is. Your goal, however, is to set yourself up so that you don't have to work as hard over an extended period of time.

Chapter 5

Micro-Business "No-No's"

"The essence of strategy is choosing what not to do."

- Michael Porter, Harvard Business School Professor

There is no sense in you re-inventing the wheel when it comes to developing your micro-business. I have been down that road already, and am glad to share with you what I have learned along the way. Don't make these mistakes.

Giving Up Too Soon

An app development or online business can be quick to start, but it is also fast-changing. So if you only have one product or one idea, it can be hard to earn high profits. It takes time and a lot of patience to get an online micro-business recognized. So often, people give up within just a few months and, sometimes within a few weeks, of opening a micro-business. I've seen it time and time again. They lose their drive and don't have the time or the energy to keep it going. Out of her frustration, my friend almost sold me ThePerfectContract.com for only $750. I saw the value in this start-up, but my friend was prepared to pack her bags and sell me her online business. To her credit, after some encouragement from her colleagues, she decided to give it 2 more months. It was the best decision she ever made. Just a little more marketing took that company from flat to fabulous. Throwing in the towel too early is a common reason for failure of a micro-business.

Don't Dump A Solid Job (Right Away)

Though you love doing your own stuff, it may be necessary to maintain full-time employment to ensure a stable income. Remember, a micro-business, just like any other business, is an experiment in its initial stages. Until you are profitable over a period of time, you cannot count on your micro-business as your main source of income. For most people, managing a full-time job, along with their own business, is a tough routine. It all depends on the level of commitment you have to the business. Often, once the commitment or the motivation fizzles out, the business starts to rapidly decline. Therefore, be very sure to evaluate whether or not you have the necessary motivation and incentive to get going (and keep going) with a micro-business.

Bad Management

"Bad management" is, obviously, a vague term that can include any number of poor choices and/or approaches. In the micro-business context, the term refers to an overall lack of attention and diligence. As I have previously mentioned, treating your new business like a hobby can yield unimpressive results.

Though a micro-business sometimes is not as involved as other full service businesses (in that it does not have high start-up costs, major inventory, etc.), it still needs focus and attention. This is true especially if you want to increase the possibility that your micro-business grows. You are the operator-owner of your business; hence you must make the decisions, and take full responsibility for the outcomes of those decisions. Because a micro-business owner is usually the sole operator, he often finds himself managing a lot of moving parts. From marketing to buying and selling, from monetary transactions to customer service, it all has to be done by him. Lack of focus in any of these areas could lead to failure. One unsatisfied customer can mean trouble for the business. I effective marketing strategies aren't helpful. So, if you start up a micro-business as a sole operator, be prepared for the possibility of rough sailing. Without the right tools, the right motives and the right action plan, success may elude you.

Poor Planning

As with any type of business, in order to succeed, one has to provide something that the market wants. If no one is buying what you're selling (be it a product, service or information), you will not have much of a business. We all know there are no guarantees in life, including in business; it is best that you try to set yourself up for success. Why do they need your product? Why do you think your service is good for them? How will you attract them to your business? Conduct a market analysis that will give you an idea of whether or not what you plan to sell will be marketable. Ask for feedback from knowledgeable friends and associates who will give you an honest opinion. When it comes to the initial planning for your business, this is the most critical area to consider.

Because I'm a serial entrepreneur, over the years several of my friends and colleagues have come to me for my opinion on their business ideas. Full of excitement, they present to me their vision for a business that does not even pass my simple, "Who's gonna buy that?" test. Even if there is a potential market for their business, more often than not, they have not clearly identified their consumer market. This information is too critical to not have seriously contemplated it. Remember, it doesn't need to be an elaborate plan (because micro-businesses don't deal with elaborate plans). There just needs to be some kind of approach for how you will reach your target market.

Failing to Control Costs

You might be surprised by how often new micro-business entrepreneurs let costs get out of hand. This typically happens when one treats the business like a hobby instead of like an enterprise. What tends to happen is that one gets so excited about the project and making it successful, that they simply stop paying attention to the bottom line. They start buying things that they've convinced themselves the business needs, and, sometimes, the costs go unchecked and unanalyzed. More Facebook ads here... more Google Adwords there... add in a fancy new business location and... soon enough, your overhead has become much more than expected.

No matter how you go about defining the term micro-business, the idea to take away from this discussion is that 1) a micro-business is one that is very do-able and 2) a micro-business should be manageable. It is a low-risk, potentially high-yield business vehicle in which anyone can engage if their desire to do so is strong. Often it can be built while you continue in your current employment or continue to operate your existing business. It offers a tremendous amount of income potential, as well as added flexibility and time. In other words, you can make a go of this thing and, it can work. This way of doing business can change your life.

Chapter 6

Business Failure, Business Success

"You cannot afford to wait for perfect conditions. Goal setting is often a matter of balancing timing against available resources. Opportunities are easily lost while waiting for perfect conditions."

- Gary Ryan Blair, Motivational Speaker and Author

As you know, my first business, BioFit and Wellness, was a failure. The failure with Biofit and Wellness did not, however, discourage me from doing business. Even though I was completely in the dumps because of my not-so-successful endeavor, I was still convinced that I wanted to be in business. Sure, I hadn't figured out how to do it, but I wanted to change my life. Having had a taste of what it is like to experience the gratification of bringing my ideas to life and knowing that I controlled the success or failure of my operation was such an intense rush, I knew I no longer wanted to live life under the control of anyone else. I could see the kind of lifestyle that business ownership would afford. I wanted to be my own boss. I wanted to run the show. I wanted the power of freedom. I wanted to control my own destiny.

While being a formal educator wasn't at all a bad way to make a living and express myself through my work, I knew that, for me, it wasn't the optimal method. I wanted to have vast opportunities – limited only by the bounds of my own mind and my own willingness to work. I refused to give up. After the failure, I retreated for a few months until I was able to evaluate what had gone wrong with Biofit and Wellness. After the initial sting of the business collapse was over I looked forward to finding another opportunity – one that I could actually make work.

In the end, if there is one thing I have learned, it is that true business people think differently – even if they have not yet succeeded in business. They recognize that failure should not be considered a losing proposition; f failure just gives one more insight into was doesn't work. If someone truly wants to be a businessperson, he does not give up when he first meets defeat because the bottom line is this: you won't win 'em all. We can and should all learn from failure. Most of us have heard (or experienced first-hand) that the early versions of the Microsoft operating system sucked. Or, that animation giant, Pixar, while under the direction of George Lucas, was on a downward spiral until Steve Jobs tweaked the focus of the company and made it profitable. Now these two companies are industry leaders. There are many well-known stories of businesses and business people who were, initially, colossal failures, but who later turned things around.

My story is no different. In fact, my story is remarkably similar to Justin's, except that, unlike Justin, my first business did not work out so well. Because I was determined to, eventually, succeed in some kind of business, I set out to identify and learn the principles that I needed to adopt to be successful in my future business attempts. I will share with you in this section my personal experiences with particular businesses that I have developed and currently run. My purpose in sharing this information with you is to give you an illustration, using my first-hand experience, of how businesses (and a business portfolio) develop. I also want to give you an idea of how, once certain business principles are learned, they can be applied to a variety of ventures. Going from where you are to where you want to be is as simple as starting the process – making a move. Trust me, there is no better time than the present to position yourself to capitalize on your ideas and seize opportunities.

National Property Institute (www.theNPI.com)

A few years ago, when the real estate market in the Unites States was at the front end of a major uptick, I found myself contemplating an entry into this totally new and dynamic area of work. Remember, with Biofit and Wellness behind me, I was looking for ways to transition in my life. I was hungry. I was eager. But with little capital, it was hardly a time one would call optimal for starting a business.

However, born from a late-night infomercial on real estate investment, National Property Institute was the second business I started - and my first successful one. I'm not kidding; the seed for it came from an infomercial I happened upon on a random sleepless night. As I watched the Robert Kiyosaki program, "Choose to Be Rich," I realized quickly that the real estate industry represented an opportunity for a successful business venture. I'm a natural skeptic but Kiyosaki's infomercial program seemed to make sense. The business plan was well-thought-out and seemed like something I could do. According to the infomercial, people – regular people like me – were making solid incomes as investors in the real estate business. Why couldn't I do it too?

With my ears peaked up and my heart pumping a little faster, I ordered his instructional CD program and listened to it intently several times. The model presented by Kiyosaki looked like one that could work. The steps laid out by the program were logical. It seemed to make good business sense. Buy good quality properties at a low price, add value, create cash flow and later sell at a profit.

Overall, it sought to teach an inexperienced person how to succeed as a real estate investor, using very little cash (but, definitely, some cash). The program stated very clearly that one of the keys to success in the real estate investing industry required tenacity and perseverance and I had that part down. I knew that I had both the stamina and work ethic required and could succeed with a bit of practice and diligence. I also had some start-up capital; not much, but some.

Before making any purchase, I viewed well over 100 properties and I researched four times that amount. My first purchase was a single family, three bedroom, two bathroom house in Decatur, Georgia that needed a good bit of work. All of this was calculated before I selected the house. I was meticulous! Remember, I was a novice investor; I had never been in the business of buying and selling homes. Although my father was in construction, I despised construction work as an adult. I had never even done so much as a major renovation on my own home. I thought everything I knew or even saw about construction was lost from my memories as a young boy. I felt I was learning an industry that was totally new to me. However, what I did have going for me was (1) I believed in myself and my ability to make the business work and (2) certainly, above all else, I would outwork the competition. So whatever I may have lacked in experience, I made up for in sheer grit and work ethic. Within 4 months after first seeing the Kiyosaki infomercial, I purchased my first property and soon after that National Property Institute (NPI) was born.

My initial business model with NPI was threefold. First, I identified properties that were distressed, but had lots of potential. I looked for properties that were in working class neighborhoods, but were in need of some work – particularly aesthetic and finishing work. Second, I would purchase the property, renovate it and refinance it to pull out the equity dollars available (either by virtue of having picked an undervalued property to begin with and/or through the renovations we did). Lastly, I would secure a renter for the house, whose monthly rental payment exceeded the amount I was paying in mortgage and taxes for the home. This is what is meant by "cash flowing" a property. I set-up this cash flow system using the monthly rental income, and would apply the difference toward the purchase of other properties. After renovating the property, I would refinance the house at the higher appraisal value. Then, I used the refinance dollars to finance the purchase of other houses, and, thus, continue to build the business. My overall strategy was to buy and hold. At that time, "flipping" did not appeal to me because I was seeking long-term assets and an increased personal net worth.[1] I could then leverage a solid net worth in other transactions. Slowly, I was building a business in

---

1 "Flipping" refers to the process of purchasing a house, renovating it, then quickly selling off at the higher appraisal price.

which I was a landlord and asset manager.

I continued to purchase, renovate, and hold houses in a landlord capacity – and I did well. Over time one thing became clear; a good bit of money could be made from the renovation portion of the process, without having to deal with the trouble that comes with managing assets on an ongoing basis and/or dealing with tenants. I discovered this by accident. On occasions when my renovation crews were working on my own projects, owners of neighboring homes would ask me if I would be willing to renovate their homes. Emphatically, my answer would be "absolutely not." I had no interest in renovating other people's homes. After all, I was not in construction per se. I was a landlord and asset manager.

After the bad childhood experiences with my family's business, I barely wanted to deal with the renovations of the homes in my own portfolio. I definitely did not want the headache of dealing with anxious homeowners with unreasonable expectations. But then... I woke up. What was I thinking? This low-hanging fruit presented an excellent opportunity for my company. By not seizing these opportunities, I was breaking one of my own fundamental rules. As I always say, "Go after the money!"

Having done the renovation process several times at this point, I had a team of skilled professionals that did great work. These workers knew my expectations, and would give me good prices because of our existing relationship and the prospect of more work. With the knowledge I gained and a strong team, I could do house rehabilitation work without actually purchasing and owning the homes myself. This would take little to no adjustment to my existing business model. Why not go for it? I did.

I started renovating the houses of individual homeowners, in addition to maintaining my own asset portfolio. The more jobs we got under the company belt, the more proficient and efficient we became at the process. During any given month, I would have up to six or seven rehab projects going on, while still managing and rehabbing the properties my company owned. Overtime as we got my team got better, I felt comfortable in pursuing the ultimate client - the government. This has evolved into the bread and butter of my business. I quickly began renovating houses for county, city, state and even federal government agencies. The company took off faster than I could have imagined. You never know where your life may take you. I was fully in the business that I loathed as a young boy. I was fully entrenched in the construction field.

As I said, I started off wanting to be an investor. However, I transitioned into being a contractor and, soon, the operator of a full-fledged contracting company. I had not set out to be a contractor and, in fact, I would not have even imagined that I would end up going from being a classroom educator to a work boot, jean-wearing construction guy. When I look back on the whole process, I see that even though it wasn't planned out, it involved a series of logical next steps - each of which moved me from one thing to the next good thing. As I gained familiarity and exposure to one area of work, I was able to identify ways to better position myself and my company. For example, if I had not been seen renovating my own properties, I would not have been exposed to individuals who would ask me if I would be willing to work on their homes. While doing one thing, an opportunity arose to do another. Had I not gotten heavily involved in the general contracting business, I would not have seen the opportunity in doing this kind of work for the government. Once I saw steady growth in my business from government contracting, I was forced to become more efficient. From the need to become more efficient, I was determined to get into mobile app development.

Over time I realized that, with more efficient operations, I could be highly competitive, without becoming an organization drowning in overhead and administrative red tape. I just had to find a way to use my time more effectively – to run a more nimble operation. As the company was growing, I quickly determined that there had to be a better way to get bids estimated and submitted without me having to physically go home and put pen to paper each time. The rapid growth of NPI forced me to think of a better solution. This is how my mobile app development company, iQuick Tools, came into being.

iQuick Tools for Estimating (www.iquicktools.com)

It started as an elaborate office-type spreadsheet that I would use on my phone when I was on site. I could quickly plug in the project specifications, and, based on the formulas in the spreadsheet, I could determine, almost immediately, what my estimated costs would be for the project and whether it was one on which the company should bid. I no longer needed to go home to prepare bids because, with my calculations in hand, I could submit a bid to a potential client, using the e-mail account attached to my Smartphone. During pre-bid meetings and project walkthroughs, my fellow competitors noticed that I didn't arrive on site with pen and paper – just the spreadsheet on my Smartphone. Several of them asked me – flat out – "How can I get that?" Can you say "light bulb moment"? I had in my possession something in which others found value. Surely, they'd be willing to pay for it.

Would they really want to pay for a spreadsheet, though? Yes, it was helping me be very efficient, but even I found the spreadsheet to be cumbersome to maneuver through and manipulate. Having it conveniently on my phone was awesome, but scrolling from cell to cell on a hand-held device was not. Being the business information junkie that I am, I was aware that there was an emerging industry, specifically related to the development of applications for Smartphones. I had seen a documentary on how developers in this niche were making tremendous income developing apps for these devices. It became obvious to me that if I wanted to optimize my phone to improve my work, I ought to use a platform designed specifically for the phone.

While I did not have the technical know-how to actually build an app and make it operable, what I did have was the real world experience that gave me informed insight on how to build a tool that would be useful to someone like me – someone in the construction industry. I knew what calculations I used most often on projects sites. I knew what information I needed most when trying to get bids done quickly and efficiently. I already had the elaborate spreadsheet I had been using, so that gave me the basis for the calculations that would be embedded into the app. I also had some familiarity with apps that I had on my phone and how they functioned, so, once I spent some time seriously thinking about the functionality of the tool I wanted to create, I had a clear picture of what I wanted. I knew how I wanted it to look, what I wanted to see on various pages of the tool, and what kind of outputs the tool would produce. What I didn't know, however, was how to make the picture I had in my mind, appear as a workable tool on a Smartphone.

I've made it clear by now that I'm not a techie nerd, right? So, I knew that there was no way that I would even think about learning how to code mobile apps. First of all, I didn't have that kind of time. Secondly, I had no interest in learning how to do it. I just wanted to create the app and needed someone to help me do it. The bottom line is this: I have neither the time nor the interest in developing and mastering the skills needed to make my projects successful. (Who really does?) The skill I need more than any other is the ability to assemble teams that can get the job done, under my vision, guidance and direction. Remember, with my full service business NPI, I was definitely a "construction guy," however, I had very little skill in doing construction work myself. Plumbing? Ehhh, I know a little something. Electricity? Hmmm, I know enough to not get electrocuted. HVAC? Forget about it. With each of these skilled trades, what I learned was who I worked well with and how much it would cost me in each instance to get the level of work quality I needed from these people in the timeframe by which I needed it.

Taking the advice of Tim Ferriss, the author of *The 4-Hour Work Week*, I began to research outsourcing options for the development of the mobile app. Elance.com proved to be a remarkable tool that put me in contact with potential app developers all over the world – from India to Russia, China, and the United States, as well. It was exciting to see how many contractors quickly responded to my request for proposals. Communicating back and forth with these potential contractors was enlightening: I was learning how to do business differently... Globally.

My first completed app was iQuick estimator – a simple estimating tool that included various estimators for flooring, concrete, paint, roofing, framing and miscellaneous services. It was designed for the small contractor who needs to make quick calculations. The app is not at all complex. It is a tool that can be used "on the go" by anyone needing to create estimations on a construction project.

As with any endeavor, the majority of the true learning comes from the doing. As a businessman, I am in a constant state of improving and learning what works well and what does not. There are, however, some very clear lessons I learned through earlier stages of my app business that I've continued to build upon over the years.

My method for starting and building my app business, iQuick Tools, was similar to the one I applied with NPI – I started by studying, then I built upon what I already knew. Most of my initial apps were within the same family – the same "space," as I like to call it. Since I knew construction and businesses, I built various apps that would be of value to those looking for tools relating to those industries. So, instead of having one app that related to, for example, accounting, another that related to concrete and another that related to goal setting, I focused on the area that I knew best and made various apps within that one genre. I made the apps robust enough to be useful to construction professionals but simple enough to be used by anyone embarking on a home remodeling project. Then, instead of limiting myself to just the Apple platform, I expanded to the Android platform as well. Again, same product, just packaged differently.

What Works?

Identifying and Focusing on Common Needs

My focus was on what the majority of people would find useful. In doing this, I recognized that there would be potential consumers that would not find my product attractive or valuable. For example, those who worked on very unique projects that required unusual or complicated calculations would probably find my apps to be over simplified.

Those on the other end of the spectrum, whose home projects would be considered more as arts and crafts than as construction, would deem my apps to be too complex. I did not concern myself with those on the far ends of the spectrum. I followed the model that Apple has successfully applied for years – keep it simple and concentrate on the majority.

Developing for the World, Not Just Your Country

Incorporating the metric system exponentially added to the reach and utility of my apps. Even though the metric system was not one that I grew up using or that is generally used in the United States, it is the predominant system in many other countries around the world. When I upgraded my apps to include the metric system into my app development, I significantly increased the number of people who could use the product. Sales quickly increased and my ratings were more positive.

Staying Focused

Even though I have had several ideas for apps outside of the construction and real estate genres, at the time of the writing of this book, I have not made the development of them a priority. Instead, I focused on more and better apps for the construction industry. By going about it this way, my company has become recognized as an authority on apps for the construction and real estate industries. Several large companies that provide products for homes, like flooring and windows, have solicited my help in creating apps for their companies. Staying focused on these areas has helped me develop better products and expand my expertise. I wholly subscribe to Steve Jobs' philosophy, as stated in a 1998 *BusinessWeek* interview, "... That's been one of my mantras - focus and simplicity. Simple can be harder than complex: You have to work hard to get your thinking clean to make it simple. But it's worth it in the end because once you get there, you can move mountains."

Thinking Outside of the Box

Since a mobile app business is a wholly different type of business as compared to construction, I had to rethink my approach to marketing and advertising; I had to find different ways to connect with my customers, who would be geographically further than the customers with which I had been dealing under NPI. I set out to learn how mobile products were being marketed by other app companies. What seemed to be working? What was not? My goal was to merge what I already knew about traditional marketing with new methods and approaches. To go with my online product, I created a strong online presence. I became well-versed in the use of social networking tools like Facebook and Twitter. I saw that some app companies were using giveaways to promote their apps and it seemed to produce impressive results. So, what did I do? I copied them and did the same thing with my apps. I had never done a press release for NPI, but, with this different type of business, I knew I had to reach people in a different manner.

Self-Promotion

I cannot stress this enough. Talking about your products, services and skills is extremely important. You are your business. You must be prepared to talk about it at any given moment. Share your excitement about what you have to offer with those with whom you come into contact. My friends often harass me about how I'm always eager and ready to promote my projects. I even ask the ladies who work at the counter at the smoothie shop I frequent to download my apps and tell me what they think. I don't care! I make no apologies for being excited about the work I do and being proud of the products I bring to the market. Listen here: if you're not excited about your stuff, who will be? Furthermore, if you're not talking about it, you're missing valuable opportunities to increase your business success.

What Doesn't Work?

Mimicking Desktop Applications

By trying to mirror desktop applications, one can quickly lose the interest of an app customer. The mobile app environment is a different environment – one with greater limits of screen real estate and movement. By virtue of it being on a handheld device, the user's attention is limited and often narrowly focused. With mobile apps, you have approximately 30 seconds - from the time the user first opens the app – to win the person over. If you fail to grab their attention within this short window of time, you risk the user closing your app, giving you a bad rating, forgetting who you are, and never using it again. Therefore, the app cannot be one that requires the attention that one might have while working on a computer. Since there's no ability to use a mouse, the app cannot require complex navigation, which would be more acceptable on a desktop.

Too Complex

The purpose of a mobile app is to give the user valuable information quickly. Therefore, the app should not be too involved, requiring extensive instruction or guesswork. It has to be designed for a person with an average to low level of technical experience to be able to quickly figure out how to get desired information from the app. If getting that takes too long, the opportunity to connect with the user can be lost.

Complex App Names

Having a long app name is something I would not advise. When it comes to this part of the project, I learned that simple is best. At iQuick Tools, I did not reinvent the wheel. I simply continued to improve upon my own ideas and products, a process that has become commonplace in today's business world. Take Robert Kiyosaki, for example. His original *Rich Dad Poor Dad* book has evolved into a franchise that includes dozens of books and other products. Each of them relates, in some fashion, to the foundational premises of the book, but the products and services target different markets and offer different tools. This is, precisely, the approach I have taken with my app business.

Rock City Birds! and Monkeys & Bananas

A business principle is one that can be applied to a range of different businesses, but be expected to produce a similar outcome. In expanding the scope of my app business, the principle I applied was the following: make something that is already good... better. The idea for Rock City Birds! came from the extraordinary success of Rovio Mobile with the Angry Birds franchise and Half Brick with the Fruit Ninja Smartphone game. For a small mobile app development company to reach profits of $1,000,000 per year is pretty good. But for such a company to profit $6,000,000 per month is mind-blowing! Before I ever considered developing a game of my own, my curiosity simply from a business standpoint, was how these companies had developed such successful products. True to form, I began to study.

In gist, what these companies did was keep things simple. Instead of focusing on the development of a complex game strategy, they made a beautiful looking product – something that people enjoyed looking at. They also created a product that could be used and enjoyed by a range of people – not just people who tend to play games. The games are simple enough that anyone in just a few seconds can easily figure out how to play and could pass the time doing so. Who would have thought that such simple games could be so widely successful all over the world?

One of my goals is to build a portfolio that consists of businesses that do not rely solely on the success of any one particular market (i.e., businesses that have global reach), so coming up with a game seemed like a great idea. Since Rovio and Half Brick designed a blueprint for how to do it well, I designed a plan that followed their lead. My games would (1) have beautiful graphics, (2) be easy to play and (3) appeal to a very wide range of individuals.

I spent about 9 months thinking about the Rock City Birds! concept and 4 months making Monkeys and Bananas. Unlike the estimator apps I developed, these game apps would be different because they would not appeal primarily to people in a particular industry. They would have to appeal to people of a range of ages, sexes and interests. Once I had a general idea of the game concepts, instead of focusing primarily on the functionality of the game (as I did with my estimator apps), I focused on how I would market the apps. How would I, having no experience in developing games for a smartphone, get people interested in playing these games? What would be an engaging story? How would I get people to love these games?

I solicited the help of some overseas developers and, over a period of 9 months or so, created the Rock City Birds! game for iPhone and iPad. Again, I did not reinvent the wheel. I did what had been demonstrated to work. Beautiful graphics? Check. Easy to play? Check. Can easily be understood by individuals in a variety of languages and countries? Check. Check. Check. The process involved a lot of Skype conferences with my developers and, let me honest, quite a bit of frustration. As I have said several times, being an entrepreneur is work. Don't let anyone tell you otherwise. It's just a matter of whether or not the same level of work will continue throughout the operation of the business, or whether you will properly design a system that will make the work less strenuous over a period of time. Getting Rock City Birds! to look and function properly was an exercise in patience, diligence and extraordinary project management. Sometimes my developers would engage in what I call "freestyle coding," where they would totally veer off the design plan that we had developed. I would have to reel them in to keep them on track with the vision that I had for the game. Or, they would be late in delivering a version of the app, which would slow the development process for days or weeks. Then, of course, there were times when I, being distracted with other businesses, would inadvertently miss some modification that needed to be made, which would require design changes that could have been made earlier in the process. Getting Rock City Birds! from idea to fruition was a helluva lot of work, however, to date, it has been the most fun I had during the development phase.

Very Simple Ads (VSA) and FrugAds
(www.VerySimpleAds.com *and* www.FrugAds.com*)*

With Very Simple Ads, I found something good and...made it better. Have you ever seen those animated ads that Google uses to explain their new services – like those for Google Checkout and Google Voice? Or, those short and concise emercials that Groupon uses on their website? That's what I have termed a "Very Simple Ad," also known "VSA." What I have noticed is that, in this economy, where even large corporations seek to cut marketing costs, affordable and effective advertising is critical to the success of a business. Lean, but powerful, advertising campaigns have replaced many big budget, hit or miss programs. With the prevalence of the Internet and social media in today's culture, companies are utilizing methods of communicating to and connecting with customers that were once considered too edgy, but are now considered necessary.

Seeing this trend toward unconventional advertising, it seemed that putting together a business that would make great-looking animated advertisements for regular business owners at a great price would be a good idea. As was the case with NPI and with iQuick Tools, I knew nothing – NOTHING! – about the advertising business. I have never taken so much as an introductory marketing course in college. All I knew was that there appeared to be an emerging trend toward businesses reaching out to customers and clients using this unique and creative medium. I wanted to see how I could capitalize on that by providing value for other business owners like myself. Remember, part of my success in creating my first apps was that I was familiar with the industry and understood what kinds of tools would be helpful to someone in that industry. So, while I did not know anything about the advertising business, I did know about business, in general, and how it is to be a business owner in need of affordable advertising solutions. From this perspective, I could relate to my potential customers and provide them with the type of product that I would use in my own businesses.

Again, through NPI, I learned how to run a successful contracting business, without having been a skilled tradesman myself. I became adept at building and managing teams of people who had the skills I needed for my projects, even though I did not possess those skills myself. By developing apps, I refined that way of doing business. I would come up with the ideas, and I would find people with whom I could work with and would help me execute those ideas. With Very Simple Ads, my process was the same. Having developed several apps by this time, I had become a pro at finding contractors on Elance. With VSA, I, once again, sought individuals who could help me bring my vision to life.

Once the concept was clear in my mind – a completely online company that provides short (i.e., between 30 seconds and 10 minutes) animated ads for businesses and individuals at a fraction of the price that they would pay to a larger or more traditional advertising company – I found someone on Elance who could create the animated pieces at a price that was low enough to allow me to charge reasonable prices to my customers, but high enough to ensure the quality that I required. Within a period of 3 months, VSA went from conception to fruition.

To capitalize on economies of scale, I created inter-competition for VSA, before things with VSA were even finalized. That's when I started working on FrugAds. I was developing two companies that provided functionally the same service, but would target two different markets. I adopted the business model of auto manufacturers – I created two similar, but different, products that would appeal to two different markets. Most of the large auto manufacturers have both a "practical" line of automobiles as well as a luxury line of automobiles. For the person who wants more pizzazz and comfort, Toyota makes Lexus. For those who do not need some of the extras provided by Lexus (and who do not want to pay the cost of a Lexus), a Toyota Camry is just fine. In my business portfolio, VSA is my Lexus and FrugAds is my Camry. While both businesses provide reasonably-priced animated advertising, the latter is a lower-priced, less frills opportunity for those with very small budgets. Remember, these companies were created at the very same time. Each was designed slightly differently in terms of website and business model, in order to appeal to different markets.

Working with offshore developers was much easier on this project than it was on the Rock City Birds! or Monkeys and Bananas game project. While the ongoing operations model was more involved (meaning that there would be more ongoing interacting with customers), the general business model was simpler. The business would be entirely online, so having comprehensive and functional websites for each was the most critical element. With a robust website in place, potential customers would (1) learn about the business, (2) view samples of our work (i.e., the VSAs put together by my overseas developers), (3) order either an ad with customized features (through Very Simple Ads) or one with standard features (through FrugAds), and (4) have the finished ad delivered directly to their inbox. Getting the websites set-up was much, much easier than building a mobile game app.

My biggest challenge with VSA and FrugAds was creating two such similar companies that were still different. To do that in an organic fashion, I assembled two separate teams, explained to each the particular concept on which they were to work, and had them develop ideas independently of one another. Neither team interacted with the other. In essence, it was one business model, with two different looks and feels. These companies had to legitimately compete with one another. We had to approach the process as if the two entities were truly fighting to secure their space in the marketplace. Going about the business development process in this manner was fun.

VSA and FrugAds have proven to be both profitable micro-businesses as well as creative outlets for me. While I don't play an active role in getting each of our customer's ads designed (my team does that for me), I do enjoy participating in the process when time permits. What I love about these businesses is that they have provided further confirmation that not having experience in a particular industry does not have to be a barrier to your entry into it. If it's an industry worth getting into, you just have to learn the best means to get there. Notice that my entry into the advertising world was through a micro-business. I did not attempt to set-up a traditional marketing agency to compete with agencies that have been in business for decades. I stuck with an emerging form of advertising that is web-based that did not have a large amount of competition. I went into something that was consistent with my business philosophy and that was a manageable micro-business. It turned out to be a great decision.

CTQ – Critical to Quality

Critical to Quality (CTQ) is another idea that emerged out of my observations of a changed economic climate and corresponding market trends. As we all know, in recent years, many people have found themselves out of work and in need of additional or new skills. It's tough out there these days. Many jobs are being outsourced, so even highly-skilled people feel the need to be more competitive. Even for highly-skilled workers, there is no such thing as job security – it doesn't exist anymore. People are seeking to reinvent themselves, transition, and create alternative ways of generating and/or increasing their income. With the prevalence of technology as a tool, schools and educational companies are making skills training programs more flexible and accessible to those who are unable to embark upon a traditional educational path – often due to time and/or financial limitations. Training courses ranging from associate's degrees to Ph.Ds are being offered online, as well as various certificate and certification programs. CTQ is another one of those programs.

CTQ offers an online Six Sigma certification that one can earn either by taking the full online course, or by simply taking and passing the certification exam. Six Sigma is a popular quality control methodology that many companies use to streamline operations and control costs. With a Six Sigma certification, there are, generally, four levels of achievement that can be attained –Yellow Belt, Green Belt, Black Belt and Master Black Belt. When I found out that there is no standard certification test for any Six Sigma certification, I had another "light bulb" moment. Since one can develop their own certification test, as long as it adequately addresses each of the essential elements of the certification, that's what we did – we created our own.

It seemed clear to me that there was a plethora of individuals looking for an affordable, convenient means by which to enhance their skills.

I did not, however, rely solely on my "gut" feeling and casual observations. In deciding to create CTQ, I researched the market thoroughly. Who would be in need of such a program? What companies and organizations were already supplying the product? What would make someone want to buy my program? Most importantly, how much would they be willing to pay for it?

In my research, I found that there were way more Six Sigma programs being offered in the traditional classroom setting than in an online setting. Knowing that many executives and other busy adults do not have the time in their schedules to attend a series of structured courses, I knew that for this type of program, the online vehicle presented an excellent opportunity.

Though CTQ is not my favorite among my micro-businesses (just being honest here), it has proven to be a terrific idea for a bad economy. From a business operations standpoint, CTQ fit well into my typical business model – low overhead, internet-based, and low maintenance. Once the product was developed, it could be used and sold repeatedly. As with my apps, this one product could be useful to a range of individuals in locations around the world. With it being internet-based, my potential market was much larger than it would be if I were conducting local courses. I could reach people who were in different geographic locations and who are unable to attend courses during typical class time hours. Additionally, developing CTQ would not require me or any member of my team to go out and acquire a new set of skills – we could simply expand on existing knowledge. Having a team member with a strong Six Sigma background was the foundation for the building of the online product. I surround myself with intelligent, productive people and, in doing so, I am able to draw upon the various skills and abilities they bring to the table. I have mentioned previously the importance of knowing how to assemble and effectively utilize human resources. Without applying this principle, CTQ would have not have come into being.

My biggest challenge with CTQ was in creating the project infrastructure. Much of the development would be outsourced (i.e., the training module system, the voice over work, and the payment system), but I had to put together a project plan that would successfully pull together each of these moving parts. When I first got the idea, I jotted it down on a napkin in a restaurant. After that, I developed a detailed PowerPoint presentation, so that I was clear on the various steps that needed to be taken and when these steps should be taken. Remember the quote I mentioned by Steve Jobs about clarity? My purpose for going through the process of creating the PowerPoint presentation was to make sure that I was not overcomplicating things. I wanted to make sure that I truly understood what the heck I was talking about. Once I had a presentation ready, I showed it to some business savvy friends of mine to see if my idea made sense to someone besides myself. This was no formal process; I did this while my friends were at my house for a Super Bowl party. With confirmation that I was on the right track and that my idea made sense, I was able to create a detailed project plan for CTQ.

With so many moving parts involved, CTQ's development was far from linear; multiple things were happening simultaneously. While the website was being developed, we worked on the content pages. As the content pages were being developed, we were interviewing voice over professionals who could provide the audio content. Some portions of the project went slower than expected. When the voice over artist prepared the audio files in the wrong format, our time frame was pushed back by a few weeks. When there was a glitch in functionality of content slides in the course portal, fixing the matter involved a series of Skype meetings with our developer in Indonesia. As was the case in each of my prior businesses, the upfront legwork was extensive. Lots of time was spent developing the idea and communicating it with clarity to the team (including the offshore team members), and making the system functional. Over a period of 8 months, there were a slew of Skype conference calls, even more chats, emails, and many revisions to and "do overs" when it came to the content. In short, we busted our asses to get the thing up, running and profitable. But as I've said over and over, once the business system was in place, the amount of work required was considerably reduced.

App Millionaire's Greatest Concern – The What

Here's what you should take away from this conversation: Again, an App Millionaire's greatest concern is not how to go about taking a particular course of action, but whether or not the particular course of action should be taken at all. Notice that with several of my businesses, I did not have any direct experience in that field. Before starting NPI, I was an educator. I didn't have any experience investing in real estate. Before building apps, I had zero experience in and a virtually non-existent technical background (I actually had to buy a Mac computer while developing my first app because I didn't know that I wouldn't be able to see the app on other platforms). Along the way, there was plenty that I needed to learn. However, when building my first apps, I had a strong understanding of my target market because I was a member of it. With Rock City Birds! and Monkeys and Bananas, I knew nothing about the target market, and made it my business (pun intended) to learn enough about the market to make my vision come to life. Once I determined that a certain course of action ought to be taken, it was then that I went about figuring how to do it. The key is not letting the learning process seem so daunting that you're discouraged to move forward. Know that learning is just a part of the process. Be ready for it.

After identifying certain business principles, I learned to apply these principles to each of my business endeavors. Once I learned to operate under certain principles, I was able to apply these to a variety of areas. Notice that, after NPI, my businesses had common elements: (1) they were low maintenance, (2) they capitalized on a recessionary economy, and (3) outsourcing was used to develop them. Notice also that my business portfolio, even when you take NPI into account, is diversified. On no given day and in no given year are all my eggs in any one basket. Some of my apps are for business, and others are for causal gamers, two completely different target groups. If one business is slow, the other businesses can pick up the slack. If my creative juices are flowing more in one area, I focus on that area and let the others coast along until I am able to redirect my focus to them. There is a certain level of balance and juggling that goes along with all of this.

Sure, I always give some level of attention to each of my businesses. At certain times, however, some projects get much more attention than others. My model is set-up to function in a manner that my businesses can continue to run and generate income, even if I am not focusing directly on them. That is the beauty of the micro-business.

Notice how my progression was similar to that of Justin's: I started out as a traditional Joe Schmo educator. From the knowledge gained through that traditional, local business, I created a micro-business that had global reach. I started with one thing, which led to another, and then another. You, however, can skip some of the steps that both Justin and I took. With what you learn in this book, you can skip the step of a traditional business and move immediately into a micro-business operation that is systematized, profitable, low maintenance and global. It doesn't need to take long, either.

Let me assure you: As you learn more about business, in general, things get easier, the further along you go. Once you learn how to successfully run one business, the principles you applied to succeed in that business can be applied to your other businesses. Inevitably, you will learn from your mistakes. The key is getting started. Do something! Pay attention to what is going on in the market, consider what you know and what you're good at doing, and develop an idea that will provide value to the marketplace. Do not get wrapped up in how you will go about doing it. First, figure out if you have a good idea that can be profitable. Remember: think about keeping overhead low, keeping the business low maintenance (which is why I wholeheartedly believe in micro-businesses), and finding a way for your product or service to reach a large range of people. I strongly recommend that you not limit yourself to your geographical area. These days, there are just too many opportunities for global business to limit yourself in such a way.

Chapter 7

Base Hits and Other Realistic Expectations

"Dreaming is one thing, and working towards the dream is one thing, but working with expectations in mind is very self-defeating."

- Michael Landon, American Actor, Writer, Director and Producer

"I want to win every race, but I know that's not possible."

- Roger Staubach, Heisman Trophy Winner, Former Dallas Cowboy Quarterback and Hall of Fame NFL Quarterback

A common theme I've noticed among many would-be entrepreneurs is unrealistic expectations. They fail to act because they envision a certain outcome. To the extent that they feel uncertain about their ability to achieve that outcome, they do nothing – or virtually nothing. Instead, they read more, plan more, analyze more, talk about it more, and ponder on the idea. What they really should be doing is acting on their idea. "What if it's a flop?" they ask themselves. "What if I lose everything and everyone who had doubted me says, 'I told you so'?" They get paralyzed by their fear of not achieving a particular, expected outcome. Sure, it is extremely important to start an endeavor with an end goal in mind. Even though that end point often gets modified along the way, I still know that it is important to know what one's desired destination is before embarking upon a particular path. I acknowledge and embrace that. I also acknowledge the important role that a healthy level of fear can play in motivating one to act. When that fear, however, is at a level that becomes paralyzing, there is a problem. One's commitment to a desired result should not keep them from taking necessary action.

Many new app developers set out to produce a mobile app with the same level of success as the popular Angry Birds. (It is reported that in 2012, "Angry Birds Space" was downloaded 50 million times within the first 35 days of its launch.) Success like this is, obviously, achievable – given the fact that it has been done – but it is very uncommon. When you look in the Apple App Store or the Android Play Store, what do you see? Of course, you see the Angry Birds, Fruit Ninjas, and Cut the Ropes of the world, but what else do you see? Thousands of apps that are totally unrecognizable. They may not be popular apps, but they might be… profitable apps. They may not produce millions of dollars each year for their makers, but… they may produce several thousands of dollars a year for their makers. Most of us would, of course, prefer to have a project produce millions; but would you throw it away if only produced thousands? That's my point. The reality is that not everyone will produce a Facebook or an Instagram. But that doesn't mean that producing isn't a worthwhile and profitable thing to do.

It's easier to produce projects that create thousands. That's the bottom line. These projects can be mobile apps, desktop apps, Facebook apps, or other micro-businesses that produce sleep money. The more of those projects you produce, the more likely you are to earn thousands. Get the idea of achieving mammoth success out of your mind. Why? Because it can be debilitating. Hold tight to the idea of achieving consistent, productive results over a period of time. Why? Because that's something you know that you're able to accomplish. If the mammoth results occur, then you've received the best icing on the cake that you could possibly imagine. If those results do not occur, you've still achieved something – something that has, hopefully, put substantial money in your pocket.

If you think I'm being cynical, look at it this way: what is the likelihood that Mark Zuckerberg knew, before starting what was initially called "The Facebook," that it would change the way the world communicates and, as a result, he would become the youngest billionaire in history? Do you think that was his aim when he started? If you are familiar with his story, you know that was not his aim at all. Do you think that when Bill Gates dropped out of Harvard University as an undergrad to pursue his idea of creating a home computer, that he knew he would, at one point, be the richest man in the world? What is the likelihood of that? These results were unexpected and incidental to the fact that what mattered most was producing the product. I am certain that the possibility of not becoming the youngest billionaire in the world would not have stopped Mr. Zuckerberg from following his idea.

Here's my point: don't always expect extraordinary results. If you get them, *great*. However, if you don't, you still will have achieved results of some kind. I suggest that you aim to make consistent, reliable returns on multiple projects that you can run simultaneously. What you're aiming for is a series of base hits; not a grand slam. Over time, those base hits will become the strong foundation of a solid enterprise. (By the way, did you know that "Angry Birds" was the 52nd game developed by Rovio Entertainment? None of the games that they developed prior to that became particularly popular. Notice that they didn't stop making games after the first 30, 40, or, even, 50 weren't hugely successful. Even *they* lived off of the base hits until they hit their grand slam). Perhaps you'll come up with a grand slam idea at some point, but don't just focus on that. Focus on your ability to accomplish realistic goals over a period of time and maybe a grand slam will occur.

Consider this: You develop your first app and, after 6 months, it consistently produces $25 per day. Using a 30-day month, that is $750 of revenue per month on this one app. Is that a lot of money? To most of us, it's not. Assume that your initial development costs for the app were $2,000 and that, over the 6-month period, the app has already fully recouped your initial investment.

Now imagine that you take that same app and put it on an alternative platform. This time, your development costs are lower because the app had already been done on another platform. In this case, then, let's say that you recoup your initial development costs to put the app on the alternative platform within a period of 3 months, instead of six. So, by month 9, everything you earn from both of these apps will be sheer profit. If they each earn $750/per month, you're earning $1,500 per month on just these two apps. (These figures are reasonable, by the way.)

Ok. Let's take another step. Let's say you repeat that same process and develop five more apps and, in short order, they start to perform at the same level as the others. At this point, with 7 apps under your belt, you would be making $5,250 per month. Is this starting to get your attention? After you have them up and available in the app stores, you wouldn't be doing much work at all. Wouldn't you like to earn that sleep money, on a monthly, repeated basis, without having to work for it every month?

To take our scenario even further, let's say you build over 30 apps over 3 years at an average development cost of $2,000. If you develop 10 apps per year, your development cost would average $20,000 per year, for a total of $60,000 over the 3-year period. If we continue to assume that the development costs of each app are recouped within 3 months, and each earns an average of $25 per day, once all the apps are done, you would get to the point of making $750 of sleep money per day. That's $22,500 per month, and $273,750 per year!

Now, imagine you were to have 60, 90, or 200 apps in your portfolio. Or, you could even have one group of apps that you duplicate on the Apple, Android, Microsoft Mobile and Blackberry IOS systems. With this model, you've become highly efficient, having duplicated your efforts without having to reinvent the wheel.

Do these figures seem unrealistic or outrageous? They're not. Over a period of 3 years, I developed 32 apps, while operating my full-service construction company. Remember, I'm no special guy. If I can do 32 of them over a period of three years, I don't doubt that you could do

30. Now, do my apps produce anywhere near the amount of money that Angry Birds produces in a month? Hardly. But, producing your money this way, through several different apps, is much easier than producing one Angry Birds.

Notice an underlying theme through all of this? By creating multiple products and putting them to work for you at the same time, you are not only creating multiple streams of income; you are also duplicating your efforts without starting from scratch each time. You are efficiently utilizing your time and resources by capitalizing on what you already have and what you already know. Once properly developed, apps require minimal maintenance. So, what you ultimately have is a low-maintenance system that continues to produce, even when you aren't putting much effort into it.

Again, on an individual basis, your apps (or projects) may not be a grand slam. In the aggregate, however, they can be a nice home run. The key is to build, little by little (as I say, "move it forward"), and develop your portfolio until you have a slew of profitable projects.

This is the business model under which I operate – multiple projects, producing at the same time. I am constantly in a state of thinking up new ideas for apps and refining the existing apps to the extent that I need to. I am constantly developing projects because I enjoy doing it. If I did not enjoy it, however, I could very well rely solely on the apps I've developed thus far, and simply live off of the sleep money that they produce for me. They are already complete and on the market. So, if I decided not to touch them again, they would still be available on the market for anyone to purchase. I just choose not to do that.

None of the apps I've built thus far have come anywhere near the success of Angry Birds or Fruit Ninja. I don't need them to, although I would like that. I simply need them to be profitable. And all of them are. Sure, I would love to one day create an app that produces millions of dollars for me in a period of months. If I don't, however, I am still making the kind of money that affords for me the lifestyle that I enjoy.

The micro-business model makes business easier. That's not to say that there isn't plenty of work to be done or that you won't have to work hard to make the business succeed. You just, in most cases, would not have to work as hard as you would in a traditional business setting. I say this from experience. And I know what I'm talking about.

PART II
THE CAVALRY

"Leadership is the art of getting someone else to do something you want done because he wants to do it."

- Dwight Eisenhower, 34th President of the United States

"The very essence of leadership is that you have to have a vision. It's got to be a vision you articulate clearly and forcefully on every occasion. You can't blow an uncertain trumpet."

- Reverend Theodore Hesburgh, President Emeritus, University of Notre Dame

Chapter 8

Master vs. Mastermind

"When you hire people who are smarter than you are, you prove you are smarter than they are."

- R.H. Grant, Canadian Farmer and Politician

Do you remember the old Bruce Lee movies from the 1970s? In classics like *Fist of Fury*, *Game of Death*, and *Enter the Dragon*, there was always both a master (usually played by Lee) and a mastermind. The master was the one who possessed superb skill while the other, the mastermind, orchestrated the skills of others. The word "master" conjures up images of a prolific expert at the very top of his game. He is wise. He has outthought, outperformed and outshined all of his competitors. He is the go-to guy in his discipline – the leader of the pack. He can tell you from where the art originated and execute every single move to perfection. He has an intimate understanding of and respect for both the art and the discipline of Kung Fu. He knows every sequence of movements inside and out. He is the master.

Now consider his arch rival, who very often has graduated from, at one time, being a master to being the mastermind. He's the guy lurking around in the background, guarded and virtually untouchable. He's an idea, a phantom, an enigma. He makes all of the important decisions in his organization. He knows the art, but he's rarely provoked to fight. He's more of an organizer of people. As I said before, he is an orchestrator. This man is calm, cool and collected. He knows how to draw just the right mix of talent for whatever challenge or foe he may face. But when it comes time to go to battle, the talent he's chosen will fight for him while he's safely tucked away or making his grand escape.

Now consider your business goals and how you want to operate. Are you going to be the master ... or the mastermind?

Masters are masters because they have gained incredible insights into one or more specific areas. They are very learned and highly experienced in their line of business, but their knowledge base and understanding is generally limited to their particular field. They are professionals, gurus, PhDs and others who have achieved the highest level of expertise in their industry. Masters are those who trade their time for money. While their level of expertise affords them the opportunity to place a high premium on their time, for each moment they work, they are still limited to performing a single task or a single set of tasks in that moment. Masters spend their time performing duties perhaps not even truly considering the fact that time, once spent, is spent. In that way, being a master is actually not the most effective use of time. A master will use up a significant portion of his life trapped in a cycle of trading nonrenewable time for money.

A mastermind, on the other hand, is an expert at recruiting and assembling masters. In the truest sense of the word, masterminds are entrepreneurs and thinkers, movers and shakers. They are team-builders, coaches and CEOs. In business, they excel in two specific areas: (1) generating money-making ideas and (2) pooling the talent needed to take those ideas from conception to production. Masterminds do not trade their time for money. In fact, using a more collaborative approach, they create causes for which they are able to recruit the expertise and input of masters. They then synergize the energy and talent of the masters to accomplish their desired goals. Often masterminds are exceptional at multi-tasking. With their hands free, so to speak, they can utilize their mental energy to conjure up creative ideas then delegate the responsibility of manifesting those ideas to the talented folks who trade their time for money. Masterminds are able to conceive and bring to fruition many ideas, products and projects at once. This is why outsourcing is so important (we'll talk about that later). In that respect, being a mastermind becomes a far better use of time and energy than being a master.

If you're at all familiar with the concept of life design, you've probably wondered how you can transition from a 9 to 5, Monday through Friday kind of existence into one where you're checking your email only once a day and still earning a comfortable living without all the late nights at the office. Here's the short answer – learn the ways of the mastermind.

Mastermind Paradigms

Don't think of the mastermind as being a vague, unusual concept with which you are not familiar. American society is replete with fine examples of those who operated their lives and businesses in mastermind fashion. You don't have to wander the backwoods or arrange interviews with eccentric and elusive geniuses. You can open your history books or turn on your television to find masterminds at work. You may find that the mastermind approach is more common than you realize.

Benjamin Franklin

Take for example, Benjamin Franklin, Founding Father and inventor. His association with the Enlightenment Movement rightfully positioned him as a philosopher and a thinker. He was a politician. He was a businessman – a printer and store owner. Franklin was full of ideas and smart enough to recognize and support the great ideas of others. He successfully transitioned from master to mastermind by learning to leverage his relationships and take advantage of the talented people to which he had access.

Some of the brilliant ideas for which Benjamin Franklin recruited supporters included an effort to pave Pennsylvania roads and organize community restoration He recruited several financiers to buy large numbers of books from England to provide a local collection of subscription-based resources for a public library. He organized a localized place for the ill and infirm to get medical attention (Pennsylvania Hospital), a community victim fire protection fund (fire insurance), and an independently operated printing companies network (newspaper franchise, the first of its kind). He is also credited with conceiving of the flexible urinary catheter, the simple odometer, the glass harmonica, swim fins, and bifocal glasses. As such, he was one of the country's first great entrepreneurs. C'mon now, do you think it possible that Franklin was well-versed in each of these different areas? Or, is it more plausible that he leveraged his time and network to identify and work with those who were masters in these respective industries? I would go with the latter. He outsourced talent and put together effective teams. Benjamin Franklin was a mastermind.

Phil Jackson

The mastermind knows how to manage and motivate people. He understands the importance of vision and is a natural at getting people on board with that vision. Phil Jackson, the former coach of the Los Angeles Lakers and Chicago Bulls, is arguably one of the greatest sports coaches in history. During his more than twenty years coaching National Basketball Association (NBA) teams, he was able to consistently motivate and train some of the most talented players in professional basketball. Over the course of his career, he led his teams to 11 NBA titles. Although he was never a star NBA player during his career, Jackson didn't shirk the challenge of working with the most elite players. In fact, his legacy is one of shaping already highly-skilled players into even better athletes and sportsmen. He understands the entire game. More importantly, he understands the people who play that game. He knows the importance of giving exceptional talent both the guidance and the freedom to be exceptional. He knows how to balance flexibility with discipline and structure.

Steve Jobs

Now, let's go digital. Steve Jobs is credited with helping to usher the world into the Digital Age. His claim to fame was not in the work of his hands, but rather in his tendency to trust in the viability of his great ideas and recruit capable, dynamic people to bring those ideas to fruition. He said in an interview once that there are two requirements for success. The first is passion because passion precipitates perseverance and perseverance is necessary to face the challenges that will inevitably arise in any endeavor. The second is the ability to scout good talent. No matter your level of intelligence and creativity, you need a team of great people. According to Jobs, you have to be able to "size people up fairly quickly... make decisions without knowing people too well." Being the visionary he was, he would know how critical it is to have a clear vision around which a smart team can rally and produce. His strength was in predicting trends, assessing voids in the marketplace, and imagining the products that should be available. Once he conceived the product, he succeeded in getting people to create those products.

During his life, Steve Jobs was known as an inventor, although he never invented anything. He was the "what if?" guy. What if cell phones played music and surfed the web? What if we could condense the size of the laptop and have people type right on the screen instead of connecting a keyboard? What if people could download only the songs they wanted to hear from a digital music store online? Jobs was a builder, building upon existing ideas and adding to constructs that were already firmly in place. Although he wasn't an engineer or designer, he was credited with building some of the best consumer tech products ever made. Can you name who his chief engineer was? Anyone from his product design team? Probably not. They are the masters. Steve Jobs was the mastermind. He was able to organize the best technical talent in the word to work in harmony towards his vision. He was a master of integration and helped to build a company steeped in the idea that the whole is in fact greater than the sum of its parts.

Sean Combs

When it comes to the entertainment industry, Sean "P. Diddy" Combs is the quintessential mastermind. Regardless of which name he chooses to go by at any given time – Diddy, Puff Daddy, or Sean John – Combs is a man who perfected the art of using old songs to make new music hits - super hits. Oddly enough, Combs was not a musician and probably will never, legitimately, be considered one. He didn't start off as a kid with a guitar in the basement. He, instead, began as a party promoter while in college. After dropping out of Howard University, he got an internship at an urban music record label, where he later transitioned into an Artist & Repertoire (also known as "A&R"). He was a hip, young marketing genius who could spot talent and predict hits. Armed with marketing ability and with his finger firmly pressed on the pulse of the urban music market, Combs was able to raise an entire army of talented artists and clever music producers who quickly dominated urban radio with their brand of music revivalism – new lyrics and voices set to familiar old tunes that may, or may not, have been popular when they first reached the radio waves. His approach and operation were brilliant.

The success of his record label and production company, Bad Boy Records, was not based on his own musical ability, but on the collective talents of those he assembled into teams. Various producers, engineers and writers followed his direction, applying their knowledge to the creation of his vision for a particular song or music video. When you think about it, he operated in typical App Millionaire fashion - he outsourced. He outsourced both the recording and the production work and earned himself the appropriate moniker of "music mogul." Again, these accolades were not a result of his own raw musical talent, but from the artist, engineers and writers that he used to produce his music. He is considered by many to be a musical genius, while others do the majority of the musical heavy lifting.

Like Combs, New Orleans businessman, Percy "Master P" Miller, grew No Limit Records using a similar method. Outsourcing the actual creation of the product, Miller's No Limit Records consistently populated radio playlists in urban markets with a selection of music classified as hip hop, but with a distinctive sound branded "the dirty south." With a stable of personable and intriguing artists and producers who created music designed to sell, Percy Miller orchestrated the rise of No Limit Records as a musical force in the urban market.

Michael Dell

Michael Dell utilized a similar approach with computers. Dell built a technology empire by tweaking the business model used by his competitors. While he was a college student, Dell followed a hunch that he could find success in the personal computer business by selling the computers he built (and rebuilt) directly to the end user instead of selling to retailers like other computer companies were doing at the time. He was right. Starting out of his dorm room, and then moving his business to a condo before officially incorporating Dell Computer Corporation, Michael Dell's "manufacturer selling" business model made him the youngest CEO to have his venture ranked as a Fortune 500 Company. He was 27. Like Sean Combs' outsourcing of musically talented people to create musical hits, Michael Dell outsourced computer manufacturing and customer service to successfully operate his business. This is what masterminds do in order to build their business interest. They find the true masters and convince them to work towards their Mastermind goals. It's ingenious!

* * *

As you embark upon your personal entrepreneurial journey, remember that you are most effective as a leader and manager. You can always find people to do what you need to have done; you cannot, however, find people to create your vision. Only you can do that. So direct your efforts toward that – toward generating ideas, developing new products and services and, otherwise, being a visionary. Learn how to rally individuals in support of your cause so that you can focus on the bigger picture.

Chapter 9

Getting Started In Business – How to Build a Micro-Business

"I have been impressed with the urgency of doing. Knowing is not enough; we must apply. Being willing is not enough; we must do."

- Leonardo da Vinci, Renowned Painter

"The way to get started is to quit talking and start doing."

- Walt Disney, Film Producer, Entrepreneur and Philanthropist

As an educator, I encouraged my students to apply a particular motto throughout their entire educational career. It is the same motto I employed, not only through the process of my formal collegiate studies, but also in my quest to become an entrepreneur. The motto is this: *ask a lot of questions ... listen ... and don't forget.* As simple as it sounds, this axiom, when applied consistently, can produce amazing results. Its main premise is that, if one diligently seeks to obtain certain knowledge and actually applies that knowledge, there can be no other outcome other than growth and development. You cannot help but become better when you continue to seek and apply what you learn. Keep this precept in mind as you embark upon your own personal entrepreneurial journey. Trust me, it will not fail you.

How to Build a Micro-Business

Small businesses are the backbone of the United States economy. Historically, this has been the case, and, despite the economic instability many of us have experienced over the last few years, small businesses are still the primary support for the U.S. economy. In fact, since the economic downturn, the number of active small businesses operating in the U.S. has actually grown in number. If you have recently been laid off, have a criminal background that makes job acquisition challenging, need a new challenge, are just plain bored, or for any other reason are thinking about joining the millions of other Americans that have started businesses across the country, you are on the right track. In this chapter I will lay out a road map of how to start a micro-business.

Starting a micro-business is easier than ever. Part of the beauty of it is that you do not have to operate from a brick and mortar location, or sign a long-term lease. You also don't have to hire full or even part-time employees who come with all of the headaches of payroll and benefits – especially when you are first starting out. If you want to run an online business you can now take care of most of your technical and content needs by using freelancers. In fact, virtual workers can help you with almost any part of your business that doesn't require direct face-to-face contact with your customers.

Start with a Good Idea

Every new thing starts as an idea. Every new game, new song and consumer good starts as a thought running through somebody's mind. When the idea originated, the person with the idea had the option to capture and develop that thought or just let it go. A business, therefore, is just an idea that has been brought to life. I would venture to say that more often than not, people have a tendency to let their good ideas go. But the ones that are captured, developed and supported through hard work can make it to fruition.

Ideas are the lifeblood of the business world. Without ideas, there would be no products. Without ideas, there would certainly be no technological innovation. Everything from the chair you are sitting on to the landscaped scenery you may see out your bedroom window is birthed from an idea. Every social organization and professional sports club is someone's good idea. Ideas are bought, traded and sold every minute of every day. They are valuable and the people who can generate good ideas are also seen as valuable. Those who can find a way to consistently integrate several good ideas and turn them into a handful of great ideas will go from being valuable to being invaluable. Whether you ascribe to the notion that ideas are created by individuals or that they are gifts from a higher being, one thing is sure – good ideas are an essential factor in moving a business forward.

I hope you understand that I am emphasizing the importance of ideas for a reason. Without an idea, you don't have a business, let alone micro-business. It's really just that simple. So from now on when you get a good idea, you would be well-advised to pause for a moment and consider the ramifications of the idea being fulfilled. What could you reasonably expect to see if you took the time to expound on that idea and bring it to life? What is there to gain? What is there to lose? What are the benefits? Who benefits? It takes just a few seconds to ask yourself a set of pointed, intelligent questions that can help you to distinguish between a random thought and a good idea. Commit to doing this before letting another good (possibly great) idea leave your mind and disappear into the ether. After you've done that, the last question you need to ask yourself is, "Now how do I make it happen?"

Getting an idea from conception to production begins with writing it down. Taking the time to write your ideas down accomplishes several things. Writing things down gives you direction. The way the human mind works, what you think about and document becomes real to the mind. We tend to direct our day-to-day lives by what we think, say and do. So if you have an idea and you take the time to write it down, you are more likely to come back to that idea later.

Writing things down also brings about clarity. Something happens in that mind-to-notebook transfer that will help you to organize a solid plan quicker. You can create a big picture for a new idea in seconds and map out the details in just minutes if you write it down. Writing your ideas down will help you to sort things out.

An additional benefit of putting pen to paper is that doing so helps to minimize fear. When you put ideas on paper, you can better see the realities present in the opportunity before you. Writing brings a certain level of finality and accountability to ideas. Once the script is written, all that is left for us to do is to act it out.

But what if it doesn't work? The threat of failure can seem monstrous when an idea has not been fully analyzed and reviewed objectively. That is why putting your thoughts, ideas, and plans on paper is so helpful. We have a tendency to make matters bigger than what they are when we create various scenarios in our head regarding every aspect that can go wrong. When we take the idea out of our heads, and put it in black and white, somehow, it can be easier to gain perspective. What seems big in the human mind can look very small and quite manageable on a piece of notebook paper.

Once you have your idea mentally developed and scripted on paper, you want to protect it. Not every person should be privy to your plan. Once you have made the decision to move forward on an idea, your focus should be on how you plan to execute the idea. At that point, the people with whom you should communicate the most are those who will support you in your endeavor and can help you get your idea from inception to fruition. Note that some of the people closest to you may be among those with whom you should not be sharing your idea. So, be careful.

Next, you want to give your idea time and attention. When I say develop the idea, I mean take some time – even if it's just a few minutes every day for a week – to write down the details surrounding your idea. Fully explain the concept of what it is you see yourself accomplishing by pursuing this idea. Remember that the idea originates in your mind. It's what you are imagining a business to be. So be thorough about what it is you have imagined. Write down everything – your product, how it works, the people who will use the product, the people who will like the product, how the product will be made, what your sales will be like, what your website looks like. Anything that relates to this idea you have, write it down. Don't be deterred by nay-sayers. Not everyone is going to like what you are offering and that's okay.

Once you are done thinking, it's time to start planning. The planning stage of your new business is crucial. Many businesses fail not because they run out of money, but because they are either poorly planned or not executed according to the plan that was developed. So the planning phase could literally make or break your business.

Research the Market

If you don't know what type of product or service you want to sell, try observing different market places for ideas. The best way to do this is to do some introspection and research on the type of customer that you want. Then, focus on the needs and desires of that potential customer. Once you know what that segment of the market needs and wants, you can start a business that truly caters to the customer you desire. Justin did just that. He was familiar with the customer base because he had been serving them for years. He realized that there was a need for a website that provided them with a user-friendly forum for particular types of organic lawn care products and information, and he decided to create a website that would serve this need. When he decided to use the website as a platform to sell his lawn care products, he successfully supplemented the existing business he had by applying his knowledge of the market to provide that market with what it desired.

Justin was fortunate to start his business at the right time – during the age of the internet and social media. Most of the obstacles associated with a conventional business were eliminated and he didn't have to do traditional market research to pinpoint a speculative trend. After all, there is no question that the internet and social media are here to stay, so, for him, it was simply a matter of how he could best utilize this tool in his business. He got the idea for his global lawn care information service and store just by being a keen observer of what people who were utilizing his lawn care service seemed to need. He really did not have to engage in extensive research to find out what the market desired. Instead, he leveraged the power of the internet to develop a business that produced an ideal product for his target market.

There are many ways to explore an idea for a business and learn whether it would satisfy market needs. You can actually do all of your research and planning without spending much money. A company like Persuadable Research Corporation can do your research all online for you. They can provide you with a written report on the feasibility of your business idea.

Your main goal during the planning phase is to gather as much information as possible about the business you are going into and the people who will utilize your service or purchase your product. Learning the ins- and- outs of your business is going to give you some insight into what it will take to run the business. Find out everything you can about the market you are entering. Know the other businesses (competitors) currently providing the same or a similar product within the market. Find out if there is a need for the product or service you are providing. It very well may be that you came up with the idea because you saw that there was a need. Maybe your own frustration even led you to start a business simply out of necessity. That was the case with Dave, a start-up entrepreneur who went from buying windows to wholesaling windows online in a matter of minutes.

From Frustrated Buyer to Successful Supplier

Dave worked in the Pittsburgh construction market for nearly a decade as a residential contractor. The installation of new windows was among the services he regularly provided, particularly in vacant properties that were being rehabbed. Many of his customers requested security bars be place on the windows at the basement levels of their houses. Through his years of experience, Dave learned that glass block windows were actually a better choice for keeping energy costs down and maintaining curb appeal for a property. Dave, and other members of the Pittsburgh construction community, all used the same glass block supplier – the only one that serviced the Pittsburgh market, in fact. A common complaint amongst the construction community was that supplier was unreliable. The glass block company was managed by a father and son team whose management style left much to be desired. The store was sometimes closed during the posted business hours and the father was known to change the prices of the products he sold on a whim.

Because they held a virtual monopoly on the Pittsburgh market, there was little contractors could do besides tolerate the inconsistent and poor service. Without fail, just about every time Dave went to purchase glass block, he ran into problems with the owner of the business. "You should be grateful I'm selling to you at all!" the owner yelled across the counter of his business one morning, as Dave tried to negotiate a price break on glass block that had gone up 35% in price. Frustrated and infuriated, Dave's response was, "You don't have to sell me any block! I'll start my own glass block company."

Armed with the knowledge that his former supplier's biggest liability was a lack of professionalism, Dave contracted with an online sales team of professionals and opened an online store right out of his home. Initially, his company catered specifically to the needs of local contractors. He was able to match his supplier-turned–competitor's price and capitalize on his ability to offer great customer service. More importantly, Dave never touched his product. Every glass block was drop-shipped from another manufacturer and fulfillment service. By his second year of operation, he became the number two supplier of glass block in the state of Pennsylvania and the primary glass block window retailer in the Pittsburgh market. Since he was online, he quickly was able to expand his market to include other parts of the U.S., as well as Mexico and Canada. Although his business had the appearance of a midsized company, what he was really operating was a successful micro-business.

Finding out if there is a need for your business in the market may not (and probably won't) be as cut and dry for you as it was for Dave. But, there are simple ways for you to test the validity of your idea. First and foremost, talk to people. This is not a complex process and there aren't any tricks. Just ask four words: Would you buy this? Then, follow up with, "Why?" Or, "Why not?" If you approach people in a manner that demonstrates that you want a sincere response, and can handle whatever they tell you, people will usually be honest. That will at least give you some idea of whether or not people are interested in your business. Market research is based on the opinions and habits of people just like you and me. Much of what we don't get is because we don't ask. So start asking.

If you are thinking about selling a product, you can set up an online store in a matter of an hour for under $20. Using providers like HostGator.com or GoDaddy.com, you will have access to dozens of e-store templates where all you would have to do is upload the images, descriptions and prices of items you are selling and the shopping cart feature would allow you to take orders for products before ever having to purchase any inventory items. The initial investment would include $2 to $10 to own your domain name for a year and another $10 for an online store that you can stock with virtual products. Usually when you open a web hosting account, the provider will offer incentives like free photo credits and free online advertising tools such as Google Adwords and Facebook. With the free ad credits, you can drive a bit of traffic to your site and use web analytics to find out how people are using your site.

Most importantly, you can also gauge interest in your idea by creating content that drives people to a web site or launch page about your product or service where you can capture email addresses by offering information, free e-books or newsletters. I'm sure you've seen web pages where something interesting is being advertised as a free offer if you would subscribe to the newsletter. You can do the same thing for your product or service and find out a bit about your target audience.

Try to sell your product even if you don't actually have it on-hand. You can use an auction site to find out the real-time value of just about any item. EBay and Amazon are amazing that way. You can always issue a refund later if you need to, should you find that you were unable to get the product shipped to your customer. Or, you can stop the sale before it goes through. The idea is to find out if people are interested before you are up to your eyeballs in inventory that you cannot sell.

Keep in mind that these tests are just starting points. They don't promise to deliver sales, but are designed to give you an idea of the level of interest that you may be able to translate into actual sales.

Identify your Unique Selling Proposition

What makes you better than your competitor? For Dave, his unique selling proposition was good online customer service. Also, he benefited from being online and having customers everywhere instead of only servicing his local area. Often, your unique selling proposition is going to be dictated, at least to some degree, by your competitors' weaknesses. When you can identify what it is you offer that your competitors will not offer, cannot offer, or do not provide as well as you, you have found your unique selling proposition.

Sometimes figuring out what you can offer is simply a matter of just watching the activity in your market. Watch what people are buying and then develop a version that is different in some way. Add functions, or narrow the focus of the product. Can you find a way to make it less expensive without compromising the quality of the product itself? Can you find a way to make it better without making it expensive? Can you find a way for the customer to get it faster?

If your idea is for a new product – a desktop app for instance – you build a demo and present it to potential customers for feedback. You can learn a lot just by the user feedback and reviews you get on a new product. Encourage your customers to be honest and let them know that you are relying heavily on their opinions of your product. Even doing a stripped down version of the product without all the bells and whistles will give people the opportunity to connect with and provide feedback on the basic premise of your product. They can then recommend ways to make it better. Don't be afraid of the crowd. Honest criticism is a friend to the entrepreneur.

Assess Your Competitors

Another important part of market research is a comprehensive assessment of your competition. To properly assess your competition, you should answer some basic questions about them. You should know how large their share of the available business is, how well they are doing, what they are doing well, and what they are doing badly. Please understand that your competitors cannot be ignored. If they are true competitors, they are selling something that is, at least, similar to what you are selling and, therefore, vying for the same customers. Your job is to craft a strategy that meets your customer's needs in a way that is better than your competitors. In order to do that, you are going to need to know who your competitors are. For web-based businesses, you can perform a keyword search for the primary service or product you provide and see who shows up in the top results. Go to a site like Alexa.com to see what kind of traffic these sites are generating. Check out their site, taking a very close look at their content, and noting any promotions they are offering. Are there things your competitors are doing that you could do better? You can use audience-measuring tools like Quancast.com to assess your competitor's demographics. This will also help you to identify your own potential customer base.

You would also do well to tune in to online chatter. You can learn a lot about your competitor's strengths and weaknesses just by "Googling" their name. Social media is a powerful tool for establishing brand recognition. If your competitor's presence is online, there is a good chance someone is talking about them – and much of that talk is likely to be online. You can find out what is being said and who is doing the talking. Outlets like Twitter can also be helpful. If your competitor is engaging with prospective customers on Twitter, for instance, you can find that out. Information on whatever product or service your competitor is providing will likely be found online. You can gauge their reputation and the influence they have within the market by finding out who they are connected to in social media. You can even go so far as to sample their products and familiarize yourself with their face-to-face or online customer service practices. The bottom line is that you want to learn as much as you can about what is already out in the market so that the product or service you are introducing is one that would be of value – not more of the same.

Look at how your competitors market themselves and how their corporate image is maintained. How are they getting business and what are they doing to keep it? Are they engaging in e-mail marketing or are they using pay-per-click ads online? If you are competing with a "mom and pop shop" that has no digital, that can be quite telling as well. It lets you know that their customer base is predominantly local and the core of their business consists of in-store transactions. How is your competitor meeting the needs that exist in the market? Can you meet the need presently in the community and expand by utilizing the web to provide your product or service on a larger scale? Do your research. Find out all you can. Find the press releases they have issued as well as any media coverage issued by local and national outlets. Follow them on social media networks. What is their story and how did they start? Where have they been successful and where have they fallen short?

Having this information gives you the benefit of being able to avoid making the same mistakes they have made. As well, you get the opportunity to capitalize on their successes. In other words, you get to capitalize on their good ideas and use them to your advantage. At the very least, you want to be able to provide a level of service and a quality product that is comparable to what your competitors are providing. Remember in the beginning of your start-up, often you will be measuring your business by your competitor's standards. They set the bar. You will raise it.

Quick Questions

If you take this process seriously, you will gain a pretty good idea of what it is you are getting into – whether you have a reasonable chance to succeed with your business. You should have vetted out any parts of the original idea that don't work and quite possibly replaced them with other ideas that can better assure your chances of success. Before you go on to the next stage, take a few seconds to evaluate the viability of your business by asking ten important "yes" or "no" questions just to make sure you have covered all the bases during the information-gathering phase of starting your micro-business.

1. Does your micro-business fulfill a market need?

2. Can you readily identify your customer base?

3. Is your micro-business designed to capitalize on a trend or designed to outlast a trend?

4. Have you identified your top competitors?

5. Does your business have a unique offering that gives it an advantage over your competitors?

6. Have you designed a business model that leverages your competitor's successes and avoids their pitfalls?

7. Have you tested your product in the market?

8. Is your product safe and does it meet any applicable regulations?

9. Did your market test prove that the product has an audience?

10. Have you been able to identify a price point that works for your product?

    Bonus Question: Can you operate this business as a micro-business?

If you have been able to honestly answer "yes" to all of the above questions, read on. If not, go back and find the information you are missing.

Develop a Business Strategy

You may have the brightest idea for a business, but if you don't know how to attract customers then you better give up the idea of starting that business. A business needs customers. Without them, your business is surely doomed. Regardless of the type of micro-business, it is your customers who will bring in money to your business. Your goal as a micro-business person is to get customers and keep them. Make them raving fans.

Unfortunately (even if you're developing games), creating customers is one of the most difficult parts of starting a business. Having a fantastic product that you know people want or need is just not good enough. Your potential customers will not find your website or your product without you actively seeking them. The only way to ensure that you get your customers in front of your product is by developing a business strategy.

You are planning your business strategy. That may sound bigger than what it is. A business strategy is not a stack of papers with charts and graphs, though it can include those things. Your business strategy is basically the method you are going to use to run your business and remain profitable. Strategies are developed for the sake of competition. Your business needs to be able to compete in the market and your strategy should be built around the thing that gives you an advantage over your competitors. Your business strategy should be so clear that it can be communicated in just a few sentences. In fact, often with a micro-business, you need to be able to sum it up in a single sentence. That sentence is what you are going to refer to over and over again as you plan your business. Your business strategy may evolve over time so that you can maintain a competitive edge over your competitors. It should be regularly reviewed to ensure that it lines up with the current mission and vision for your business.

Define Your Offering

There are seemingly as many products and services to sell as there are ideas. But remember that, when it comes to building a micro-business, the objective is to keep your load light, and as you learn and develop, make it lighter. I strongly encourage you to consider a web-based micro-business. Many of the goods and services provided in the physical market can make their presence known in the online market as well. Additionally, there are ancillary services that can generate profit for you, without you having to set up an e-commerce website. Among these services are, for example, mobile apps that dealerships use to generate sales with online banner ads. Once a potential customer clicks through to the dealer's website, the interested customer can go through the credit application and qualification process right online. If they qualify, a local dealer will follow up within hours. Even though the customer may have to visit the dealership to take a test drive or sign documents, and receive delivery of the vehicle, much of the purchase transaction was handled in the virtual realm.

Alternative Ideas

Besides models where you post inventoried products for visitors to purchase (think online stores and eBay), there are various other business models you can use to launch a web-based micro-business. Ad supported content is big with the content provider community. Content providers include bloggers and freelance writers. Ad supported content is content that contains in-text hyperlinks to other websites, blogs and online retailers. So, let's say you have a blog site that is fairly popular. You may get a thousand or so unique visitors every month that read your blog and recommend it to other people. By using a tool like Clickbank.com, online marketers (people selling products) are able to connect with content providers that can promote their products. You, as the content provider, would get a percentage of every product sale that originates with one of your blog readers clicking through a hyperlink to the marketer's site to make a purchase. It's called affiliate marketing and it can become a profitable business for you. Now, the links have to make sense, of course. Otherwise, the value of your content is diminished and your reputation along with it. So, a fashion blogger could reasonably recommend a site that sells discount high-heeled shoes. A micro-business blogger may recommend a productivity app and, within the context of the content the blogger provides, a hyperlinked recommendation for a productivity app makes sense; A random link to a retailer who sells organic dog food may be nonsensical.

Freemium content is another business model that is becoming more popular. If you have ever gone to CNet.com and downloaded AVG Antivirus or played a limited-feature online version of Scrabble for free, then had the option to upgrade from the basic free product to an enhanced version with more features, then you know what freemium content means. The draw of freemium is that it gives users the chance to sample just enough of your product for them to want more access to it - access they are willing to pay to get.

Hulu's basic service includes a limited selection of television shows and movies to watch online at any time. The menu of sitcoms, dramas and available movies changes from time to time and only ten or thirty-second excerpts are available of some shows. Their subscription-based service, Hulu Plus, offers a much wider selection, as well as full episodes. You can access new episodes, old television dramas and just a better, more comprehensive service for a fraction of the cost of cable television.

Credit reporting agencies offer online subscription services which alert subscribers to changes in their credit reports. Subscribers also get access to their credit reports and FICO scores as needed. For a small monthly fee, Gevalia coffee sends customers two imported products – either coffee or tea – every month. Subscribers to Melissa Dawn Johnson's BrandMeLive.com community get to engage with other members of the community for a small monthly fee. Plus they can get VIP access or discount admission to local events and information products (e-books, newsletters, etc.) delivered to their inbox on a regular basis.

I do understand that Hulu and credit companies are not micro-businesses, however they serve as good examples of how subscription services work. You can offer any number of things from information products and consumer goods in order to create a subscription based micro-business.

Fulfillment services are often used by online retail and wholesale businesses that are set up to accept orders from consumers on behalf of another company. Many small businesses use these services to handle product shipment and handling. When using this type of service, you would either pay a one-time or monthly fee for each sale generated.

Drop shippers are wholesalers who fulfill product orders for various retailers. If you operate an online site populated with items from a drop ship company, you can just stock your eStore with only virtual inventory. When orders come in online, you contact the drop shipper (or just forward the invoice) and pay for the item at a reduced rate. The drop shipper will ship the order directly to the customer for you. Drop shippers will usually offer your address and company name as the sender. Drop shipping works because you can fulfill orders without ever having to stock inventory and you buy product based on sales you have already made. If you don't have your own product, you will usually get a substantial discount on the retail price paid for the item and the customer generally covers his own shipping costs.

Network marketing often gets a bad rap, but as any woman driving around in the familiar cotton candy-colored Cadillac with the Mary Kay stamp on the back will tell you – the model works. There are dozens of products available for sale through multi-level marketing and the model works just as well online as it does face-to-face. One of the primary advantages of this particular business model falls in line with the franchise idea – you are selling a product that already has an established reputation and you have the support of the person who brought you into the business because they have a vested interest in your success. The more money you make, the more money they make. That's the key with network marketing – building a strong network of like-minded individuals who are as committed to building their businesses as you are to building yours.

E-Distribution is another popular business model for running a web-based micro-business. The distribution of digital content is still a growing business. It's the same format that has virtually leveled the music industry. It's the format that allows you to buy a book for your mobile reader instead of going to the bookstore to buy the paperback version. Smartphone applications like iQuick Estimator, Lease Maker, Invoice Pro, or Monkeys and Bananas, are just a few apps developed by my company. These apps are, essentially, electronically distributed products as well. Downloading digital versions of physical content from online sources rather than purchasing them in stores is at the core of e-Distribution.

Assess Cost

The next step in starting your micro-business is to assess the start-up cost. If you know how to manage your budget, your start-up cost for a micro-business can be relatively small. The most common costs will include the cost of developing a dynamic, interactive website, creating a unique market-tested product, developing an effective and innovative marketing and promotion strategy for your high- quality product and company, web hosting, registration of domain name and setting up a merchant account. Even though this sounds like a lot, it really is very minimal when compared to other types of business models.

It pays to shop around and ask for referrals for good providers of these services. For instance, some web hosting companies ask for a minimal one-time set-up fee of around $25 to get the space for your site ready, while others do not. Fees associated with merchant services accounts also vary from provider to provider. Therefore, take the time to research those services that are best for your business model and wallet. One of the biggest start-up costs for an online business is building the website. An easy way to find a good web developer is to use a service like Elance.com. More on Elance and other outsourcing work stations a little later.

Set a Budget

As is the case in all areas of life, in business you need to get in the habit of using the resources available to you. That means setting a budget for your micro-business and operating your business in accordance with the funds that you have available. If you have done your research, you should be able to get a pretty good idea of what it will cost to launch your micro-business. If you are launching a website, you may be able to use any number of money-saving techniques, including the use of templates available through sites like Wordpress and Go Daddy. You can also hire well-priced contractors in other parts of the world to design your site for you. If you have content for e-distribution, what will it cost for you to promote the book or music online? What would be the most effective marketing medium? Banner ads? Social media advertising? Affiliate marketing? If you are starting a blog and don't have the time or the skill set to populate the site with content, what is it going to cost you on a per article basis to hire someone to provide you with content? You need to have a realistic idea of what it will cost to start this endeavor, but also remember that you want to use just what you need to get the site launched. Try not to overdo it. If you don't need the bells and whistles, don't put them in the budget. Part of the advantage of owning a micro-business is that when it's done right, you can run it with a relatively small investment of time, human resources and financial capital. Think small, and direct your resources to only those items that matter the most.

Set Up An Outsourcing Account

Welcome to the development stage. Once you have done your research, decided on your business type and strategy, and set a budget, you are ready to start looking for the talent you need to get the work done. There are several resources you can use to get access to freelance contractors from all over the world. Every day, tens of thousands of talented web developers, writers, graphic artists and administrative professionals submit competitive bids online for thousands of available projects. When you post a job description, you don't have to spend time looking for someone to do the work. They come to you. By using virtual marketplaces like Elance, Guru, oDesk, Freelancer and more to employ contractors for specific projects, you have the advantage of being able to review a contractor's biography, work history, average pay per project and work portfolio. You also get actual feedback from the contractor's previous clients on their work performance and habits. Many of the talent sourcing platforms offer a rating system for both contractors and employers. On Elance, for instance, contractors can earn from one to five stars in different aspects of their performance such as timeliness, ability to follow directions, and professionalism as rated by previous employers who have worked with these contractors.

Elance is pretty much the gold standard of virtual contractor sites in the U.S. Elance has solid systems in place to protect the interests of both employers and contractors. As an employer, you can set up hourly jobs using WorkView (their job monitoring system) and Elance will take regularly scheduled screen shots of your contractor's desktop to ensure that your contractor is working during the time for which you are being billed. WorkView is also a great tool for tracking the progress of a project. Elance provides conflict resolution and you can opt for either manual or automatic payments for any job you commission. There are plenty of other conveniences designed to make the process of hiring and working with a contractor as seamless as possible. It really is a fantastic system and setting up your outsourcing account is simple.

Build a Team

Your business will be your baby. Sometimes it is hard to let go of control. You will have to, at some point, get the assistance of others as you build. If you want your business to operate smoothly and efficiently, there are times when you will need to have a team.

The key to building a team is knowing exactly what you need from your team and clearly communicate their roles and responsibilities and your expectations of them. Building a team also involves sharing with them your vision for your business and making them own that dream. Before you build that dream team, determine first what aspect(s) of the business you want to do yourself. These tasks should be the ones that you can do just as well or better than anyone else. Next, you should determine what tasks can be done in-house and what can be outsourced. If you are not adept in web design and maintenance, you will need a web designer to ensure that your site is always updated to meet your clients' needs. When I needed a website for my first micro-business, I hired a brilliant web design company from India. Outsourcing this part of the development saved me a lot of start-up money. My development cost was only $400 for a professional and beautiful site.

The most amazing thing is that you can build a virtual team right online. Once you have made decisions on which contractors to use, continuously evaluate them to determine who is good and who is not. When you find someone good – hold on to them. As your business grows, add more members to your team, such as a virtual assistant or a bookkeeper, if necessary. Keep your team small, manageable and within your budget. Sometimes you need several contractors and sometimes you don't need any. Hire only who you need.

One of the best ways to get a qualified contractor for your project is to make sure your job description is thorough and clear. I have mentioned the importance of writing things down for clarity and direction. Your project description is no different. You want whomever it is that you hire to help you launch your micro-business to understand exactly what is expected of them. The details of the job need to be specifically outlined. Your providers need to know what you want them to do and how long they have to get it done. If your contractor is helping you develop a project that has not yet been pushed to the market (as opposed to them making modifications to an existing website or product), you will also need to take legal precautions by having your provider sign a non-disclosure/confidentiality (NDA) agreement. Remember, one of the first rules of building a business is to protect your idea - even at the development stage.

When you submit a project proposal to a virtual marketplace, contractors will, in turn, submit their bids based on the requirements of the job and their skills. Take into account that, like anything else, the more qualified the contractor, the higher their bid will likely be. If you're in the U.S, England or any other major developed country, having access to international talent however, means that you have a greater possibility of getting the work you need completed for much less than you would normally pay for a domestic contractor. Still, choose your work provider based on more than just a cheap rate. Review all offers. Make sure that the contractor you choose has the qualifications needed to do the job. Look at the feedback they've received and their work history. Great feedback on twenty jobs trumps great feedback on two jobs. When it comes to Elance contractors, most of them will have feedback that ranks somewhere in the 4s. I only work with contractors who have a feedback score of 4.6 and above. However, don't be afraid to use new contractors. Although this may be a gamble, many of them are hungry for the opportunity to prove themselves and are willing to work hard to deliver (and sometimes over-deliver) on your job.

Below you will find a sample of a post I made for two logos that I needed done. This is just an example for you see.

> I need 2 (but similar) icon logos. The first one should look like a general "invoice" with the one corner of the bottom page turned up. The words "Invoice" should go diagonally across the page with a raise shadow and light red see through color. A small signature in blue should be at the bottom.
>
> The second icon logo should look like a general "contract" with the one corner of the bottom page turned up. The words "Contract" should go at the top of the page. A small signature should be at the bottom in blue. Also an ink pen should be laying at the bottom of the page.
>
> The icon logos should be made high-quality. The logos should be designed using vectors that are scalable.
>
> The icon logo sizes that I need are: 1024x768, 512x512, 320x480, 114x114, 72x72, and 57x57.
>
> Please send sample work. If chosen please show different variations of the concept. NO IMAGES

SHOULD BE BLURRY.

This project should be simple, and go fast.

Depending on the length and complexity of the project, you and your contractor will need to negotiate a project price and a payment schedule. You can create milestones where the provider agrees to complete a certain percentage of the project or hit a certain benchmark, in exchange for a predetermined amount of the total contract value. So, if you are contracting with a web designer to complete a website, you and the designer can agree that once the mock-ups for the site pages are complete, the first half of the total contracted price will be paid. Whatever schedule the two of you agree upon, keep up your end of the agreement. That includes your payment schedule. Elance advises contractors not to begin work on a flat-rate project unless the employer has already put money in the Elance escrow account. That protects the contractor from investing time into working on projects that go unpaid by the employer. The money will not be released from escrow until you authorize its release. There are exceptions to that rule, but the system is designed to keep everyone honest. Conduct your business ethically. That's not to say you should be careless or foolish. You want to make sure that the job has been done according to the proposal you laid out and the agreement the two of you made. But if you have received a service from a contractor, you should have no qualms about paying for that service. Be fair and pay on time. Be aware that contractors get the opportunity to leave feedback for you on Elance as well.

When you enter into a contract to get work done, allow your work provider enough time to deliver on the contract. Don't be too anxious to get it finished. You want it done right and you want time to review the work that's been done. Ideally, there should be enough time for your contractor to do the work, for you to review the work and then a period where you can submit revisions or edits in accordance with the contract, if necessary. If you are developing an app or other programming product, the revision and edit period needs to include time for debugging and repairing any programming glitches. Always thoroughly test your product build. If you are commissioning the development of an app, the entire app doesn't have to be done before you start testing functionality and seeing if the graphics fit within the scope of your original vision for the project.

Product Development

Sometimes product development efforts fail. The product may not exactly meet the buyers' expectations or doesn't offer a high-level of buyer satisfaction. This is a very expensive waste of time and resources - two critical elements in product development - since time to market is vital and your resources are not limitless. In most cases, this is due to a very unsystematic approach to product development. Customer satisfaction is a strategic component of product development. You need understanding of your potential customers' needs and desires. You also need to make sure that all these needs and desires are taken into consideration when developing your product. The best way to proceed with product development is to create a prototype or a teaser model of your product. You can have this done by someone else or, if you have the capability, you can do it yourself. Building a prototype or teaser model (i.e., one single item) may prove a bit expensive since it is mass production that usually brings down the cost of a product. The benefits will more than outweigh the investment.

If necessary, another method to get a virtual product to market is to have a virtual teaser model of your product. There are computer programs that can simulate a teaser model of your product in 3D. The programs can test if the product works. A virtual teaser model can be inexpensive to produce when done by a professional. This professional should even give you a CD or video animation of your virtual teaser model in operation. In the case of digital products, developing a virtual teaser model is more practical since you will need it for product testing.

Test the Model with Your Team and Friends

Teaser model testing is one of the most satisfying and exciting stages of your product development. This allows you to test how your product will be accepted by the market. The best way to do market testing is to put your teaser model into use in situations where it will be required to function. Identify the features that are vital to meet the needs and requirements of your customers and test those features repeatedly.

You can use your friends and team members as the first target of your market testing. Let them use it and solicit comments and suggestions from them. If you want to and can afford it, you can even enlist the services of a market research group to help you analyze the reactions and comments of your friends and team members. Once you have analyzed the comments and suggestions of your team mates and friends, accept the feedback, even if it consists of criticisms, and go back to the drawing board. Iron out or debug whatever needs to be fixed. Improve your product, based on the feedback you received. Take this opportunity to make your product as desirable as possible to your potential customer, focusing on the product functions, its physical appearance, or design appeal.

Begin the Preliminary Marketing

Once you have completed market testing, processed the feedback, and made the necessary changes in light of the comments and feedback you received, the next step is to begin preliminary marketing. Preliminary marketing involves validating the desirability of the product to a wider audience before you decide to put it into production.

Preliminary marketing can give you an idea on how to price your product to be competitive, but still profitable. It also lets you know what other changes the product needs, and helps you identify where the right outlets are to sell your product. This stage in starting a business is very important. The unbiased opinion of a wider buying audience other than your team and friends in the development stage of the product will help you avoid the possibility of having it modified or at worst, scrapped when production is already complete.

To fully take advantage of the benefit of market testing and preliminary marketing, you should have an adequate number of prototypes manufactured and sold to a test market. This will give an indication as to how it will be accepted by the public and how it will perform. This should be done before full-scale manufacturing starts. Of course, with digital products, this becomes a much easier task. There is very little cost to distribute a digital product like an eBook or app. The biggest upfront cost for a product like this is development. If you are selling a digital product, don't skip this stage though. The market feedback you get is invaluable.

Finalize Your Product

You are now in the final stage of product development. Once you've gathered all the comments, suggestions and criticism, you need to sit down with your development team to finalize the product. Valid comments, suggestions and criticisms should be taken into consideration in this final product development stage. If you have outsourced your team, you can still do this step by using a virtual meeting room online. That way, all of you can get together and share ideas and be on the same page.

Iron out all any bugs and test all systems. When creating a product, this can be done by doing a pilot batch launch or a final beta run before full-scale production. A pilot batch launch or final beta run can detect some other defects of the product that were not uncovered on the prototype. This will also give you an idea on how real production will really go or how the digital product will actually function. It gives you a chance to iron out any problems and bugs before the product reaches the market.

Build a Website

While your contractors are busy getting your product developed, now is the time to build a website that is both compatible and manageable on mobile devices. One of the things that tend to get overlooked in website development is the compatibility issue. You want to make sure that your site is fully functional when accessed using any of the major web browsers - Internet Explorer, Safari, Chrome, Opera and Mozilla (Firefox).

It's also important, particularly for the web-based micro-business that the site functions on mobile devices as well. In fact, you may want to have a mobile version of your site for marketing purposes. You may want to use the domain .mobi when setting up your site for mobile devices, as I anticipate that this domain will become more popular in the near future. Online purchases using mobile devices are steadily increasing. It has been reported that 11% of online sales during the 2012 Christmas season originated from mobile devices and 59% of smartphone users made purchases from their phone. These numbers are expected to steadily increase over this decade. You want as many people as possible to have access to your product or service and nothing says "do not buy here" quite like an improperly functioning website.

If you can, launch your site ahead of your product and advertise like crazy using banner ads, affiliate marketing, Google Adwords and social media marketing. With your fully functional site launched, set a price for your product or service and enable users to purchase your goods. Again, you don't have to go through with the sale if the product is not yet available. You do, however, want to perform a "ghost test" to make sure that during the ordering process, everything works the way that it should. Make sure that you are receiving notifications of product orders immediately and that the transaction is being processed properly by your ecommerce provider. This will serve the double function of making sure that your site is functional and again monitoring the interest of your audience. During the ghost testing phase, you can program your site to let your customer know that the item they are attempting to buy is out of stock. The point is that you want them to complete the sale before making them aware that the product is not available. This will allow you to accurately gauge their propensity to purchase your product without allowing them to spend the money doing so.

Back in the old days, being able to take credit cards was a process involving lengthy phone calls to call centers, credit determination departments, decision letters and quite possibly being turned down. When it comes to ecommerce today, many web-hosting providers will recommend or include ecommerce solutions in their web design packages. PayPal is the most widely used ecommerce service provider. Unlike traditional merchant accounts, you don't need a business account or Tax ID number to get a PayPal account. There is no merchant credit check. All you really need is a bank account, debit card with a credit card logo and an email address to get a PayPal account. Google Checkout is another solution that offers an easy setup to just about anyone with a Gmail account. Authorize.net is another payment gateway that allows you to accept electronic payments. Authoize.net also offers a free mobile app to users for accepting payments on the go. Intuit, most well known for the QuickBooks line of accounting software, offers a pretty user-friendly online merchant system that works with your version of QuickBooks software to accept electronic payments. Sam's Club offers several merchant solutions for professionals including point of sale systems, ecommerce and online merchant processing systems.

Dual Testing

Another action you should take is to perform what's called a dual analysis. Dual testing analysis is when you build two versions of your website, with two different looks, two different taglines, and a bit of difference in the functionality. You also use two sets of Google Adwords to find out which keywords drive the most traffic to the differing sites. You will be selling the same items on both sites, but the duality allows you to identify the keywords and key phrases that are most effective for what it is you need to accomplish. The keywords that you identified during this testing period should be within the written copy on your website. As well, you'll be able to get some idea which web presence is most effective in creating sales.

Once your dual analysis is complete and you know which keywords work best, decide which site to use. Once you've selected the site, start the pre-marketing process. This is not the same as the ghost test where you aren't actually going through with the sales. Pre-marketing is the process of priming the market for the launch of your product. Have a press release crafted and get some sales copy for the PR page of your site. Start engaging in conversations and facilitating relationships with other members of the online community who may have an interest in what you are doing. If you have time, start blogging (or hire someone to do it for you). There are many marketing companies like Duct Tape marketing or My Social Agency that will do this for you. So if you are developing a social app, start participating in those blogging communities to let people know that your product is going to market.

By this point, your product should be in the final stages of development. It's time to compare the finished product to the original vision you had to make sure that what you have is what you initially set out to create. Wrap up all testing and make sure your program is completely debugged. Your product should be fully functional.

Marketing

Now is the time to really organize and invest in an online marketing campaign for your product. You may already know about your audience on a broad level. But who are your potential customers – the people who will actually buy what you're selling? Women? Men? Children? Seniors? College students? Ask yourself these questions. A difficult thing to understand is that not everybody in your audience will buy your product or is your potential customer. The challenge is to determine who your potential customers are because you will be directing all your marketing efforts towards them. The key to the success of your micro-business is your ability to identify that specific customer group and build an on-going relationship with them.

You know how to find them online and you have had at least some level of active participation in an online community that is interested in your product. A full-scale marketing strategy is an important part of getting the word out about your product. The web is saturated with stuff – consumer goods, information products and applications. You want to be sure that what you're offering does not get lost in the shuffle.

People buy products or services to either satisfy a need, make themselves feel good or to solve a problem. You need to know the reason why people will buy your product. Will it satisfy a basic need, entertain them or will it be a solution to a problem? Your product may even answer more than one reason about why people buy goods and services. The best way to differentiate your product from the others in your market space is to tell people what's different about it.

Side note: I've heard some business people speak highly of blogging and a lot of them say that if you are going to use a blog as a marketing tool to drive traffic to your site, it's a good idea to host the blog separately using a free tool like Wordpress or Blogger and provide links back to your website within the content of your blog posts. I'm no expert on blogging, but it seems very sensible to have your blog be separate from your main product site. That way, you create backlinks to your main site through the activity on your blog site.

As a low to no cost resource, social media always offers great marketing tools for almost any kind of product. Create a Facebook page for your project. If you have the budget for it, you can hire a page designer to create an attractive Facebook landing page that can capture email addresses for direct marketing purposes. Tell your friends and family about your page and start collecting '"likes" from the people you know, as well as those you don't. Twitter and Google+ work well with promoting products as well. Currently, Google+ is still growing in popularity and use while Twitter is pretty much a social media staple.

Use social media to engage potential customers by, basically, conversing with them. Talk to them. Engage with them. You can easily tweet upcoming promotions, advertise discounts, offer coupon codes, present free trial periods, and promote new product releases. When it comes to Twitter, you want to be followed as well as one who follows. This is how you get engaged on multiple levels. The more you engage with people on Twitter, the more likely they are to follow you back. Most of the people you follow on Twitter should be in the same field as you. Those who follow you should be a larger group of people.

YouTube and Vimeo

YouTube and Vimeo videos are a good way to add a bit of personality to your marketing campaign. Instructional videos, views on trending topics and program demonstrations are all great ways to leverage the power of visual presentation. Not everyone wants to read and type. Some people respond better to visual representations such as cartoons, diagrams, and animations. Use of these video tools will help you appeal to that. Once the video is done, start posting links to it on Twitter, Facebook, Google+ and on your blog. We will talk more about marketing in a later chapter. Let this serve as a brief introduction.

Assess the Product

The next step is to do an assessment of your product. You have a beautiful product; it passed the technical and market testing with flying colors but all products need continuous improvement to stay relevant in the marketplace. Some points to consider are whether there is a possibility for repeat business from a customer and whether the product is a frivolity or a necessity (if it's the former, don't expect repeat customers). Does your product come with or need accessories? How do you market for an upgrade or an up sell? Does it need to be serviced? Is there a change in the marketplace to which you will need to adjust?

When you assess your product, honesty is crucial. Specific facts will help you build or develop the best product, which is the foundation of any successful business.

How Will You Earn Money?

My strategy is to build a profitable micro-business that will need very little management and supervision, but will provide me with enough income to support my lifestyle. There are several ways to achieve this goal in an online or mobile business. Once you have successfully set up your business system – one which has one or a combination of these online money-making models - and it is running efficiently, you are moving forward. From there, I suggest you identify several different ways to make money from your new micro-business, then you can choose the one (or more) that are the best fit for you. You will then be on your way to becoming a business owner who has created true sleep money. Here is just a list of some business models that can become profitable entities online.

Ad Support – You can earn money from your website in ways other than from the sale of your product by leasing ad space directly to advertisers. This is called monetizing your site. Before you can earn that extra income, however, you need to attract advertisers first. Independent advertisers will only come to your site if your site is popular and has a consistent flow of traffic. The experts have stated that you need at least 500-1,000 distinct daily visitors to your website before you can see a noticeable amount of money from advertisers. This will not happen overnight, so don't count the money from advertisers yet. You have to build the popularity of your site and have a loyal community of fans before you will see money from advertisers flow. While you are developing your traffic, you should also use AdSense or AdMob to place ads on your site or app. These products are a hands-off solution and you get paid every time someone clicks on an ad.

Subscriptions - Subscription income can be a very important source of income for any online business, whether it is subscription to a product, a service, or to information. This is one place in your business where you can make sleep money really happen. The Apple App store has one of the best subscription business models. Users can download a magazine app for free then the developer can offer new content weekly or monthly for the users to purchase. It can be very profitable to have a subscription-based business since it is a continuing mechanism for selling your product. You can also ask your visitors to subscribe to your site for resources and content; this is especially true if your business offers web-based resources or software. Offer them quality free content and the best premium content can be placed behind a subscription wall. Make sure that your visitors see an outline or an abstract of the premium content. This is a great way to get them to subscribe. This is very similar to an "in app" purchase on mobile phones where the user can buy additional app products at any time from within an app. Many developers are beginning to use this method to up sell their customers. This method provides a dynamic and evolving app experience where the app is always changing and offering new products without becoming stagnant or stale.

Fees or Commissions - Fees or commissions are the principal source of income for a huge number of reseller websites and affiliate sites all over the world. Affiliate marketing companies such as ClickBank.com, Commission Junction, and Paydotcom have created a relatively easy affiliate marketing network model where you will be paid a commission or fee whenever a customer you referred to another site buys from that site. This is an avenue that has the potential to be very lucrative, as affiliate marketing is now a billion dollar industry. If this isn't the epitome of sleep money, I don't know what is. While this serves as an easy way to generate income, it is one that will take time; don't expect to earn a livable income quickly. If you want to concentrate on affiliate marketing as your main source of income, you need to attract a large number of visitors to your site to earn a decent living from it. You can also create several small sites to connect to more people and earn yourself a decent income. Although affiliate marketing will earn you a smaller percentage of the profits than if you sell your product directly, it can still be a good source of income.

Retail - Online selling is another lucrative e-business; proof of this is the volume of sales at sites like Amazon.com and Newegg.com, as well as the existence of hundreds of thousands of online stores on the web. When you go through the process of apping your business (more on this later) you will likely be operating in a similar fashion as these monstrous sites. This means of ecommerce is a great way to move your product without investing in a physical store to display and sell your products. Unlike selling from a brick and mortar location, where you need to keep an inventory that is restricted by warehouse and shelf space, you can sell a wide selection of products and sell them directly from your online store's producers to buyers anywhere in the world. The internet offers tremendous market exposure and sales opportunities, even for obscure and unusual products. The internet is the most level business playing field where a new micro-business can compete with the giant global retailers. Without ever owning a single product, you can sell most anything you can think of and have your product drop shipped to your customer by just forwarding a purchase order to a fulfillment house.

Build a Competing Site

As odd as that may sound at first, this is an idea that actually works. Competition is always a good thing because it makes consumers believe that they have options. It's the American way and, since you are going to have competitors, it's a smart idea to be one of them. There's an urban legend that surfaced around the turn of the century that, if true, exemplifies the benefits of competing against oneself. Back before digital downloads shook the music industry, street pirating was its kryptonite. Street entrepreneurs (that's what I'll call them), would somehow get copies of new music before it was officially released and they would make hundreds of illegal copies of the CDs. They would then sell these illegal copies to the general public at a discounted rate. Well, back in the 90's an east coast hip hop group by the name of Wu-Tang Clan reportedly started flooding the streets with these bootlegged copies of their own music and videos. If anybody was going to make illegal money off their music, they decided it would be themselves. This turned out to be a great marketing strategy for the group. To this day they are considered to be one of the most popular underground hip hop groups of all time.

The TJ Maxx (TJX) Companies specialize in closeout apparel and discount designer fashions, and they do so at multiple price points. Until a few years ago, the company had 3 brands, including Marshall's and another called AJ Wright, which were stores that specialized in urban apparel. All three stores were run by the same parent company. All three stores focused on discount fashion, just at different price points. Same company, different stores.

So once you create your product or service, think about a competitor product or service, and create that as well. It's an ingenious strategy that allows your customers to shop various brands within your own company. Monitor your product's performance. If it's selling, find out why by asking your customers. Offer incentives (freebies and discounts) in exchange for their willingness to take surveys. If your sales aren't good, do the same kind of research because you need to find out what's going wrong. Check and double-check your AdSense keywords to figure out how much traffic is coming to your site as a result of specific keywords. Separate keywords that perform well from the ones that are underperforming. Swap out the keywords that are underperforming for new ones. Never stop testing the effectiveness of your marketing strategy.

Also, check on the functionality of your website and make sure everything is working the way that it should be. If you have developed mobile apps, it may be time to debug again and upgrade your system to work with Apple, Windows or Android upgrades. Your customer comments and reviews will usually give you a pretty good idea of anything that goes wrong. Keep your ears open and follow any online conversation about your products. Quick answer questions and respond to inquiries when possible.

Set Financial Goals

Based on what you see in the first 120 to 180 days, you should be able to make reasonable projections relating to your product's performance. Create a growth plan for the next 6 months, two years and five years. What goals do you want this particular product to accomplish within that time? What benchmarks (annual sales, number of subscribers, downloads, frequency of visitors, growth of product inventory, etc.) must be reached and surpassed for this project to get where you want it to go? You want to set quantifiable goals so that you can measure your growth. Without having any goals set, you could be limiting your potential in your business' success.

Don't be afraid to tweak your business or marketing strategy a bit and be flexible in doing so. The digital world moves quickly and being able to adjust your plans as needed can make the difference between your micro-business having longevity and it being a flash in the pan. Remember the once popular social site, MySpace? Well, compared to the popularity it held years ago, it is considered a dinosaur now. Once your great system is in place, your product is generating profits and you have done a performance assessment, you can take another great idea and do it all again.

Re-Assessment

You've done everything that is required to start a micro-business – develop a business strategy, do market research, build your team, identify how you will make money, and market test your product. Now, if you're going to sell a product, this is the stage at which you prepare to have your product made. The last step in the process is to fine tune your business design and your product. If necessary, tweak the business design. Review and assess your business design by answering several questions. The two most important of several are: (1) is the direction of the company clear enough and (2) is your goal clear enough? If you want to continue the growth trajectory of this micro-business, make sure your business structures are clear and concise.

Other questions that need an answer would be: whether you have a clear idea of what the opportunities are to take your business to the next level and what steps are required to take advantage of those opportunities. Are you and your team aware of the strengths and weaknesses of the business at this stage? How will you capitalize on the strengths and find solutions to address the weaknesses? Is the business strategy good enough for the business to withstand a changing marketplace? Your business strategy should be focused enough to get results and flexible enough to change as the marketplace changes.

Chapter 10

Outsourcing

"Do what you do best and outsource the rest."

- Tom Peters, Co-Author of In Search of Excellence

"The other part of outsourcing is this: it simply says where work can be done outside better than it can be done inside, we should do it."

- Alphonso Jackson, 13th U.S. Secretary of Housing & Urban Development

What Is Outsourcing?

Let's take a closer look at what outsourcing is. Outsourcing is simply paying someone else to do a job for you that needs to be done. It doesn't have to be offshore from where you live – although it can be. It is an excellent process for getting single jobs or a series of similar jobs done. You can leverage the best talent from anywhere – including right next door neighbor or from the other side of the globe – at very competitive prices.

Outsourced workers can work on long-term and short-term projects. If you find outsourced workers who are professional and competent, it is a good idea to provide them work on a regular basis so that they keep time open to work on your projects. The best workers are often in high demand and their time books up very quickly.

Freelance sites like Elance.com, oDesk, and Freelancer make it much easier to find the right person, because they offer feedback and ratings from previous employers. This not only gives you an indication of past performance, but also gives your contractor a huge incentive to do a good job for you – they want good feedback.

Before developing iQuick Tools, the first thing I learned was if you don't already know how to build apps, don't try to learn how to build apps yourself. It will be the biggest waste of precious time. I know that may be contrary to common belief but it's true. Don't waste your time on it. As an example, did you know that many real estate developers don't know how to build a house? Yes the same developers that come and hack down all the tress in your neighborhood, cut in the streets and… voila… a new subdivision appears. Many developers understand that learning the details of how to build a house is not a cost-effective way to utilize their time. It's much easier and more cost-effective to find a project manager and bid out the contract for experts like the framing specialist, excavator, electrical tradesman, HVAC contractor, etc., to piece together the house. The developer is not an expert in any of these particular areas; instead, he is the mastermind who assembles teams of experts (i.e., masters) to get the project completed.

Not to mention that bidding out each piece of the housing puzzle puts the developer in a better position to get the very best price from the subcontractors. How? Through competition. In each project, these contractors are bidding against each other for the work, knowing that they must perform the very best at the very best cost to continuously work for the developer. All the developer is doing is managing the big picture, while ensuring that the ultimate goal is met – a house is built. This is the same process you can easily employ for app development. So knowing how, who and where to outsource the development is key.

Outsourcing the entire development to the right company will save you time, energy and money. You can just use their knowledge and skill that they have acquired over the years. So, again don't try to build or learn how to build your apps or develop your website yourself. I know for some people this sounds counterproductive, but actually it is the exact opposite. Good developing and programming takes a lot of time to master. Plus, it's just not necessary. It's like trying to become a real estate investor, but feeling like you have to become a real estate agent first. This is not necessary. In essence, it takes away precious time from building your business. That's ultimately what you want to do - build a business, not just build things. So focus on building your micro-business and let the developers develop. Remember, you want to be the mastermind not the master.

Don't get me wrong, it is good to have some basic knowledge on how to develop the apps, website or whatever it is you need to know. Trying to become an expert, however, is not necessary at all. When you need an expert developer, there are thousands of developers around the world who are more than willing to become part of your team while you are developing your projects. Remember, time is money. Your time is your money. By outsourcing some of your development, you'll be saving money in the long run by saving your time.

Let's take a closer look at my process of app development. I post most of my projects on Elance.com. For one project for our iQuick Tools apps, a company from India came to us with a tempting proposal. After they sent their proposal, I was a little worried because their price was really low. At that price, I wondered if they were capable of providing a good quality product. Although I had some concerns about their price, I decided to give them a shot. In the end, they did a fantastic job. Over the past year, they have built apps for me for as little as $500. So which was the better approach: use my time trying to learn how to code, or contract out the development at $500? My time is worth much more than that. It is far more cost-effective for me to outsource the development of a quality app overseas where I can get more "bang" for my buck. Contracting overseas is done all the time in big business. Why do you think Apple builds the iPhone in China? Where do you think Microsoft builds the Xbox? Not in the U.S. Both products are outsourced to Foxcom, a company in China. The big companies like Apple and Microsoft understand the strength of outsourcing, and you should too.

Leverage Your Time and Money with the Power of People

When most people think of the word "outsourcing," they think of jobs being lost and get mad – like seriously angry. I completely understand. When you see jobs being shipped overseas, it can be disheartening – especially if you are dependent on one of those outsourced jobs for your income. It doesn't have to be that way. If you choose, you can be on the other side of the equation. It can be you who is hiring the best talent from all over the globe to make your ideas a reality and make your dreams come true. In turn, you will be the one hiring people for things such as marketing or fulfillment here in the states. The possibilities of what you can accomplish by outsourcing are endless. Many mundane tasks that you are doing now yourself or are paying your domestic staff to do can and should be outsourced. This frees up your resources and the time your team needs to work on critical projects that only you can do. In fact, I would say to you that if you want to start earning sleep money, learning how to effectively outsource is essential. It's easier than you think.

My friend, Heather, is a great example of how simple it can be. Heather runs a successful web publishing company. People find her content on business and entrepreneurs online, read it, like it, and sometimes click on her banner ads. Although she makes no money from the content, the ads make her money – whether she is working or not. With the influx of readers and contributors, she has a pretty good gig going. When Heather started out, she was writing all of the content for her web publishing business herself. It was really a full-time job. That was okay with her at the time because she wanted to be around for her kids, and her business structure let her do that. As we all know, there is only so much time in the day, and only so much writing a single person can do (kind of sounds like Justin, right?). Heather knew that, if she wanted her business to grow, then she needed to do something different. She decided that the best thing she could do was hire full-time writers to take over part of that task for her. She had already done some outsourcing on a per job basis and saw how much that had helped her business.

It was a little rocky to start out because she had never before hired full-time writers. The first one or two writers didn't work out (more on that later). But after a couple of false starts, she found a freelancer from Romania online who could write on business very well. She started giving her assignments and feedback and within about a month, Heather's writer was paying for herself and within six months Heather's income had tripled.

Heather was, obviously, pretty happy about this. Her current goal is to work herself out of writing completely, only oversee the content production, and run the marketing side of her business. I think she is well on her way. As you can see by Heather's example, you can outsource more than just the technical side of things. You can outsource writing, customer service, and many other administrative duties as well. What you can outsource is often only limited by your imagination.

Outsourcing works so well because there is only so much time in the day. Just as in any business, you will quickly learn that you can't do everything yourself. It is often smart to hire someone else with more expertise in a specific area to help execute your idea. By building a team of experts, you can leverage your time and money to accomplish more than you could ever imagine. Let me tell you a secret - it doesn't matter how good your idea is – if you can't get it done, then it's not going to make you any money. Moving your ideas into reality, where they can make you a profit, is what outsourcing is all about.

Let's take a look at what outsourcing isn't. Outsourcing isn't like hiring a full time onsite worker. Outsourced workers are contractors; they are not full-time employees. As such, they will not make the kind of investment in your business that a full-time employee might. Because they may not know your business structure and goals like an employee would, it is, therefore, important to provide very specific instructions to your contractors so that they can properly complete the task that you wish to have accomplished. Most outsourced workers specialize in one area, so it is important to find someone who has established proficiency in the task you want completed.

Please understand that there are benefits and pitfalls of outsourcing. There are a ton of reasons to outsource. You can get things done that you don't have the time or skill to do. You can get the very best people from around the world working on your ideas and projects. You can also save a ton of money by outsourcing work (especially technical work) to various places in the world from a country that has a strong currency to a country with a weaker currency. But, there are some pitfalls as well. It takes time and skill to find and manage the right people for the right task. You have to know when to work with people and when to cut them loose, Sometimes jobs don't go quite the way you would like. The language barriers can present a problem when constant communication is necessary. The good news is that when contracting you never have to pay for inferior work or work that is not done to your expectations.

Whether it's across the street or across the globe, do not feel obligated to pay for unsatisfactory work. If you need to fire someone, it is way easier than it would be if you had hired someone on a full-time basis. Using a platform like Elance, GURU or Freelancer to hire contractors protects you so that you only pay if the contractor does satisfactory work. The flip side of this is that if your contractor is doing a great job for you, then they deserve to be paid promptly. This keeps them happy so that they will be willing to work for you again. That's always a plus when you've found an excellent worker. When outsourcing, the benefits far outweigh the negatives, and I will teach you how to avoid some of the inherent problems that come with hiring people as contractors.

What You Can Outsource

A lot of times people tell me that they don't have anything that they're able to outsource. This is actually a pretty common response when I talk about the power of leveraging others to help you. Most people want to maintain control over their enterprise and fear giving control over to someone else. This can be a huge mistake. Outsourcing can greatly increase your ability to get multiple things done. It can be the difference between the deferment or realization of your dream. So don't think that outsourcing means losing control. When you do it right, it actually gives you more control over your destiny.

Let's do a quick exercise to help you identify how much of your current and future tasks you can outsource. Ready? Good. Grab a clean sheet of paper. Now, draw a line down the middle and on one side write down "current task" or "business" at the top. On the other side, write down "my task" or "business idea." Next, write down all of the tasks that you do on a daily basis. Then write down all of the things you need to do to take your business idea from concept to reality.

The next part may be a bit challenging. It was challenging for me when I started outsourcing, but has gotten easier as I go along. I want you to take a critical look at your list and put a star next to the things that only you can do. There should only be a few things starred. If there are more than 4 or 5 (and preferably only 2 or 3) on the whole list, look at it again and see if you can take some off. For all of the things you haven't starred, you should be hiring help to get them accomplished. That means outsourcing. As a micro-business or a future micro-business owner, you should be focused on growth, ideas, and making sure that your ideas get executed. Your plan should be to work yourself into a position where everything else can be delegated or outsourced.

The best way to do this is to take the task at which you are least skilled and start there. This will dramatically free up your time to focus on the things that only you can do for your business. Once you've decided where in your business you should start outsourcing, the next thing you need to do is figure out where to find an outsourced worker.

You can find your workers in a variety of ways. For web developers, you can post fliers at a local technical college. Yes, not all outsourcing jobs go to companies overseas. Think about Justin; he outsourced his web development to a local neighborhood teenager. I, instead, go online to sites like Elance, Freelancer, and oDesk for temporary or long-term workers. You can hire a personal virtual assistant full-time through these same sites. For very small jobs, I go to Fiverr.com. I love this site. All jobs start at only five dollars. Many start-ups even post an ad on Craigslist.

There are advantages and disadvantages to each of these methods. If you don't use one of the hiring platforms I've mentioned, the number of providers to which you have access is more limited. On the other hand, by hiring through a platform like this, you may not get the benefit of personally meeting the person you're hiring and getting a feel for them through an in-person meeting. Nevertheless, if you are in need of technical development, I would recommend you start with a site like Elance. To me, they are the gold standard by which all other outsourcing sites are measured, and there is good reason for this. Quality workers are attracted to quality employers and both the best employers and best workers are often found at Elance.com. In addition, their system is really easy to navigate, and they actually have live phone support if you run into issues. They also have a feedback system for workers and an escrow system for employers that protects both parties.

Since I use Elance all the time to find qualified workers for the different projects I have going on in my business, I thought I would give you a broad overview of how the system works and what is important to know. Let's start with hiring. One of the great things about the Elance system is how easy it is to use. To find qualified workers, you just need to post a project description on the site. Make your ad as specific as possible to attract the right candidate, and you will get competing bids from people interested in that job. Before choosing a good contractor, there is a very useful feedback feature you should employ. As contractors complete jobs, the employers give them feedback and let them know if the job they completed was good. You can see this feedback, and this can help you decide whether or not to hire someone. This is my favorite way of determining if I want to hire a contractor, and it is a pretty good indication of whether or not they will be successful for you. After choosing a contractor, you should verify that you have the funds in your account by using the escrow service. You will get a more serious working relationship if you do this first.

The next thing that is important is managing your workers. There are two ways to do this within the system. The first is through time tracking. If you hire an hourly worker, then they will track their time with the time tracker widget. This is a little desktop program that they set when they start work on your project and it takes screen shots of all their work as they complete it. This makes the work verifiable and you know what your worker is doing.

The other way to manage your team is hiring them on a fixed price basis. This is the method I use most of the time. These jobs are exactly as they sound. I hire for the development of a specific program that I need done as a single job. Then, I set up milestones (or checkpoints) within that job to monitor progress. This allows me to get excellent results and to make sure that my contractors are delivering before the escrow (payment held by Elance) I set up is released to my contractor. That is really all there is to it. Using the system is simple and you are likely to get excellent results with outsourcers hired at Elance.

There are some absolutely amazing people that want to work for you. These people are smart, dedicated and experts in their fields. On the other hand, there are people who will lie to you about their skills, never meet a deadline, and give you a sob story. The key is figuring out the difference quickly so you can get the work done that you need to get done. That being said, there are some best practices you should follow when hiring workers.

This reminds me of what Heather told me about the first full-time writer she hired. She had already used services like Freelancer and TheContentAuthority.com to get writing done and was figuring it wouldn't be much different than that experience. Heather had heard about onlinejobs.ph where you could hire full-time workers from the Philippines for less than $400 a month (which is a decent wage there) and decided to put up an ad on the site. She got a lot of responses and selected someone who went by the name of Bob to work for her. Of course she thought the worker would be great, but the worker was terrible. She gave him a list of assignments and he would only do half of them. He wouldn't send in his daily reports, and working with him was, overall, a nightmare. She kept him on for about a month, which was 4 weeks too long according to her, before finally throwing in the towel and starting over.

You may wonder why I even tell you this story. After all it sounds... depressing. Don't forget the other part of the story that I told above. When Heather found the right person to work with she was able to outsource so much of her work that her income tripled within 6 months. Therefore, it's worth getting through the learning curve for those types of results.

I interviewed Heather a while back and asked her why she thought her first experience was so bad. It turned out that she made three classic mistakes that nearly everyone does when they start outsourcing. Let's take a look at what she said and how you can avoid the same mistakes.

(1) Don't Let Emotions Cloud Your Judgment. This is a huge challenge when hiring people. Heather liked Bob and wanted to give him another chance. And another chance. And another chance. So she kept working with him, even when he made the same errors over and over again. The rule of thumb here is to assume the first problem is a result of you not making expectations clear, but if the same problem comes up repeatedly, then the person you hired just might be the problem.

(2) Don't Make Your Project Post Broad. Make your project post as specific as possible. When the ad was first placed for this position, Heather stated that she put together a very brief ad that was, basically, a broad overview. Because of this, the candidates she got for the ad weren't prepared to actually do the job. Be sure when you are writing ads to let prospective contractors know exactly what is required, so that you can attract contractors whose skills are properly matched to your needs.

(3) Don't Be Wishy-Washy. Have clear expectations. When she was selecting the person for the position, Heather conducted an interview in a casual, chat-like manner. When Bob asked how many articles she needed written per day, she responded that she was "flexible." This set her up for failure from the beginning. Avoid this mistake by being clear in your expectations.

If Heather had been better at conveying clear expectations and following through quickly when the expectations were not met, she would have greatly increased her chances of finding a high-quality worker faster. In fact, that is exactly what she did the second time around. She created a very detailed project posting and was very clear about expectations. This helped a great deal and she got a worker that really benefited her business.

How to Use Outsourcing to Create Sleep Money

Let's take a look at a past college friend named Rebecca. Rebecca owned a gift basket business that was making her a nice income. The only problem was that her storefront allowed for limited expansion. She decided that she wanted to start selling gift baskets online, but needed a shopping cart for her website that was easy-to-use and intuitive to visitors. With all of the gift baskets companies out there, you may think that creating a virtual storefront wouldn't create much revenue, and you would be right. It's where she took her business after the virtual storefront was created that is so interesting.

Rebecca found a web development company that made 3D graphics and custom shopping carts. This was before things like 3D graphics were commonplace. Rebecca had them tweak their web design to meet her needs. It is important to note that she didn't start from scratch here. Instead, she outsourced a particular aspect of her site with a tech company called SynapseIndia. This company had already developed the technology that she needed to improve her site's appearance as well as the shopping cart. She had SynapseIndia design the tools to meet her needs.

After Rebecca got the 3D design and shopping cart technology that she wanted - she re-launched her site. The site graphics had the look and feel of a real 3D basket. The users could change and mix and match different products into their baskets. Instantly, her sales increased. It worked so well, that she wondered if other brick and mortar stores could use the same technology to get online. She contacted the company that developed this shopping cart for her, and she got the rights to sell it under her own brand. She used the contacts and marketing savvy she had built in her online gift basket venture to market the technology. Other retail shops needed software like this too, and they were happy to buy it from her, because it was already done and they didn't have to do it themselves. Selling this technology was a great way to increase her bottom line.

Rebecca is a perfect example of how to take something that you have developed to make your business run more smoothly or expand, and then market that solution to other small businesses to create additional income. Rebecca identified a technology-based solution to expand her business. She outsourced the creation of the technology-based solution to someone else, then put it into practice. Finally, she decided to market the same solution to other businesses that could use her help. This is a very common way that micro-business owners learn to create sleep money. The best thing is that with the kind of technologies that there are today, you can do the same type of thing in your business with just a little creative thinking.

Here's another bit of outsourcing advice. Even if I have a provider that I really like working with, I will still sometimes make them bid on projects in order to get the job. I used to use a company for web development, videos and graphics out of Indonesia that has done a great job for me named Bread 'n' Beyond. Although I like their work, sometimes I will have them bid on projects to let them know that they have continuous competition for my business. This assures me that I'm getting the very best price for my project and assures me that I'm getting the best price per project. Don't ever let a contractor get too comfortable and take your work for granted.

Elance is just one of many outsourcing companies available, but it happens to be a favorite of mine. As the world's leading platform for online employment, Elance helps businesses hire and manage on the internet. For businesses looking to staff-up a team on an hourly or project basis, Elance offers instant access to qualified professionals who work online and provides the tools to hire, view work as it progresses and pay for results.

If you are looking to jump-start a project, broaden your reach or just simply get things done, you will find that Elance is faster and more cost-effective than job boards, staffing firms and traditional outsourcing. You name it and Elancers will deliver great results – from writing code, crafting a marketing plan, designing your website, managing your day-to-day schedule to a thousand other projects. There are other outsourcing companies you can try – it often comes down to personal preference. Here are a few other options:

37signals Job Board
www.jobs.37signals.com
37signals has a dedicated section for posting iPhone developer jobs. It currently costs $300 for a 30-day job posting.

CocoaDev
www.cocoadev.jobcoin.com
With 2,000 unique visitors a day and job listings priced at just $99 for 30 days, you can reach a large number of developers for a small payment.

Craigslist
www.craigslist.org
Craigslist is still a valuable resource for those looking to find work and is a great place to post jobs.

Fiverr
www.fiverr.com
No job over $5. I use this work site all the time for small and quick jobs. Have you ever seen the promo video for Rock City Birds! on youtube.com (go to www.youtube.com/rockcitybirds)? Well I found the guy who did the voiceover work for that on fiverr. He only charged 2 fiverr's ($10) for this job.

Freelancer
www.freelancer.com
Similar to Elance, and their biggest competition.

GetAppsDone
www.getappsdone.com

There are always quite a few jobs listed on GetAppsDone. Your listings will also be shared via their iPhone app.

Guru
www.guru.com

Guru allows companies to find freelance workers for commissioned work.

oDesk
www.odesk.com

Operates similarly to Elance, but focuses more on hourly work, not fixed-price projects.

Chapter 11

How to Build an App Business

"Teamwork is the ability to work together toward a common vision. The ability to direct individual accomplishments toward organizational objectives. It is the fuel that allows common people to attain uncommon results."

- Andrew Carnegie, Industrialist and Philanthropist

*I*n case I have not made it perfectly clear by now, an app business is simply a type of business. Fundamentally, it is a business which should be operated in accordance with certain principals. Additionally, in the vast majority of cases, an app business is a micro-business, and, as such, can be made successful through the application of the same sound business practices that would be applicable to any other type of micro-business. That said, I went about my App Millionaire journey as a man with no technical ability to build apps. I went about the process by putting together teams that could help me bring my vision to life. I will explain to you how to go about building an app business, using the method that I employed. This will not be a useless chapter for those who have technical ability, though. If you are able to build the app yourself, you should simply skip over the parts that do not apply to you. Let's get started.

Come Up with a Good Idea

Ideas are a dime a dozen, right? Since you're reading this book, you're probably one of the millions of people who have an idea for some business, some app, or some other blah blah blah. Let me tell you: having an idea is not enough. You need a really, really *good* idea. With hundreds of thousands of applications available in the various app stores and on the internet, how do you come up with something unique? Or, how can you execute an idea better than everyone else in the market? Besides game apps, the most successful apps available today either offer something completely different, or solve an existing problem in a very extraordinary way. A well thought out idea is the key. If you can solve someone's problem in a simple fashion, or entertain a user in a completely novel way, you're definitely on the road to achievement. A good idea is the gateway to a successful app. Think Instagram. Think Voxer. Refer back to Chapter 9 for a framework on identifying and fleshing out your ideas.

Build a Team

I cannot stress enough the importance of building a quality team. If you try to do everything yourself, your chances for failure are inevitable... simple as that. In other words, if you try to make all the money, you'll end up making no money at all.

I've made good income from projects such as iQuick Tools, Very Simple Ads, CTQ, and other mobile apps. None of that would have happened if I hadn't created effective partnerships with developers and suppliers overseas who are willing to work for me like an on-call partner. One of the reasons that I like freelance contracting companies such as Elance, Odesk, GURU and Freelancer, is that they give you the opportunity to develop a relationship with someone in a "safe" environment. Most of these freelancers have their own business as well. If you choose to work with them independent of these platforms, later, you can. In the initial stages, when you are evaluating their performance and building the relationship, you have a trusted and safe platform through which to take them for a "test drive" first.

Online Freelancing Contractors

I've made it no secret that Elance is my outsourcing platform of choice.

Elance is not the only outsourcing portal but I think it's the best. (Odesk comes in strong as second place.) If you choose to go another way, that's fine, but you need to get your account started and ready to go. To use Elance, you'll go to www.elance.com and create an account under the "I want to hire" portion of the front page. From there you will be guided through setting up your account and the selection of the appropriate membership level.

Be sure to take the time to complete a detailed profile. Service providers will want to know as much about you as you will want to know about them. If you leave large gaps of information out, it looks like you are on the shady side. If possible, include any recommendations or testimonials from clients or providers that have worked for you in the past.

Make sure you take care of any financial parts of your account. You do not want to get the point where you are ready to hire someone but you have neglected to properly set up the escrow account. You will look suspicious to them. Ensure that your financial account on the site is linked to your bank account, and you have enough money available to fund the project. No money will leave your escrow account until you approve the work, however, most contractors want to be able to see that you are able to pay them for their efforts.

When you finish a job with a provider on Elance, be sure to (1) pay them promptly and (2) leave positive feedback (as long as they have done a good job). This will ensure that they will be willing to work with you again when you have another job that needs to be done.

Develop a Short Test Project

If you're new to the online contracting process, I suggest you try a small test project before you jump in to a fully-loaded app project. Maybe try a small logo project first to make sure you understand the ins and out of the online contracting process. That way, when you're ready to hire your first app developer, you will feel more comfortable with the process and your judgment in selecting contractors and managing your projects. My first test project was a single page website.

Create a Detailed Job Description

Not sure how the job description should read? You're in luck...there are plenty of them on Elance, Freelancer, etc. I included a sample that I have used in Chapter 9. Peruse through the mobile app job descriptions and see how they are worded. Remember, the more detailed the better. You will see some that are as generalized as "Need an iPhone App for Children's Game." It would behoove you, however, to provide more detail, so that expectations on both sides of the transaction are aligned.

Feel free to be very specific in what you require and what you expect. If proposals come in that don't meet your specifications, it is very possible that the provider is not paying attention. Another way to ensure you are not getting "robot proposals" is to ask for a specific keyword to be put in your proposal such as "blue pumpkin". It may sound ridiculous, but again, this gives you assurance that that people are actually reading your proposal and not just mass responding.

Finally, ask for examples of previous work. Keep in mind that past non-disclosure/confidentiality agreements may preclude some providers from showing some of their prior work to prospective employers. They should, however, be able to show you something in their portfolio that supports their claim that they know what they are doing.

Review Your Proposals and Ask Any Clarifying Questions

Remember, you don't have to just throw a dart and pick a provider. Also, don't pick a provider based on price alone. Sometimes the old adage is true - you get what you pay for. Other times, you can get a real bargain with a provider who needs the money and is in between jobs. Take a complete look at their work, and ask as many questions as you deem necessary. Most online contracting sites will give you the opportunity to converse with the provider through messaging before you actually choose them. Make sure you feel comfortable with their abilities to meet your work expectations and due date.

Choose the Provider & Set Clear Milestones

Once you have chosen the provider, make sure you set clear milestones for due dates and communication. If the project is going to be longer than 2 weeks, consider making milestone payments for progress along the way. This keeps your provider motivated throughout the process. If there are any issues that come up as the project progresses, inform the provider

The purpose of having milestones is to be able to control the progress of the project. If you are not happy with how the project is moving along, having set milestones provides you with distinct indicators of progress or the lack thereof. If you see that the project is not moving as you would like it to, be sure to talk to your provider and course correct early. This will keep frustration to a minimum on both of your parts. Remember to pay promptly and leave feedback at the end of the project. You want to have a good working relationship with any provider that has done a good job for you. Since you are likely to need help for additional projects down the line, you want to establish a good reputation on the freelance platform.

Basic Tools

There are a few basic technology tools that you will need in order to build your micro-business and your app. Again, I'm not talking about any high-level specialized knowledge. But, you do need to have some familiarity with these basics.

Skype. As you are building an outsourcing team, communication will be critical. Skype is a communication tool that allows you to connect with your team members across the country and across the world. You can instant message an individual team member or connect with several of them at the same time. You can also speak to one another via voice and video communication. You can place international calls to another Skype user at no cost over your computer. In addition, you can share files and even share screens. It's a great no-cost collaboration tool. Simply go to www.skype.com to download the application. They even have an app so you can use Skype when you are away from your computer and on a mobile device.

Google Voice. Google Voice is a service that allows you to have one phone number that can be applied to all of your phones. This one number can reach you whether you are at home, on the beach, or anywhere else in the world. Perhaps the best feature of it is that it allows you to make free calls throughout the United States and to Canada, and low-cost calls to other areas of the world. When you're doing business with people around the globe, this can be an excellent resource.

A Mac and PC. You'll want to have both a Mac and a PC to ensure that your apps and any other programs operate properly on these systems. The same is true when working with team members. Some will have Macs, some will have PCs. You'll want to be ready to interface with anyone and everyone.

It is vital that you know your how your app looks and feels on different platforms. You won't want to limit yourself to just one platform (we'll be talking about that later) – so you'll need to test on all platforms. Although you will have a team of developers, the app will, ultimately, belong to you. It is, therefore, up to you to decide if the look and feel is what you had it mind. Does it convey what you thought it would? Is the user experience what you envisioned? You won't know if you can't see it the way the end user would see it.

Make It Beautiful

Give your customer a good product, and they will come back and support your business. Although you may be small, you don't have to look like you just threw something together in a pile of junk. We no longer live in the days of "Pong" and "Pacman" (although retro is cool); graphics are much more sophisticated and customers now have high expectations.

One of the best ways to market your apps is to use good graphics. Better yet, make that sexy graphics. Yes, this will cost more and will take more time, but it's worth the investment. One of the biggest mistakes I made in the beginning was not knowing how good graphics should look. As a result, my sales weren't as high as they could have been.

I was getting my butt kicked by a competitor app company that made similar apps as iQuick Tools. They made apps in the productivity category. The products they made were just okay, but this company's sales were really good. Why? Because the graphic design of their apps was top-notch and professionally done. It's like their graphics pulled you into their app. When you're designing your apps remember, interface design is all-important, and there are plenty of app developers capable of doing this.

Along the same lines as design and graphics, music and sound effects are other elements that can set your app apart. This is particularly important when developing game apps. Think about it...when you're playing a video game or playing in a casino, what sticks in your mind (sometimes for hours) after you've left the game? The theme music.

You may think that theme music is something that comes at a premium cost, however, you'd be amazed how inexpensive it is. You can outsource a simple theme for a nominal price on Elance or even Fiverr.com. Yes, Fiverr! Once a company made my own custom theme music for only five dollars and it was very good. So when you are creating a unique sound for your apps, what you're doing is simply additional branding. Whether you have a game or some other type of app, you are creating an additional branding process that your customer associates with your app. Sound effects can be just as important an element. They may not be missed if they are not there... but they certainly are a bonus when they are included. So don't ignore the sound and music components of your app. Make sure you have a quality intro, a theme that sticks in your head, and sound effects that are relatable and consistent throughout the app.

Take a look at some of the review sites and online forums for apps. The usability and functionality of the app is certainly important and it will always be the most important feature to the users. When it comes to overall enjoyment and the "fun factor," however, the sounds and music will often be a part of the comments. It's the "wow" factor - the element that brings the app to life, so to speak. If your app developer is not qualified to do sound effects, that's okay. Put a job request out on Elance, oDesk or even Fiverr and you'll have plenty of proposals from providers who can give you quality sound and music to suit your app.

Know Your Business Model

There are several different ways that you can make money with your app, and you'll need to decide which business model makes sense for you and your type of business. Here are some of the most common business models in the app space to consider.

Sell Your App. It's almost as simple as it sounds. You set a price for your app and sell it to those who are willing to purchase it. Hopefully, lots of people are willing to purchase it. (Of course, we'll talk more about making sure people want to purchase it in the marketing portion of the book). There are a few other considerations – namely, price. You'll see a vast majority of apps out there priced at .99 cents. That's not the only option. You need to take a look at what your costs were. Now, if it only cost you $1,000 to get your app developed, you may be able to make your money back pretty quickly at 99 cents per download.

Freemium. Sometimes offering free products can be very lucrative in the long run. Chris Anderson, the author of the book *Free* stated that offering free products is "the next big thing" in entrepreneurship. If possible, offer free items to your customers and try to upgrade your customers to paid premium products or sell them a different product. With regard to your app, you would start by offering a free demo of the app, which would be a scaled-down version of the product. You would provide for sale a full version at a nominal price of, let's say, 99 cents or $1.99 (hey, you have them hooked by that point). Or, you can start out your app at 99 cents for a good solid version and have upgrades available at 99 cents for additional levels or have the entire full version available for $4.99, which would include future upgrades.

Subscription App. This is similar to any other type of subscription. If you create an app that has some kind of continuous new content, consider having a subscription app. Just make sure you are delivering new and continuous worthwhile information to your subscribers.

Service App. Some people call these concierge or life apps. This is the type of app that combines the convenience of mobile technology with customer service. Is there a service you wish you could have available at your fingertips? For example, do you need to make travel plans or a hotel reservation? Chances are, others feel the same way and have the same needs. Build an app to fill the service needs in the area around you. From kids sport car pool services to airport rides, building service apps can be a great way to meet needs and make money. Think: Alfred. Think: Scout Mob. Think: Red Square.

Ads. Ads are another business model that you can choose to pursue. This business model is one that could have an entire chapter of its own. When you are using ads as your business model, you are giving the app to the users as a free download. Yes, free. How can I possibly make money giving away my app for free? In the app market space, there are advertisers who are businesses that pay to have their ads placed on apps. Then there are publishers. Those are people who develop the apps, and have ads placed on them.

Additionally, there are ad networks. These are basically automated networks that bring the advertisers and the publishers together. They collect the money from the advertisers, take a commission, and give the money to the publishers. The advertiser will be bidding on a keyword and paying a price per click – basically how many times someone clicks on an ad that appears on your app. So, the more people download your app, the more chances you have of someone clicking on the ads. You get revenue from the click.

At the end of the month, the ad network settles up with you and you receive your earnings based on the number of clicks the ad received. You may have heard about the overwhelming success of ads on the free version of Angry Birds on the Android platform. You may not be in the realm of making $2 million a month, but ads with free downloads can be another way of making money. If done right, you can make good money from free apps that are supported with ads.

Do some research and find out what business models have worked well for the niche you are considering. Find the success stories that are out there and allow yourself to be motivated by them. Just because someone has succeeded doesn't mean there isn't room for someone else to succeed as well. There's always another success story around the corner, and it may as well be you.

Be Diverse

As I said before, most people hear the word "apps" and the first thing that pops into their head is "iPhone." "iPhone" and "apps" seem to go together like peanut butter and jelly. But, they are not mutually exclusive. To limit yourself to the production of iPhone apps only is akin to saying "I'd only like to make $5,000 this month. Please...don't give me anymore money. I don't want anymore and I will turn away any additional money you try to give me."

Why would you do that? You already have the idea...bring it to the other platforms! Build your apps for the iPhone, but also for Android, Windows Mobile, Blackberry and even desktop, if possible. You want to gain as much exposure as you can. Just look at Angry Birds or Farmville. These games are, literally, everywhere.

In order to build on each platform, you must first become a registered developer. It's fairly inexpensive to become a certified developer on these platforms. Apple is the most expensive at $99. That is still pretty reasonable for a one- time fee. The other platforms, however, range from as low as free to $25. After you become a developer, you simply download each development kit to your computer. This will allow you to test each app on your computer within a simulator. It may be necessary to choose members of your team who are well-versed in the different platforms. However, it is possible to hire a multi-platform developer that is able to build apps on the different operating systems. This can save you a lot of time and effort. The bottom line is that you should aim to have an app that is everywhere, so that you maximize your earning potential and exposure.

When you start making sales of your app, there is no time to sit back and rest on your laurels. Once the success ball starts rolling, you want to keep that ball rolling. Just remember, when Angry Birds first started, it wasn't with a bang. Once the iPhone app started taking off, they took that success ball and started looking for ways to diversify. There was the Android app, plush toys, video and more.

How will you diversify once your success ball starts rolling? Don't wait until the ball is half way down the hill before you start thinking about it. It'll be too hard to catch up to at that point. Plan for success from the beginning. You don't have to implement everything at once, but you should have your "what if" plans on paper. What if my app sells at a rate of 100 a day? What if my app sells at a rate of 500 a day? What if my app cracks the "What's Hot" list? What's the next step at that point? Will you: Incorporate add-ons to your app? Have spin-offs of your app? Have other apps in the same niche that solve other problems that exist? Create or sell products that compliment your app?

Define early on what diversification will mean for you. What is the next step? At what point will you take the next step? Is it once you have sold a certain number of apps? Is it once you have a certain level of sustainable sales per day? Define it and plan it so you are ready to move forward when the time is right.

Stay Informed

The mobile app business is a quickly-changing one, as is everything else that is related to internet marketing. Much of what you'll be doing from a marketing perspective will be via internet marketing. Social media will be particularly useful. You will want to keep yourself up-to-date and stay educated on the latest and greatest of what is going on.

Sign up for any RSS feeds related to mobile app news. Do a Google search on "mobile app information news" and create an email alert for any new information. Find websites that have consistent, compelling articles and sign up for their newsletters. Find out how they communicate with their readership. You can always learn from others.

Know your industry inside and out. That includes not just the app industry, but the industry that is the subject of your app. You'll want to stay 2 steps ahead of your competition. That means knowing what your customers' wants and needs are, and meeting them better than anyone else. Create a system that will allow you to remain informed.

Chapter 12

App Your Business

"Business opportunities are like buses, there's always another one coming."

- Richard Branson, Entrepreneur, Founder and Chairman of The Virgin Group

In addition to creating an app, based on a random idea you have, you can also do what I call "apping" an existing business. I use the term "business" in the last sentence loosely. In this context, "business" can mean "profession," "trade" or "line of work." In other words, you can app any business – it does not have to be one that you own; it just has to be one with which you are familiar.

There is a common misconception that running one's own business allows for more freedom. That's not usually the case. On average, full-service small business owners experience less freedom and work more hours than if they had remained in their jobs. Launching a small business is not without its challenges, which is, obviously, why more people don't venture out and do it. The cost of running it - stocking inventory, covering insurance, paying employees, taxes and rent – can quickly wipe out one's personal savings. When developing a full-service small business, it's not unusual for an entrepreneur to leave their 9 a.m. to 5 p.m. job as an employee only to take on 7 a.m. to 7 p.m. hours as an employer.

One way to reclaim your time if you run a small business is to systematize your business. Incorporate a system within your business model that allows you to move away from the grind of day-to-day operations. In order to partake in that ever-elusive freedom, you need a set of standard operating procedures in place that address most aspects of the daily functions of your business. Built into the system should be a protocol for delegation and accountability – the who does what of your business.

These days, there's just about an app for everything from gaming to bartending and everything in between. In just the last few years, apps have become a pretty important part of our daily lives. Some common tasks that were once part of a cumbersome process have now become more manageable. Need to deposit a check into your bank account? No need to drive to the bank because there's an app for that. Need a new driver's license? In one state there's an app for checking in with the Department of Transportation before you even leave home. Apps have, literally, saved us time and made many of our lives simpler.

At this point in this book I hope I've made it clear that becoming an App Millionaire does not have to involve just the development of mobile or desktop apps. When I talk about apps, I'm talking about a way of doing business that is based not on a particular thing, but moreso a process – a system... small... flexible... portable. For some of you, the thing may actually be mobile app development. But for others, your transition to the App Millionaire mindset and lifestyle may be rooted in something you already know and do – something with which you are already familiar. It's probably something that is staring you right in the face. So, one way to reclaim your time is to "app your business." Apping your business is the process of taking a full-service or brick and mortar business and identify a small portion of it to market and sell online. It can also involve taking a service that one provides (usually by trading hours for dollars) and providing all or a portion of that service in a more streamlined fashion.

If you're already in business, or working a full-time job you may have immediate access to more opportunities than you even realize. With a functioning business or hobby (a hobby that can be made lucrative), you can take a portion of your business and modify, adapt or repackage a piece of your operation, and turn it into a low-maintenance, profitable enterprise. This process is one that requires, more than anything, some creativity and resourcefulness. But don't over think it, because the goal is not to make what you have bigger; the goal is to refine and focus a portion of your business and expand your reach with a particular product or service. This is where the term "less is more" applies perfectly - narrow your scope, but increase your impact.

As I mentioned before, I still run a full-service construction company and real estate firm. In an effort to streamline some of the common functions of our daily business, such as estimating the construction cost of a project, I decided to create mobile apps specifically for my industry. When I apped my business, I decided to develop an estimating app – called iQuick Estimator. To my surprise, this app sold all over the world. That was an "ah-ha" moment for me. With the success of this first app, I launched a mobile app company, iQuickTools. It wasn't long before I created several useful applications for not just my team, but for all real estate industry professionals. We've produced a job estimator app, an invoice app, a change order app, contract and leasing mobile apps and more. Because my niche market was so narrow, these apps dominated the space in the App Store.

Let me give you another example. A business partner of mine, Tanya, is a transactional attorney with her own small law practice. Much of the work she does involves helping businesses and entrepreneurs, like me, protect themselves when negotiating various deals and when entering into contracts. Having worked very closely with many business people, Tanya saw commonalities in terms of their needs. By virtue of being entrepreneurs, many of her clients were not afraid to negotiate or make deals on their own; their weakness was actually putting the terms of those deals in writing. These were folks who ran their businesses with a very "hands on" approach, but knew that they had neither the skill nor the time to create a document that was both professional and an adequate protection of their interests. Finally, these were not large companies who were willing and could afford to spend thousands and thousands of dollars on legal fees.

Tanya and I had lunch one day and she told me that she had an idea for how to get entrepreneurs like many of her clients the documents they need, professionally done, but at a reasonable price. She would make the documents commonly used by entrepreneurs and sole proprietors easily accessible and available for purchase online. After all, drafting documents was something she already did in her regular law practice. The documents would be generic enough to be used in a range of situations, simple enough to be easily understood, but thorough enough to be effective. Once purchased, the document could be modified by the purchaser to be used over and over again, in multiple transactions. As we discussed her plans, I knew, immediately, that she was onto something good. She had come up with a way to capitalize on a portion of her existing business, streamline it, and make it available to many more people than it would ever be available through her regular practice. By narrowing her scope, she was able to increase her impact. That idea became a successful online company called ThePerfectContract.com.

After the success of ThePerfectContract.com, Tanya took another step in apping her business by carving out an even smaller portion of her practice to create another enterprise. Her next ecommerce site was AllAboutLeases.com, where she focused solely on one type of document - leases. Just like Justin's lawn care website, this new site gave practical information about all types of leases. Also, users could pick and choose the type of lease to purchases from those related to commercial real estate, cars, boats, furniture, equipment and more. So, from her traditional law practice, she apped her business and created a document ecommerce website. From there, she further apped her business by selling only a particular document type. With the success of these two sites, coupled with very low overhead, she estimated that these sites would outperform her practice in terms of gross income within 3 years.

If you are in business or working at a company you should take an in-depth look at the business structure and see if you can find opportunities that are right under your nose. If you currently offer several types of products, how can you take a small number of those products, or just one product and make it available to millions of people? Can you take a service that you normally provide to a small group of people and make it available to thousands more? Really think about it. You may be surprised by what you find. There may be an "appable" business staring you right in the face.

Think Small, Then Think...Smaller

Apps usually have limited features or services as compared to full-featured software. When Justin apped his business, he took a portion of his business (organic fertilizer) and created an online micro-business with less bloat than his full-service business. Apping your business may offer your customers a bit more flexibility in how they conduct business with you. Taking a particular product that's only offered for in-person sales and selling it online will widen your customer base. This should expand your number of prospective customers to include those outside of your geographic area.

Let's look at another example from a coffee house that I frequent. Marlee's Coffee House is a quaint meeting place located near Georgia State University. Marlee's Coffee was voted by the local entertainment guide as the best coffeehouse in Atlanta, Georgia. From its jazzy appearance you may on occasions see camera crews using it as a set for television shows like *The Real Housewives of Atlanta* or *Love and Hip Hop - Atlanta*. Beyond that, it's just a cozy place to relax and work. You'll find the paintings of local artists hanging on the walls, and restored vintage furniture placed throughout the venue. The mugs are nearly twice the size of that of your typical coffeehouse and each cup of coffee is beyond excellent. The atmosphere is calm and peaceful. Jazz music plays softly in the background. The restroom is clean and the service is fast and friendly. Their clientele is an eclectic mix of college students and professionals. If you ask the customers why they patronize Marlee's Coffee, when there are several other cafes in town, they, often, say, "It's the atmosphere."

From what I see, Marlee's Coffee House does well. However, their business model is quite different than most coffee houses. Marlee's actually markets their business in a different manner than most of their competitors. This coffee shop operates more like an event center. In this coffee shop, people have utilized the space for a number of things, including talent searches, entrepreneurial events, and even wedding receptions, too. People pack this place for these events. In addition to that, most of the events are free. Yes, free! You may think they can make good money for space rental and that may be true. However, the exposure that they get from these events is immeasurable. People come back because the customer service is impeccable. The owner told me that their in-store sales profits increase substantially after every event. In essence, Marlee's Coffee has apped their business. Not in a traditional manner, but in their own way. They use a portion of their business to create more revenue for their bottom line. That segment of their business is "space." They have created for themselves an additional revenue stream that requires almost no overhead – no complimentary donut, no one to wash dishes, no one to make the coffee. Just think of how many businesses can repurpose their usable space for something other than the current business model. Art galleries and hotels do it all the time. Why can't a coffee shop, massage spa or tattoo parlor do the same? It is quite easy to benefit from the rental revenue or just the exposure. Is there a great opportunity to increase revenues right in front of you that you are not capitalizing on right now? Are you thinking outside the box? If not, tweaking your thinking just a tad bit might be just what you need.

The same rule applies if you're in a service business. Service businesses sell information and expertise. Information and expertise are perfect for a digital medium. Again let's look at Justin's Lawn Care Service. Justin built his lawn care business the old fashioned way – through great service and reasonable prices. In a short time, he was able to hire help and did what most business people do – he created a website. Occasionally, he would answer lawn-related questions on his site. The more the questions poured in, the more Justin realized that the information his customers needed was difficult to find on the web, so he decided to create an educational and engaging website for people to learn about lawn care and serve as a platform for him to sell lawn care products. In launching that second site, he was able to expand his reach from his local area to customers all over the country. The online sales component of his business became a business of its own. During the slow seasons in his lawn care business, he still made money because the online sales continued. Justin went from owning a full-service lawn-care business to owning an online retail micro-business. After a short period of time, Justin's online business outperformed his full-service lawn care business.

If you don't currently run a small business, an apped business is actually a smart alternative to a full-service firm. The traditional barriers that can keep you from entering the market are minimized and the cost of launching a micro-business is significantly lower than what it would be to launch a full-service business.

If you run a full-service business, have a job, or have a trade, take a look at the big picture and see how you can market just a small piece of it. Do you own a coffee shop? Can you brand your own line of coffee and sell it online? Do you own a barber shop? See if you can find a manufacturer who will help you develop your own line of premium hair clippers. Are you a psychologist? Have you thought of writing your own "how to run a successful psychotherapist practice" book? You will be surprised by how a smaller portion of a bigger business can be more portable, flexible and profitable, with less headache, less stress, and less overhead. In this day and age, it's simpler than ever to set up a global business and earn sleep money. It's truly a fine time to be in business.

Chapter 13

Marketing

"The aim of marketing is to know and understand the customer so well the product or service fits him and sells itself."

- Peter F. Drucker, Management Consultant and Educator

When you are creating a business or product that will create sleep money, sometimes the most important thing is not actually the product (although you have to have one), but the marketing of the product. Marketing is the strategy you employ in order to make the public aware of the value of your product. No matter how good your product or service is, if no-one knows it exists or what it can do for them, you won't make any money.

This is the mistake I made in operating my first business – which failed - Biofit and Wellness. People didn't buy my supplemental workout CDs. In retrospect, it is clear why these CDs didn't sell. There were four critical steps I neglected:

(1) I didn't find out if I was selling was something that people actually wanted;

(2) Even though I was a popular writer in the wellness industry, I wasn't an active member in the physical fitness arena;

(3) I did not ask people to buy the product; and

(4) Although the videos looked nice, the website that let people to the videos sucked.

Do not make the same mistakes I made.

After you have identified your market and have your product in development, it's time to start marketing – developing this all-too-critical strategy. It is important to start creating awareness and buzz about the product even before it is released.

For some beginning entrepreneurs, the word "marketing" may be intimidating because it brings up images of begging, cold-calling and rejections in-person or on the phone. The internet though, has so vastly changed how sellers reach buyers, that the fears associated with many of the traditional marketing processes can be alleviated. If you used to be scared of marketing, you don't need to be anymore. There are a couple of steps that work well when it comes to the marketing process.

Start Early. This is essential. You need to start promoting your business or product as soon as possible. You want to get the buzz out and let the world know about your amazing product that offers great value.

Micro-business owner, Jason, provides a great example of how to create strong buzz in the pre-launch phases of a business. Jason started a micro-business, Soar Golfing, an online golf distributorship business. Before his web-site was even ready, he uploaded a video he made out of the great-looking photo slides of a golf driver on YouTube and Vimeo and submitted photos of his products and descriptions to Google Merchant Center. Without even having a website up and running, he was promoting. Jason used his personal page and a business fan page on Facebook, as well as a Twitter page and other social media networks to inform his friends and followers about his unique products. Launching your marketing strategy before launching the business serves double duty. It starts creating buzz right away with those who are, initially, exposed to the product or service. It also provides time for that initial group of people to share information about the business with their friends and associates. By the time the business actually launches, several layers of word-of-mouth communication will have already taken place. Take advantage of this initial exposure by creating incentives, like promising a bonus offer when the product launches. Be sure to gather contact information for those you reach through the various marketing approaches you employ. Get your e-mail distribution list started. Get people excited about what you plan to offer. Give them opportunities to get on a pre-sales list of some sort. Get these people, who you are making "raving fans," into your sales funnel. I tell you: you cannot lose by starting this process early.

Build a web-site that represents your business as a highly professional company. Although your business may be a micro one, you should still create a site that demonstrates that your company can compete with the big boys. This is worth a little bit of investment upfront. You want your product or service (whether it is an app, service, eBook, or a physical product, etc.) to look like it comes from a very legitimate enterprise. This is how you can create trust within your customers. Think about it, when you go to well-known web-sites like Amazon.com or Apple.com, you see a beautiful interface with products that make you drool. Even without website design experience, this is something that can be accomplished by a micro-business owner. By outsourcing your graphics and web development to other contractors who specialize in these areas, you can now complete with companies much larger than your own. You want it to look like an established, viable business, even if you're only a start up micro-business. You do not want your website to scream, "This company was started yesterday, and I'm operating it from a card table in the corner of my basement." Jason achieved a professional appearance for his business by simply going to iPhoto to purchase some professional-looking images of his product. He then outsourced his graphic design and web development work to an expert developer he found through oDesk. His contractors prepared a well-designed layout for his website to make it look exceptional. He also ensured that his website loaded quickly on various search engines.

On the homepage of his website, visitors can see a video that will immediately answer the question, "What do you have to offer me?" He knew that he had to explain his unique selling proposition quickly, or risk losing his visitors. With most businesses it is important that your web site highlight the features and benefits of your product or service in a manner to which your customer can relate. You will work hard for your website traffic; take advantage of what you have. Because I've been doing this for a while now, I have several tricks that can help you get the word out about your company faster than you may have thought possible. These techniques take just a small amount of work, though the payoffs are huge.

Forums and Group Discussions. On the Internet, people are always talking – about everything. So, when you aim to get the word out about your business, join the conversation. Participate in forums and discussion groups on topics about your product to establish yourself as an expert in your field. Do this by submitting well-written and informative comments to the forum. Don't just talk about your business. In fact, talk very little about your business, specifically. Instead, offer to help and provide advice that the group members will appreciate, so that when they are ready to buy, they come to you. It's all about adding value to the discussion. With forum marketing, the best strategy is to become a valued member first and then work from there. SPAM comments don't work at all. So be very careful to inform and not annoy.

Podcasts and iTunes. Talking to podcasters about your product and your company is another cost-effective promotion technique. Once, I gave a podcaster a free VSA (Very Simple Ad) for use on his website. They then used their podcast as a subtle advertisement for my company. They did this by giving a review of my product and by interviewing me. Think of it like an author's book tour for a new book. People love to hear about new developments in products and services, and by offering interviews you can get a lot of exposure.

I also sponsored a podcast program and they inserted an audio advertisement of my product at various points during their show. I didn't even have to go through an ad agency to do this; I simply contacted the podcaster directly. You can try looking for podcasters that have audiences similar to the ones you are trying to reach. For the podcaster with a smaller following, I just go directly to them and ask them if I can advertise on or sponsor the show in some way. Many times, they will be happy that you want to partner with them.

Articles and Press Releases. One of the easiest ways you can generate buzz about your business or service is to write articles and press releases about your product, services and company. In order to establish myself as an expert in my industry, I make a practice out of preparing well-written articles on industry-related topics. I submit these articles to sites that accept free articles, such as eZine Articles. Because I am spreading my message out over the web, people who are looking for information about my topic can find me. Once my articles are published on a particular site, I immediately get a link back to my website, in addition to the free publicity I receive from the site that originally published the article. The more I publish, the more people associate me with a particular topic and/or area of business. With that credibility, I earn the trust of my audience. Because the audience trusts me, they trust that the products or services I present to them are ones that would be beneficial to them. The key here is to establish yourself as one who can provide solid answers to the real questions that people have, all the while building their confidence and curiosity in the products and services you provide.

I am also aggressive about submitting press releases about my company's services to local newspapers, TV stations, radio stations and internet press release sites like PRWeb. A press release is a written statement announcing a whole range of news worthy activities and events such as awards, personnel promotions, new products and services or sales and marketing exploits, including any contests or giveaways you may be offering (more on that in just a bit). If you're not good at preparing this kind of written material, be sure to hire someone who is adept at doing this kind of work. Since your release will be submitted to a large number of people in the media, who can be quite critical, be sure that it is well-written and operates as a positive representation of your company. To disseminate your press release to the media, you will need to network with reporters who work on TV, in radio and through print media. You can also distribute your press releases online. The internet provides solid tips on how to go about that process.

Interviews. I am very liberal in offering to be interviewed and agreeing to interview requests. The more I establish myself as an expert in my field, the more people what to hear my viewpoints and suggestions. This exposure has tended to have a snowball effect. The more people hear about me and my company, the more they want to speak with me.

Getting an interview opportunity is much easier than you may think. Of course, you want to get interviews with the highest profile outlets possible. But, if getting these more coveted interviews proves challenging, be sure to pursue opportunities that may not be as popular. There are a plethora of podcasts and online radio shows that are eager to have knowledgeable and interesting guests on their programs. There are also a slew of bloggers who would be interested in provided printed interviews as well. Like you, there are countless individuals who are in the earlier stages of business, who need to build a following and would be glad to present to their audience your expertise.

Contest and Giveaways. Sponsoring a contest is one very effective approach that many businesses ignore or overlook. It is such a great tool for promoting a product and a fast way to create buzz. When my company, iQuick Tools, developed a new game app called "Monkeys and Bananas," I employed this very tactic. In the description of the game in the Apple App Store, I gave potential customers the opportunity to win an iPad. All they had to do was tweet and rate the app and they would be entered into the contest. Since I had never done a promotion like this before, I wasn't sure this would be successful, but it turned out to be extremely effective. It gave my app web page major SEO benefits (through backlinks), lots of positive ratings, and got people talking about the business. If enough people are talking, a contest can create such a big viral marketing splash that it even attracts media attention and gets your business free advertising.

Sponsoring someone else's contest is another way that you can get your potential customer directly involved with your company. This allows you to build up a mailing list that will give you a wider base of customers to work with.

To ensure that your contest is exciting enough to attract people to join, you need to make the prize worth the time and energy it takes to enter the contest. Think of something that is really irresistible and tempting enough that your audience will be dying to sign up. It could be a complete set of your products, a vacation, a new gizmo or even a cash prize. In addition, you can have inexpensive giveaway items such as coffee mugs, key chains or t-shirts with your logo for all those who participate. Before you decide on the prize, though, make sure that it is within your budget.

To ensure the success of your contest, and to get more people to participate, make the contest rules and signup process as simple and easy as possible. Reach out to the media before the contest begins so that when you launch it they can provide coverage and increase awareness regarding your contest. Press releases are a great way to do this. A media outlet will be more inclined to cover your contest or product launch if they are given a press release first. Approach reporters and writers who are fairly knowledgeable in your industry and who have an audience that is similar to the one that you want to reach. If they already have an established interest in your market, they will be more inclined to give your contest media coverage.

Just Give It Away. Offering free samples or free trials of your product is another promotional strategy that is very effective, especially if your product or service is new. Some people refuse to buy something they have not tried or experienced. Giving away the product or exposing people to the service gives them a chance to determine whether or not you're providing value at no cost to them, and will encourage them to give it a try. In giving away samples to promote your product, or service you have to choose your target audience very carefully. Aim to reach people who have a wide sphere of influence, and those who are well within your target demographic. Jason decided to give free samples of his golf drivers to golfer bloggers who had large followings. In return, he asked them to mention his golf driver in their blogs. It turned out to be a brilliant move on Jason's part. The golf bloggers were as satisfied with the golf drivers as Jason was. Not only did they mention it in their blogs, but some wrote glowing reviews and even recommended the product to their followers.

Build One, Build Two. This marketing strategy is very common in the auto industry. Ever wonder why Ford Motor Company manufactures cars under the Ford, Lincoln and Mercury brands? Or, why Toyota offers both Toyota vehicles and Lexus vehicles? At first glance, it may appear as if Ford and Toyota are competing with themselves. From a marketing standpoint, however, this technique is very effective, since it means that the company is offering products that reach a large segment of the entire market. Both Ford and Toyota offer models that cover the low to middle income levels, while Lincoln and Mercury (for Ford Motors) and Lexus (for Toyota), target an upscale market. These car brands start from the basic and economical models and go all the way to the luxurious and expensive. This ensures Ford and Toyota that no customer will walk out of its show room without finding something that will likely suit his budget and particular needs.

Many companies, in numerous industries, create both high-end and low-end products. Think for a moment about the companies you know that employ this approach. Don't many app companies offer a free and "premium" version of their application? Hasn't Versace, with its world-renowned luxury brand, also offered a line of designs for H&M? You can use the same marketing model for your product. You can have a range of products that start from t the most economical and move up to the most expensive. This way, you can target a wider market segment. For instance, Justin, our App Millionaire, sold both fertilizer and grass seed. He sold varieties for basic and limited water use. Instead of creating one single website, he created two. One featured his basic brands which had understated packaging for no-nonsense customers while a separate site looked a great deal like that of his high-end competitor, which offered his more expensive brands with glossy packaging. He manufactured all of his products at the same company, but arranged for different products to have a different look and feel. Doing this sort of marketing allows you to serve the needs of different types of customers by simply modifying your product in ways that appeal to different audiences.

I've done the same thing myself. I created 2 online advertisement companies to meet the needs of 2 markets: (1) the micro to small business market and (2) the mid-sized to large business market – FrugAD and Very Simple Ads (VSA), respectively. Both of these companies produce simple animation video ads that companies place on their websites, YouTube, Vimeo and others similar mediums. Contractor Tools and iQuick Tools are both mobile apps for the construction/contracting niche that basically do that same thing. Yet, they compete against one another, by providing a similar product. You want to create this type of inter-competition within your own product and service offerings because this gives you the opportunity to reach a wider portion of the consuming market.

Regardless of the nature of your business, you can create a comparable offering so that you have more than one product or service to offer the market. Though the offerings will, and should, be fundamentally the same on many levels, there should be some differences that would add more value to a particular segment of the market. There should be something about one that appeals to a certain demographic over another. Whichever of the two your customer chooses is of no consequence to you; it's a "win-win" situation from your perspective.

YouTube Channel. YouTube is a very effective social media tool to promote and market your product in a very cost-effective way. It also serves as a platform for you to show your company's product and the credibility of your business in a visual format.

When you create your own YouTube channel, you should design videos that appeal to all types of visitors in your target demographic. It is important that you display an interesting and informative video. Using professionally-made graphics and visuals is vital to your success. Our companies, Very Simple Ads and FrugAds, do these types of video ads for many small to mid-sized businesses. When you broadcast a superior quality and entertaining video, you have a tremendous opportunity to impress visitors and potential customers. That's why it is so important that your videos look nice. Make sure that you have a high-quality video since YouTube is capable of displaying videos at a superior level, especially to viewers who have a lot of bandwidth. A high-quality video will translate into a sharper and clearer image that will be visually appealing to the audience. The videos that you post should also be informative and specific, directly targeting the needs and wants of the customers you are looking to acquire. Remember the customer profile you created earlier and tailor your video to that person.

The Usual Suspects

Facebook. This is not just a social network - it is *the* social network - that makes promoting your company a cinch. There are countless companies who are now using Facebook to market their products successfully. Besides using Facebook to create a buzz, you can also use it get new clients, keep in touch with existing customers, and even promote new sales offers and products.

Facebook offers several tools you can use to market your product. This includes Facebook pages and Facebook groups. On Facebook pages, you can give your product and business its own profile for free. You can even post photos, videos, messages and applications. Your current and potential customers can become your "fans." As your fans, they can consistently receive new information about your product and company through the various Facebook updates you post. Every activity that you have in your Facebook pages will be broadcasted to the mini-feeds of your fans which they can then share with their own friends. The beauty in Facebook pages is that every time someone becomes a fan, their Facebook friends can see that they have become your fan. This operates as an informal form of word-of-mouth advertising and a stamp of approval, exposing your business not only to those who, intentionally, decide to be your fan, but also those Facebook friends of theirs who may have not previously known anything about your business. In turn, you gain the opportunity to attract more fans to your Facebook page. You can also place ads using Facebook ads. This ad may show on the right-hand side of any number of the various types of pages that appear on the Facebook platform – whether it be your personal home page or other types of pages such as apps, groups, photos, and other people's profile pages. These are, essentially, direct marketing opportunities. Unlike how Google Adwords functions, as an advertiser on Facebook, you bid on people, not on keywords. Because Facebook has acquired so much information about each of its users (through the detailed profiles many of us build on the site), a Facebook ad can be designed to reach just those individuals who fall within your target market. If you're selling hosiery through a website, for example, you may want to target college-educated women between the ages of 30 and 55. Facebook will allow your ads to show only to females, within that particular age group, who have listed that they have attended a college. This is a very inexpensive way for the micro-business owners to advertise at a relatively low cost.

In writing your Facebook ads, make sure that your specific call to action, graphics, and other ad copy are designed to be more people-targeted than the ads you would run using Google Adwords. They require different approaches for success.

Facebook groups are just like Facebook pages except that they are not created for a product or business, but for a particular group of people. You can create a Facebook group to generate awareness of and foster discussion about your product or service. Those who are interested in your subject-matter will become members of your group, not just fans. Facebook groups are great for creating exclusive, inner circles of customers – customers who are committed to your subject. Among these people, you can develop a strong relationship between them and your business by providing them with certain advantages and benefits for being a part of your group. These benefits can be anything from special coupons and promo codes, to first access to new products and services. Customers like to be part of an exclusive club; creating a higher level of exclusivity for your best customers can be a great way to drive sales and motivate people.

Twitter. Twitter is another powerful social networking tool for promoting your business. The single most important thing you can do to ensure that your Twitter account operates as an effective platform for building your brand and promoting your product is to make sure that your Twitter user name is related to your business. Also, see to it that a Twitter badge with your user name is placed on all of the pages of your website so that your site visitors can easily connect with you on the Twitter platform. To do this, just install a "Follow Me" on twitter button. This is a great way to increase your Twitter audience.

Use your Twitter posts to make mini-announcements regarding various aspects of your business. Since Twitter posts are limited to 140 characters, this is your chance to share posts that provide a lot of punch, using very few words. You can provide teasers regarding the launch of your product and describe your product's unique and useful features. You can announce events and activities related to your business, such as contests you're launching and anything else related to your company. Share with your Twitter followers the exciting step-by-step progress of your product development, unusual and interesting experiences in building your company, and other news or facts worthy of note about your product and your company. Most importantly, develop a relationship with your followers. Build their trust. Find out what they like and don't like about your product or service. Don't limit your tweets to your product and your company. Tweet about other interesting and novel things happening around the web and around the world. This is how you build trust and rapport with your followers. Providing commentary and insight on other matters besides just your business also helps you increase your number of followers. People are always interested in knowing what's happening around them and they search for information using keywords. So, when you tweet about the latest news or other matters that people find intriguing, they will be more eager to read what you have to say. The more you provide valuable information to people, the more they will be interested in following you. The more followers you have, the more people will know about your product. One note: be patient with Twitter, as is that it can take a good bit of time to build up a loyal following.

Twitter is a great tool to promote your business, but it can only work for you if you build trust among your followers and are not perceived as somebody who is there for the sole purpose of making sales. If you aren't sure of how to do this, follow business people who have made it into an art. Follow Tony Hsieh, the CEO of Zappos.com to see what I mean. He is a good example of how to use Twitter to build trust as well as a brand.

Blogging. A blog is, technically, an online journal. These days, however, many blogs are just as, if not more, robust as traditional websites in terms of content. If a blog is one that allows for discussion among the members of the internet community, it provides you with an opportunity to reach potential customers. In building my brands and promoting my products, I have made blog posts on other people's sites. I, actively, contributed to conversations, demonstrating that I had some knowledge and insight that was of value to the audience. I also looked for blogs that contained similar content to what I wanted to promote and offered an interview or premium content to that site owner for free, in exchange for a small link or plug for my product. This is super effective. Not only does it get more visitors to your site from direct traffic, but it also gets backlinks to your site, which are super important if you want your product to rank highly in organic search engine results.

Also, I used other people's blog sites to attract targeted visitors to my website. I eventually got them interested in my product by writing informative and insightful comments and questions that would interest the viewers of these blog sites. Again, it's about building trust with a particular audience. The more someone trusts you, the more likely they are to value your suggestions and recommendations. When I blogged, I would sometimes use a screen name that was my business name. This provided an additional link to my website. Once viewers became interested, they visited my website to get a new viewpoint on the subject and learn about my product.

Blogging can help in your marketing and promotion efforts. You can find blogs related to your product and comment on these blogs. You can get free traffic to your site by using your businesses keyword names as your screen name when you post these comments. When you make relevant and interesting comments, other readers will want to know more and will find you through this link.

If you like to write, you can also set up your own blog, which is something that Jason did when he was launching his online distributorship business. He created a business blog about golf by using a free blogging platform. WordPress and Blogger are two popular choices. No special website development knowledge is required to create a blog using these free tools. All he did was create a hosting account where his blog was installed and activated. He wrote some interesting articles about his product and posted it on his site. He built a community of golf "addicts" around his blog by writing well-written, informative posts about golf equipment, the best golf courses, the top golfers in the world – everything about golf - and established himself as an expert in the sport.

Your blog can be an effective platform for your product. But this can only be possible if you are able to create a blog that will serve as a medium for you to communicate with people and build a strong following around your content. Provide authentic, relevant and reliable content, while informing your customers about the benefits of your product.

A good way to come up with topics to blog about is to go to Yahoo Answers and look at the questions that people are asking about in your industry. If you find a common theme, then it is probably a topic about which people are interested in knowing more. By giving customers information that will help solve their problems, or that will answer their questions, you can become an authority in your niche area of business. The key here is providing value to your customers. Remember to make your blog visually appealing and user- friendly. If you can create a positive emotional reaction with your blog's design, you will be one step closer to building a relationship with your visitors. When visitors find their way to your blog site, they will be impressed. That's a good start in building professional brand awareness. The key to keeping the interest of your blog community and/or Twitter followers is to always have something fresh and new to share. If you are wondering where you will find the time to consistently blast out tweets, make Facebook comments, and develop blog posts, don't fret. You can maintain fresh and new content, without you doing all the writing yourself. Once you have income coming in, you can hire a company to create regular updates for you. There are many outsourcing firms available to do this type of work, as well as many individual contractors looking for this type of work in places like Elance.

Another strategy you can employ is to post to your site articles and comments that other people have written on their sites. By providing your own commentary on the article, you are providing new content. If you are doing this, it is most effective if you tweet a lead in or bridge that connects the article to your readers. You can also post links to your blog posts on your Twitter page if they are still relevant and timely.

Keep Up with the Joneses

One very vital component of an effective marketing strategy is having a comprehensive knowledge of your competition – who they are, what they are doing, and what makes their offering unique. This will provide you with ideas on how to present your product differently so that potential customers will buy from you rather than from them. Find your competition by using a keyword search on Google Adwords. Type your main keywords into the Google search engine and see who is being listed at the top of the search results. Do the same search on Facebook. You can take a look at how much traffic your competitors are getting by using sites like Alexa.com. Just put the name of your main competitors in these sites' search boxes and you will get a ton of usable data on them... all for free.

Do not be discouraged if you find that your niche market has a significant amount of competition. Being part of a niche with strong competition means that there is money to be made. The level of competition should not be your main concern; it is the quality of your competition that matters most. Concentrate on your biggest competitors and study their sites and keywords and search for all their backlinks. These backlinks contribute to the site's organic search ranking, and will give you an idea of how much effort you need to exert to improve your own search ranking.

You can even take advantage of your competitors' popularity to improve your own ranking and drive traffic to your site by implementing what is called Piggyback Internet Marketing. One way of putting this into practice is to use your most popular competitors' name as a keyword in your posts. When potential site visitors search by company or product name, they will find your competitor, but, with proper planning, your own company's website may appear within the search results as well.

Word of Mouth

We have all heard that word of mouth advertising is the best type of advertising you can get. When people speak about your product positively, whether it be via personal conversation, Facebook, Twitter, text message, blog commentary, or other media, you are getting free advertising. More importantly, you are getting quality advertising because your product is being personally endorsed by an individual who does not have a financial interest in promoting the product or service. For the person who is on the receiving end of this endorsement, the source is credible because he is not in the business of selling the product or service. This is a great promotional tool especially if you're operating on a limited budget.

The best word of mouth advertisement comes from a satisfied customer. When they are happy with your product they will not only come back for more, but will also recommend you to their family and friends, spreading the word about the greatness of your product. Your customer service goal should, therefore, be to keep your customers happy by adding value and providing high-quality products and services. In the initial stages of your business, you should make yourself available and reachable when your customers have concerns or questions about your product. Providing a personal touch by responding to emails and telephone calls, and blog posts, will make your customers feel confident that, even after the sale, you are still around to provide them with the service they need. Once you grow large enough, this is an area of your business that can be outsourced.

Satisfied customers are not the only ones who can spread the good news about your product and refer you to more clients. You can network with other business owners, who are not your competitors, and they can recommend you to their own clients. You, your own team, your friends, and your family can also help in advertising your product through word of mouth.

This is the only type of advertising program that you don't, specifically, launch. It begins whether or not you decide you want it to officially start. Once your business has been exposed to the public, the process can begin. And, depending on how you perform in the market, word of mouth can either work well in your favor, or it can destroy your business. So, be sure that you start of on the right foot. First, believe in the product you're selling. Know what its best features are, what it can do and also what it can't do. You should be thoroughly knowledgeable when someone asks why they should buy your product and not the others. Never hesitate to put your name and your reputation on the line for your product, and be sure you are offering quality and value for your customer.

Niche Marketing

One of the biggest problems experienced by new micro-business owners is a lack of focus; they are trying to sell to everyone or be all things to all people. This is far from where you need to be. Even if you are trying to be an app developer, you need to hone in on a target group and build your app for them. Not everyone. Just them. If you say your app is for everyone, it's probably not for anyone. Universal acceptance is very rare. Niche marketing to a particular group such as tweens, paralegals or stay-at-home moms, for example, is a much better approach. Let me tell you the story about the old man, the young boy, and the donkey.

One day, an old man, a young boy, and a donkey were all going into town. The young boy rode the donkey and the old man walked beside them. Going along the way, they passed a group of people who were making comments. They shook their heads, with several people saying, "Such a shame." The young, stronger boy was riding the donkey whilst the frailer old man was walking. The man and boy heard these comments, thought that, perhaps, the critics were right, so they changed positions.

Further along the way, they passed another group of people who commented loudly, "How mean! Look at that man who happily rides upon the donkey whilst the young boy is made to walk!" Hearing the comments, they decided to both walk, and lead the donkey.

Before long, they came across even more people who remarked how stupid they were, as they were walking while they had a donkey to ride. Becoming quite perplexed, they both climbed on the donkey and continued on their way.

Next, they came upon another group who shouted about how cruel they were being putting such a burden on the donkey, as it struggled to carry two people. Feeling sorry for what they had done, they made the decision that neither of them would ride the donkey, nor would the donkey walk on its own.

So, they picked up the donkey and continued on carrying it. Coming to a bridge, they precariously continued to hold onto the donkey but unfortunately they lost their grip and the donkey fell into the river and drowned.

What is the moral of this story? If you try to please everyone, you might as well kiss your ass goodbye!

So what to do? You can't please everyone. Instead, you want to find a topic that is compelling and interesting – not to you, but to a designated segment of the population. Let's take a look at how you can start generating overall topic ideas – and come up with niches.

Start by making a list. Make a list of anything and everything that comes to mind regarding what you believe will make your project successful. You don't have to be "passionate" about your possible project; you should be motivated by the potential success of the project. Don't worry if there's a similar product or service on the market already. Just be open to exploring the possibilities of the idea. To help you with this exercise, take a look at top web searches on the topic. While exploring market trends, you may find an untapped market group. For example, the first market group for the health supplement now known as Ageless Male was young body builders. After further research, the company's manufacturer found out that active male adults over the age of 45 was a niche group for this supplement. After they changed their marketing strategy from targeting younger body builders to targeting older, active adult males, the company's sales soared. Sales to this new niche market outperformed sales to the young fitness group by more than 10 times.

Another step you can take to help you in finding a niche group is to take a field trip to the book store. This can be a really great way to get ideas flowing. Once you are at the bookstore, head straight for the magazine section. It is simply amazing how many niche magazines there are out there. If you have never taken the time to fully peruse the individual rows, you will be in for a surprise. Grab several different genres of magazines that pique your interest. Head over to a big comfy chair or the in-store coffee shop and dig in a little further. You see, when you take the time to look even deeper in to the magazines, you find sub-niches that you didn't know existed. Make sure you have a piece of paper or your laptop to jot down a list of those subjects that seem promising to you.

Now that you're armed with a list from one or a combination of several of the above idea generators, it's time to get down to business. Go to Google Trends and see the interest level of your ideas. Are people searching on the topic? What does the interest level look like over the past six months or the past year? Is it increasing or decreasing? Google Correlate is also a great tool to use when trying to determine search patterns as such relates to real-world data.

You should also use the Google Keywords Tool to help you find out what interests people around the globe. This tool will tell you how many people are searching for information, on a monthly basis, on the various topics you've captured on your list. Google provides a slew of articles and videos on how to use this tool. Spend some time with it, as it provides a tremendous amount of information. Use it to help you refine your list of potential niches.

Now it's time to do some searches for online forums on the topics you are still considering pursuing. Once you get to the forums, see which ones have the most active discussions. It's a great place to do some research. Jot down the issues that seem to stir up the most interest. Think about how you could provide solutions through an app or other micro-business. Online forums are an absolute goldmine of information!

Ask yourself whether there are enough potential customers in a particular market to justify you developing an app or micro-business that is targeted to them. We both know you'll come up with an outstanding product, but is it worth your time? You also must find out if your target customers would be willing to pay for the product you provide.

Much of what you need to know about the business you want to create can be found in forums. Look for problems that you can solve. Look for other common problems that already have been solved by other posters – all of this is ripe to include in your business model.

As you are looking through the forums, you are gaining valuable information as to who your customer is and what it is that they are looking for. The best thing you can do for your development process is to take this information and develop a customer avatar. A customer avatar is a snapshot of your "typical customer." Keep the qualities and characteristics of this hypothetical customer in mind as you develop your business.

Chapter 14

Loans vs. Credit Cards

"The new source of power is not money in the hands of a few, but information in the hands of many."

- John Naisbitt, Author of *Megatrends* and Observer/Analyst of Global Trends

A common temptation faced by many entrepreneurs launching micro-businesses is the desire to start right up, get a few paying customers then immediately go and apply for a small business loan. I am of the mindset that startups should steer clear of saddling a business with unnecessary debt. The ability to get a small business loan is one of those unspoken status symbols for many untested entrepreneurs.

First and foremost, let's be clear here – it is possible to successfully launch and run a business without getting a business loan. You don't need angel investors or banks to start every business. Many businesses, particularly micro-businesses, can be launched using resources you already have. The ability to secure funding does not somehow legitimize your business. In the long run, sidestepping the loan and using your personal credit cards instead to finance your business can work out to your benefit. I know most people will disagree with me, but it can be a good idea.

Let's say you've been operating an online retail business for a year or so. Sales have shown continuous growth and you've been able to successfully market your products online at a small cost. You have a dependable part-time employee who has been helping you run the site and fill orders. At this point, you're actually seeing a bit of profit. You have positive cash flow at the end of the month. That's a good thing. One day, you get a call from a local company interested in making a large purchase from you. You negotiate a reasonable wholesale price for your product and set your new client up to pay for any product they purchase within 45 days of them submitting the order. You're amped, right? On the heels of that win, you get a call from another company - this one in Canada. You negotiate terms, come to an agreement and hang up the phone feeling like you're beginning to turn the corner in your business.

The good news is you just increased your sales by 27%. You face one challenge though - your business is already operating at capacity and to fulfill your part of the agreements, you'll need to make some changes. Once the money from the new accounts start to roll in, you'll be fine. For the time being, though, you need to find a way to cover a shortfall in excess of $30,000 to float the cost of the additional products you'll need to get these orders filled.

This is the point at which many people will say, "Business is booming!" Or, "I'm a global business. It's time to get that $50,000 business loan." Not so fast. Maybe it's not a loan that you need. Yes, your business needs money to grow, but there are a few things you may want to consider before you go looking for that business loan.

You already know that the App Millionaire often does not need to invest a lot of money to make money. If your product is essentially online downloads, for example, there's a good chance you won't need as much operating capital as compared to another business owner who's trying to buy equipment and a three-color display ad in the local Yellow Pages for his specialty print shop. I mentioned earlier that choosing to use your personal credit cards to give you the capital you need instead of taking out a hefty business loan to give you the capital you think you want may be the wiser choice.

You've probably heard the warning yourself: 50% of all new businesses fail within the first year. You can Google that phrase and thousands of results turn up in the search. While that failure rate may be true, the reverse is also true – the other fifty percent of business do succeed. Half of new companies survive more than 5 years and 34% are still going strong more than a decade after opening, according to the US Bureau of Labor and Statistics. For micro-business owners, that urge you feel to take out a business loan to make sure you have "financial cushion" is probably because you know that covering the costs of operations is what keeps you in business. If you're worried about whether you can sell enough of your product to cover operating costs, especially in a micro-business, you would probably do well to take another look at your business strategy before you read even one more sentence.

Ask a handful of small business experts and you will soon find that the main reason businesses fail is not from a lack of funding, but rather from being poorly managed. Now, money certainly helps and it's very necessary. But don't be fooled. Both business loans and credit lines are expensive. And depending on the amount of money borrowed and the way the loan or credit line repayment is structured, either resource can nicely support your efforts if handled wisely or wreak havoc on your finances if managed improperly.

Here's the deal - loans are top-heavy. In general, the less money you borrow, the more you pay in interest on the loan. Dollar for dollar, you pay more for microloans (small, short-term loans) than you would for larger loans. The average small business loan under $50,000 is going to be repaid at an annual interest rate of about 8 – 15%. When you go to get a business loan, you apply for a specific amount of money that is to be used for a specific purpose and you agree to repay that principal amount, plus interest, by a specific date. The way most loans are structured, your loan payments will include a portion for both the interest payment and repayment of the principal amount borrowed. With front-loaded loans, payments made early into your repayment contract will be constructed to pay off the interest on the loan before paying off the principal of the loan itself. So by the time you get to those last payments, the interest is already paid and the principal loan amount is still on the last to be paid. You pay the interest on the front end of the loan.

If you use a personal credit card, on the other hand, you may be able to take advantage of introductory interest rates. Let's say instead of getting a $30,000 business loan, you opt to apply for a personal line of credit worth $25,000 and take advantage of an introductory rate of 0% interest on the card. This approach would allow you to fund your business with money from a bank for a whole year interest-free. That's a sweet deal if you only need money to float the business for a few months during a growth cycle.

There's one thing you do have to be careful of when it comes to personal credit cards and promotional offers. Whereas with business loans, you have a set monthly amount that you agree to pay throughout the duration of your repayment schedule, with personal credit cards you have a bit more flexibility. So, for example, if your goal is to borrow a set amount of money interest-free and repay the amount before the interest kicks in on the credit card, you have to be disciplined enough to stick to your repayment plan and not be swayed by the option to make just the minimum payment each month. The payment flexibility built into credit card accounts is fantastic, but it can be both a blessing and a curse for consumers.

On one hand, you can pay more money when you have more money to pay however, if you absolutely have to pay the minimum payment you have the option to do just that without compromising your credit score much at all. But beware, after that introductory period is over, the interest on your card will likely increase considerably to between 8% and 29% of the balance still owed on the card. If you have been making the minimum payment, you may find that when the interest kicks in, it's more than what you've conditioned yourself to be able to afford. This, my friends, is where many people start having problems with their credit cards. They get caught right there in that never-ending cycle of minimum monthly payments and rising credit card balances. Now, some cards do allow you to forfeit the introductory rate altogether and settle on one low interest rate of somewhere between 6 – 10%. Even choosing this option, you're still likely to come out ahead.

Having access to revolving credit offers an advantage that's not available with a business loan. When you get a business loan, you get a set amount of money one time and, while using the funds, you work to pay the loan back. So when the money from a business loan finally reaches your bank account, you allocate it for its intended purpose. Once it's gone, it's gone. Hopefully, it's done its job. With revolving credit, you can use and repay the amount of your credit line over and over again. Meaning, a credit limit of the same amount can be used and repaid incrementally and the balance available on the card remains open even as you're repaying what you've already used. During the slim months when sales slow down, you may need to use a little more of your credit line than in previous months. The point is, you can use (and reuse) as much or as little of your credit line as necessary.

Another benefit of using your personal credit cards to back your micro-business is that, by employing this method, you don't put your company at risk by using your business assets as collateral. Now this is very important. When you take out a business loan, very often you have to convince the bank or investor that they will, in fact, get their money back. You have to be realistic (because the lender certainly will be) about the likelihood of your venture producing enough revenue to pay back what you borrow on time and within the period allotted. The assurance they, typically, require is security that, in the event that the business fails, they will have the right to take the business' assets and sell them to recoup the original loan amount.

Back in the "Old America" (pre-2007), a business owner who planned to apply for a business loan in the future would establish their business as a for-profit corporation. The business structure of a corporation is a bit more complex than that of a limited liability company (LLC), partnership or sole proprietorship. Lenders saw that as a sign of commitment and were more willing to extend business financing to corporations than LLCs and other types of business entities. Business credit is tricky, though, because it typically requires both a personal guarantor (usually the business owner) as well as tangible collateral that can attach the loan to your business if you've opted to use your business assets to secure the loan.

One of the ways lenders guarantee that they'll get their money back is by having you secure the debt with collateral. What's collateral? Cash on-hand, real property (often your primary residence), your personal savings, business assets are all items that a bank would consider security when deciding whether or not to grant a business loan. Occasionally, a bank will consider a purchase order and/or other receivables as collateral, but for the most part, banks are pretty conservative when it comes to valuing your assets for the purpose of securing a loan.

In the event you successfully woo a lender and get a business loan using your business assets as collateral, if things go badly and you have trouble repaying the loan, the bank can cure the default by seizing and selling off your assets – assets you may need to pull your business out of its slump and keep you from having to close your doors.

In a post-2007 world, business credit is a bit more difficult to come by. This unfriendly business credit environment, coupled with the personal credit laws that were made more favorable to consumers in 2009, the use of personal credit cards in business became more appealing. Please understand me. All business owners should be downright anal about keeping accurate, organized physical records and digital books. Some micro-business owners fund their startups by making equity contributions to the business, so using personal money to fund a business is not an uncommon practice.

One of the primary functions of the Credit Card Act of 2009 was to level the playing field between creditors and consumers. Creditors had to make adjustments to the way they treated late payments, adjustable interest rates and blanket defaults on personal credit accounts. While business loans come loaded with interest and fees, creditors of personal credit accounts no longer have the freedom to inflate interest rates and tack on fees indiscriminately. As a result, these days, consumers have fewer sudden changes and hidden costs with which to contend. The end result is savvy micro-business owners like you can find some value in using personal credit cards to fund new business ventures, instead of being stifled by business loan applications that have been denied.

Consider this: if you miss a few payments on your personal credit card, you may be in a better position to negotiate a reprieve with the credit card company than if you were to get behind on a business loan. Many credit card companies have hardship programs of which preferred customers may take advantage. Some credit card companies will actually stop the interest from accruing on your account for a period of time if you notify them that you're having trouble paying. The option to take advantage of such a program may be a godsend, allowing you to regroup, develop a new strategy and get your business back on track. If not, worst case scenario, you take a hit to your FICO score while you sort things out, but at least you haven't lost your business because your business was not the security for the line of credit you received from the personal card. As your business continues to produce income, your cash flow can keep you operating and keep food on your table. Over time, and with diligence, you can repair your credit score.

Your business is an investment. You invest your time, energy and money into its development and growth. The last thing you want to worry about is losing it over a micro-loan that went awry. You want things to run as smoothly as they can. No monkey wrenches. That's why you implemented systems in the first place. You specialize in producing ease.

Speaking of which, the business loan is not designed to be all that easy to get. Whether you're dealing with angel investors or the First Big Bank of the Planet, the business loan process is one that demands you be transparent. The checklist for what you will need to present to a lender during the loan application process is a lengthy one. Loans are awarded for specific purposes and those purposes will have an effect on the term of your business loan and the interest you'll pay on the loan. The quickest way to see the word "denied" stamped across the top of an application is to be general and unspecific about your reasons for needing the loan in the first place.

The loan process will require both you and your business to be closely scrutinized. In addition to your business plan and cash flow projections, you will need to present the lender with your company's balance sheet, corporate profile and history, business credit, equity contributions and a detailed description of how you plan to use the loan. But wait. That's not all. You'll also need to provide your personal financial statement, a list of your personal assets and liabilities, your previous tax returns and your personal credit report. There's more. Both you and your company will have to pass a credit check and provide a tangible guarantee that the loan can be repaid either by you, individually, or by the collateral you present.

You will then have to wait for a decision. If you are approved for the loan, you will then wait for the funds to be released. It is a daunting process that involves a ton of paperwork. Here's an alternative: you can fill out a credit card application online and play a game of "Monkeys and Bananas" on your smartphone while an "instant" decision is being made. You get the point. If it's ease you're striving for, a traditional business loan is not necessarily the way to go. For most of us, it's much easier to obtain a personal line of credit than to get a small business loan. Ironically, an unsecured credit card is easier to get than a secured business loan. And, it's easier for us to manage a personal line of credit than it is to manage a small business loan, particularly since the amount of money you will generally need to fund a micro-business is pretty minimal. The average SBA micro-loan is between $10,000 and $15,000. Many of you won't even require that much.

As a micro-business owner, there's a good chance your business is either mobile or online. You're not shelling out tens of thousands of dollars for cranes, forklifts, or the other typical overhead items associated with brick and mortar locations. Often times, you can launch and manage your micro-business using resources you already have. There is certainly something to be said for bootstrapping a business, particularly in the launch and growth stages.

Bootstrapping your business is a way of controlling your expenses so that you can operate the business without having to sell off pieces of your company, take out loans or get expensive lines of business credit. It is both an art and a discipline. Finding creative ways to meet the day-to-day needs of your business is like solving a puzzle. Your business – however large, however small – feeds on resources. It is your job to keep the business on a healthy "resource diet" until it can pull its own weight. Bootstrapping requires you to develop the discipline to make the best use of your resources once you do have them.

The moral here is this: don't assume unnecessary risk that will increase your stress and strangle your business. Implement a smart operating system that will allow you to steadily grow your business using your existing resources, or resources that are easily within your reach and do not require that you give up too much in order to get them. When you're in need of a little extra capital, check your personal resources first. Your personal credit card may be just the funding you need.

PART III
MOVE IT FORWARD

"Diligence is the mother of good fortune, and idleness, its opposite, never brought a man to the goal of any of his best wishes."

- Miguel de Cervantes, Author of *Don Quixote*

"I find that the best way to do things is to constantly move forward and to never doubt anything and keep moving forward. If you make a mistake, say you made a mistake."

- John Frusciante, Record and Film Producer

"Even if you fall on your face, you're still moving forward."

- Victor Kiam, Entrepreneur and Former Owner of the New England Patriots

Chapter 15

Move It Forward

"Care and diligence bring luck."

- Thomas Fuller, English Clergyman

"The harder I work, the luckier I get."

- Samuel Goldwyn, Film Producer

*P*rogress should always be your focus in every professional endeavors. One of the most valuable skills you can ever cultivate is persistence. Your goal should be to make measurable progress on a daily basis in some area of your business. Whether it's coming up with ideas, developing concepts or finding the right team for a project, make sure you are taking incremental steps to move your business forward. There's an old truism that says, "It's a cinch by the inch, hard by the yard." But what I say is "just move it forward every day." In all businesses there will be times when you'll plow through several important tasks without so much as breaking a sweat. Other times, you'll only get one small thing done. That's fine too. Don't beat yourself up for doing less. Just make a commitment to do something... everyday! Don't let your ideas stall or get stale. Move it forward... everyday.

Great - The Enemy of Good

In his book, *From Good to Great,* Jim Collins explains that the reason we don't have a lot of great in this world is because too many people settle for just "good." He believes that it is human nature to settle for the status quo, which in turn stymies great works. I disagree. I believe that there is a time to stride for greatness and there is a time to be good enough. I find that too often people that want to become an entrepreneur strive for greatness out of fear. Yes, fear. Many would-be entrepreneurs find themselves side-tracked and overwhelmed by all of the moving parts that need to be addressed in order to get their business idea to market. In doing so, they never get their product or service off the ground. Not every great company does something great in their core business in order to be successful. Think: Taco Bell. Think: Microsoft. These companies are considered to be at the top of their industries, but have also carried products that have been strongly criticized. Actually, Microsoft is famously known for not putting out the best initial products. Their philosophy is to create a product that is good enough to present to the market; once the market has reviewed it and provided feedback, Microsoft makes changes and updates in continuing to develop the product. Over time, the product gets better and better; or, they simply eliminate it.

Eric Ries the author of *The Lean Start Up*, states that many of the perceived barriers that hinder new entrepreneurs would not exist if they would choose to start with a good product and build upon it. The process of just getting something out to the market, even if it is just okay at the start, gives the entrepreneur a sense of accomplishment that can go a long way. The key for long-term success is to not allow your standards to remain mediocre. Most successful entrepreneurs understand that they must continue to grow and improve. However, at some time you must have the feeling of completion. The feeling of completion can be something that propels you to do something great. But, if you never complete anything, you won't have the opportunity to do anything good, much less, great.

I've seen many people sit and mull over an idea for days…and weeks… and months. They'll finally bring it to the project stage and continue to tinker with it. For days…and weeks…and months. "If I just fix this one thing, it'll be better, " they say to themselves. "If I could just get the app to do this one other thing, it would be just about perfect."

Meanwhile, the wheels of progress are turning for others. The cash registers are "cha ching-ing" and money is coming in...for others – those who got something out there and available for public consumption. It may not be perfect, but it's out there and it is sufficient to suit someone's purposes. Get the picture? You can flat out fail if you are trying to make something "perfect." The goal is to get the product out to the market. You can work on continuously improving it once you have introduced it to the public. Get it out to the market and listen to what the customers have to say. They may have an idea for an improvement that you haven't even thought of yet. You may end up bypassing that next "improvement" you were going to make for something the customers really want.

When I decided to enter the game app market, I really didn't know much about the entertainment development space. At that time, my experience was with productivity apps, not games. But I was committed to learning all I could. I worked with my development team every single day. I read, I researched, and spoke to designers, developers and programmers from all over the world. Without fail, on a daily basis, I did something to move the project forward. Out of that experience, we produced Rock City Birds! for the iPhone, then Android smartphones. While my developers coded the game, I also had teams working on the game website and the promotional content for YouTube. After months of work – it finally went to market. I worked on the game and related materials consistently – each day I touched it in some form or fashion until it was at a point that I felt it could be released to the public. To be clear: the game was not perfect when I launched it, but it was good enough. Like most other forms of software, it remains a work in progress. I aimed for a standard that would, initially, get the game to the market.

I had a similar experience during the six months my team and I worked on CTQ, a learning management system that offers online Lean Six Sigma training and certification. Every day for six months, we worked. I had an idea and didn't stop thinking about it, improving upon it, and developing it until it was actually completed. There were days that I spent significant time focused on CTQ. There were, honestly, other days on which I did not want to be bothered with it at all. It was on those days that I had to push myself to do something – anything, no matter how small – to move the project forward. In those instances, I would do something like review some modifications sent to me by a team member or simply give a team member further instruction. As I write, these projects are making sleep money for me, with little effort on my end, everyday.

Act on your ideas. When you come up with an idea, move on it. Begin your research and try to discern, as quickly as possible, whether it is a good and viable idea. If it is, start working toward bringing it to fruition. Don't let the idea get stale. Keep it in the forefront of your mind and carve out time and energy to develop the idea. If you are confident that your idea is good, disregard all the nay-sayers. In Chapter 5 on micro-business "no-nos," I spoke previously about making the distinction between a hobby and a business. When you first start off with a great business idea, you rush to the table to hash out the details. Eventually, the excitement wears off and you're left with the work of getting the idea from intangible to tangible. At this point, it is easy to lose focus and let your commitment wane. So often when we hit those walls or begin to see those challenges cropping up, we use it as an excuse to take a break and sometimes scrap the idea altogether.

Ideas that are already in production, and even products you created that are already in the marketplace, may benefit from a revisit where you focus on improving the product. Take the time to explore forums, seminars, YouTube and Facebook for ideas. As an example, Facebook has more than a billion users with more than half of the users logging onto the site on any given day. People like Facebook (no pun intended). They use it as a way to forge relationships and keep in touch. Companies find it a valuable marketing tool for staying engaged with their customer base. As with most good business designs, Facebook is constantly being improved upon. New features are added, old features are redesigned. Although they are a large business, you should do the same with your micro-business. What trends and products are out now that weren't there when your product first went to market? There's always room for improvement. Every business owner must evolve as the world, technology or even as your neighborhood, changes.

Even with micro-businesses, the process of building a solid system and a strong business is just that – a process. It is a process in which one must consistently and diligently be engaged on a day-to-day basis. Don't get discouraged by the inevitable challenges that will come and obstacles that will present themselves. In fact, welcome them. They will tell you where the weaknesses are in your infrastructure. It's so easy in this day and age to just "give up" and go on to the next thing. It is, particularly, easy to do that if you maintain a full-time job that produces income that makes you feel secure. Do not allow challenges to discourage you to the point of letting go of your idea. There are solutions and opportunities abound; you simply have to find them. But when you have committed to running a business, once you have set your focus and developed a solid plan, the only thing left to do is to execute. Remember to disregard those who doubt you and don't place too much stock in the words of people who haven't been where you're going. Keep pushing and move it forward.

My philosophy is "go big or go broke." Not big as in size, but big as in ideas. With a micro-business, there is no excuse. You don't have to shell out hundreds of thousands of dollars to start this type of business. The idea is to start small. It's about spending your time and energy, not your money. It's about how much you want it, not how much you have in your wallet. Often, you don't even have to have a crazy exceptional skill set to get started. You just have to stay determined and driven.

As you move forward with your business plans, one of the biggest stumbling blocks that you will run across is not an external roadblock (even though we often try to rationalize that it is). It's an internal roadblock. It's an "I can't" mentality. It's not even "I can't" most of the time. It's more like (insert long whining sound) – "Well…I'll try." It honestly makes me cringe. Not because I don't sympathize with the fact that dreams and goals can seem daunting when you have to actually put plans in action to make them happen, but because I know people are capable of anything. They just need to believe, and then…

well, it sounds cliché, but, "Just do it."

You see, being an entrepreneur is among the most exhilarating, but challenging undertakings you will encounter. We want to achieve grand accomplishments, make lots of money, and make our dreams come true. The execution of those grand plans will seem overwhelming at times.. It is during these times that you will start to question yourself. You will wonder what the heck you were thinking when you decided to work for yourself. You will say, "Who, intentionally, puts themselves through this kind of agony? Only a fool like me." This is your internal doubter talking, trying to throw curve balls your way. The internal doubter says things like, "But what if... I'm wrong?," "... It's too hard!" ... "Someone rejected my idea," "...Nobody seems to want my product!", "...Does anyone really need this service?," "My app is getting slammed in reviews!" If you've ever started a new business, I'm sure you can think of 100 more things your internal doubter says to you on a daily basis.

The way that I combat this internal doubter is by staying focused and simply moving my project forward. One. Step. At. A. Time. I do not let my eye off of the ball. Once I've resolved to start a business or project, I commit to the idea and harden my skin against, not only the external naysayers, but also my internal doubter. Your internal doubter knows what your hot buttons are, and he likes to push them. So you have to be prepared when he shows up (and he will show up). You will have to take time to learn what works for you. Figure out how to get your internal doubter to be quiet, so you can move forward with your goal.

One More Tool for Your Business Toolbox

At this point, you should have a nice arsenal of tools, resources and philosophies you can use to help start your micro-business. So far, we covered a lot of ground in this book and if it seems like too much to remember at first, that's okay. You can certainly use this book to guide you as you begin implementing your plans. It should also help encourage you to do something every single day to move your business from the idea stage to a functional and profitable venture over the next few days, weeks and months. Once you decide to move forward you're going to trade your time, energy and your money to launch your business. Of course, one of the benefits of choosing a micro-business is that, while the initial investment is less than many other businesses, it is an investment nevertheless. I do understand that starting a business is never easy because inherent in the process is risk and most people are decidedly adverse to risk.

So what's your next move? There's a good chance you chose this book in the first place because you are either toying with the idea of starting a business or have already begun the groundwork for putting your idea into action. Well, lucky you. There's one more tool for your business toolbox.

The 5 Whys

Sakichi Toyoda (yes, founder of Toyota Motor company) was also known for developing the question-asking technique known as "The 5 Whys." This system was developed to solve problems or malfunctions within the framework of a process or system. To use this system users ask "why" five times to explore the root cause of a given problem. In doing this exercise, the goal is to identify the cause and effect relationship between the problem and the process. Let's look at a simplistic example. Say you're paying the month's bills for your new micro-business and you notice that your payables exceed your receivables for the month by $332 and you're going to have to cover the shortfall with money from your personal account.. Of course, you should want to get to the root of the problem. Your 5 Whys may look like this:

Why is there a $332 shortage this month? There is a $332 shortage this month because a client didn't pay what he owed.

Why didn't the client pay what he owed? The client didn't know how much he owed.

Why didn't the client know how much he owed? He didn't know how much he owed because no invoice was ever sent.

Why wasn't an invoice sent? An invoice wasn't sent because I didn't generate one.

Why did I fail to generate an invoice? I actually thought I had. Looks like I forgot.

In the above scenario, the problem is not necessarily the client or the profitability of the business. The problem is an unreliable billing system – one that relies too heavily on your memory

The 5 Whys isn't just a technique that works when applied to operational issues; it can be applied to a multitude of different problems to identify the specific point at which a system failure occurred. If the 5 Whys are applied correctly, once you run down your list of questions, both the problem and the solution should be clear.

As I've said before, if your idea is a good one, you should move on it quickly and stay committed to it. The keyword in that last sentence is, of course, "good." While we know that there are no guarantees in business, there are certain steps one can take to increase one's likelihood for success. Determining, on the front end, whether or not an idea is a good one is a critical part of a strong business foundation. Toward that end, I redesigned the 5 Whys approach to one that I call the Reverse 5 Whys.

Reverse 5 Whys

The Reverse 5 Whys starts with an idea, then seeks to follow a path of reasoning which will lead you to either justify or discredit the original idea. Instead of addressing a problem, as is what the 5 Whys approach aims to do, the Reverse 5 Whys approach is to be proactively applied, prior to the occurrence of any issue or problem. As a micro-business owners or would-be micro-business owner, I would highly recommend that you use the Reverse 5 Whys as a method for deciding if your micro-business is a good, sustainable idea. Use the Reverse 5 Whys as a way to prove your business before you ever launch the venture. Let's say you are considering launching a site that sells nutritional supplements. You would apply the Reverse 5 Whys technique like this:

Why should I sell this particular product? There is a need for this nutritional supplement in the market.

Why is there a need for this nutritional supplement? There is a need because men want to find an easy way to replace muscle mass lost as they age.

Why do they lose muscle mass as they age? They lose muscle mass because many men don't have time to exercise and eat healthy enough to maintain their muscle mass.

Why don't they have time to exercise and eat right? Men don't have time to eat right and exercise because many are overworked and when they get home after a long day, they don't work out.

Why won't they work out after work? Many men don't work out after work because they are tired and unmotivated. They want something relaxing, edible and simple.

For the above scenario, you're dealing with culture and economy. Working long hours is something that won't soon be leaving the habits of the United States workforce. And vanity is not going anywhere, either. In this scenario, it can be concluded that selling this nutritional supplement is an effective way to appeal to the male ego by offering a solution that will keep him looking good and will fit in his busy schedule. Perhaps this project would get the green light.

Whether it does or not, the point of the Reverse 5 Whys exercise is for you to conduct an objective audit of your reasons for engaging in any particular endeavor. It's an opportunity for you to think about what you're selling, who you're selling it to and the returns you expect to receive as a result of your venture. So before you spend time coming up with the perfect plan and getting your team together, you may want to use the Reverse 5 Whys to decide if the idea you have for your micro-business is something you really should do. The information you uncover may help you to decide if the business you are considering has enough profit-earning potential for you to continue investing your time and resources.

The main difference between the 5 Whys and the Reverse 5 Whys is that the 5 Whys is designed to leave you with a reason, while the Reverse 5 Whys helps you to identify a purpose. The benefit you gain by using the Reverse 5 Whys is that the process forces you to take a thoughtful and objective look at your business idea. Any good conversationalist can tell you that the way to engage someone is to get them to answer open-ended questions. "Why" questions require a bit of thought and expression. It's the same thing with the Reverse 5 Whys. By asking yourself why you are choosing to start a particular business, you'll be able to distinguish between an emotional choice and a rational choice. If you're honest when conducting your Reverse 5 Whys analysis, you will quickly be able to see if your business idea is worth the investment required to launch and maintain its profitably. If you find that the idea isn't worth the investment, you may be wise to cut your losses and move on to discovering your next great idea. If it is worth the investment, welcome to the wonderful world of business or micro-business.

In the initial stages of your business development, you will have to keep your nose to the grindstone. This will easily be a time when you will feel overworked, tired and exhausted. After a while, you may feel out of balanced as well. Often, you will find that you have inherited too much work, not enough play, fatigue and stress. Don't worry, as this is common. In these initial stages, you may be working on several aspects of the business at one time, in addition to handling all of your other obligations including, quite possibly, a full-time job. Add to that the likely possibility that the projects you will be working on will be new to you. The whole thing could be overwhelming and you (like myself) will probably find it very challenging trying to manage all of these things at one time. Every great entrepreneur goes through a period like this. Basically, what I'm saying is that the quest for "sleep money" or any revenue is one that is based on urgency and continuous momentum, at least in the initial stages, when one is laying a foundation. But believe me, if you have a good idea and perseverance, there is a light at the end of the tunnel.

When I wrote the book *FIT: A Roadmap to a Better Body*, my main goal was to educate people in the area of health and nutrition in order to keep balance in their lives. It seems to me that the key to making the process work is recognizing (and embracing) that not everything can or will be done at 100%. There simply aren't enough hours in the day. Being momentarily off balance can be expected. Instead of doing a 1.5 hour workout, for example, one might need to compromise with a 30 minute workout and spend the other 60 minutes working on a project. Instead of holding a leadership position on a committee at your child's school, you might have to, instead, be a member of the committee, until your business foundation is laid.

The key here is that you have to keep moving. Some days you will accomplish a lot; other days won't be as productive. Take care of yourself and do your best to balance all of your obligations. Do. Not. Stop. Move it forward.

Chapter 16

The Lazy Businessman

"A successful man is one who can lay a firm foundation with the bricks others have thrown at him."

- David Brinkley, Newscaster for ABC and NBC

We have all heard that you need to work hard to be successful at business. Yes this is true, and for the most part you should work hard. The key phrase in the last sentence is "for the most part." Hard work is the catalyst for success in business. For most of us, the process of developing a plan and finding the right personnel and suppliers while simultaneously creating a good, working system can be draining. Believe me, I did it - been through it all. It's a grind that's fit for only the most committed and mentally prepared among us. The process is one-part boundless joy and one-part chaos that I wouldn't wish on my worst enemy.

But what if I said that you may be going about your business philosophy all wrong? What if I told you it's the "lazy businessman" who may be in the best position to create his own opportunity for success? Let's take a quick look back. Some of you may remember the parable of the ant and the grasshopper. If you don't, let me refresh your memory. The grasshopper spends his time lounging around in the summer sun, singing, while the ant works diligently to store up food for the winter. The ant is steady, methodical, reliable, and the more the ant toils, the more the grasshopper sings. When winter finally arrives, the grasshopper, starving, remembers the way the ant gathered up all that food and goes to the ant for help. But, all the grasshopper gets is a rebuke from the ant for his laziness. Back to this story in a minute.

Now, in this fable, the crafty ant has found an effective method of ensuring his survival. He works and works and his hard work gives him the resources he needs to survive. The ant is steadfast and wise. If you're like the ant – working to survive – you are like most people. That's not a bad thing. But, perhaps, you would like to do a bit of singing in the warm months like our friend the grasshopper. If so, you may need to modify your methods a bit.

Many business people think like the ant. They are the first ones to get to work in the morning and the last ones to leave at night. They firmly believe that if you work hard, be a good person, and pay your bills and taxes, everything will work out in the end. Or, in the "sweet by and by." or, in their retirement years. Or, after the kids leave. My question is, "Why wait?"

I hate to break this news to you, but the Industrial Revolution is over. I hope I haven't offended you by removing the veil from your eyes on this. The days of toiling at the mill or in the factory day in and day out, saving up sick days and getting pension contributions are long gone for many of us, even though the work habits of yesteryear remain. We are officially in the Digital Age and the mantra these days is "work smart." It is the smart worker who is able to sing during those warm months and still feast heartily during the winter months. I'm not trying to get you to modify your work ethic. A healthy work ethic is essential to running even a micro-business, or keeping a job for that matter. But there is a difference between your work ethics and your work habits. A good work ethic says, "There's work to be done, I'm getting paid, let's get it done." Your work habits determine how you will get the work done and if that work will take you an hour to complete or a day to complete.

I know what I'm about to tell you is contrary to the entrepreneurial beliefs held by most people. Still, it's an idea worth looking into. Are you ready? Here goes. Let's all try being lazy for a change. Let's just not report to the office at all for days or even weeks. We're not checking any emails, not running any errands, not printing any invoices. Let's go fishing. Or, go visit family in Florida. You don't think that's the greatest, most novel idea you've ever heard? Some of you will think it sounds silly, reckless, or ludicrous. Micro-business owners may say, "If I don't work, I don't eat." If that's your response, you may need a new perspective on your business.

Let's talk for a moment about the lazy businessman that I'm asking you to consider becoming. This guy, who doesn't report to work or check his emails, is a hero. It sounds almost unfathomable in our current society to be unreachable for a few hours, let alone a few days. I'm asking you to give yourself the option to be just that. The lazy businessman is a man who has given himself the gift of choice. If you've ever reported to work sick or missed your kid's noontime school play because you have a business conference, you could benefit from having more choices where your work is concerned. Believe me when I say this: the lazy businessman is no sluggard. He's not irresponsible. He's not flaky. On the contrary, he's smart. He's strategic. He's got a plan. He's the master of his time and captain of his day. He has created for himself a way out of the never-ending race to retirement. While you're still working 12-hour days, he's at the beach or golf course. While you're burning the midnight oil to deliver reports, he's sitting at the nearest coffee house wooing clients over mochas. He's not a rocket scientist. He's not some business anomaly. He's a regular guy who just made a different choice for what he will do with his time on a daily basis.

If you believe this is "pie in the sky," allow me to present you with a challenge. When you have some spare time, go to several fast food franchises near your house and say these words to the cashier: "Hey, I really like this place. Food's good, service is great, things are organized. I'd love to meet the owner. Is the owner in by chance? I want to tell him what a great job you're doing." I'd be willing to bet you that the friendly cashiers in 8 out of 10 establishments will say, "I'm sorry, but the owner is not here right now." Yet, the business will be functioning, food will be getting served and money will be changing hands. Now, why would a business owner entrust the operation of his business to a bunch of teenaged employees?

Because he's lazy. Not lazy in the sense that he is slothful or a bum or no-good. He's lazy in the sense that he has systems in place that afford him the option to show up for work only if he chooses to do so. I know it's strange for you to think of being lazy as an ultimate business goal, but it actually should be. Most people who go into business for themselves do so to give themselves more options. We want freedom and the ability to do what we want when we want instead of having our day dictated to us by upper management. So we swap out upper management for our own customers who pay us to have the right to dictate our day to us. That's, essentially, what many self-employed people do. They leave their 9 to 5 jobs where they report to one or two people and go to work for themselves from 8 to 8 where they report to all of their customers – however many they may have.

Therein lies the importance of having a detailed, effective system in place for everyone in your organization. You see, when there are good, working systems in place, the business owner doesn't need to be at his business all hours of the day, opening the shop in the morning and flipping the lights off at night as he closes. He doesn't need to stand around barking orders to his employees or checking the bathrooms multiple times a day to make sure the stalls are being cleaned properly. He doesn't have to micro-manage the routine tasks being performed at his business day in and day out. That's the benefit of having systems in place.

In this particular case of the fast food businesses, the owners were smart enough to buy into a successful, ready-made system that's proven to work - a system that does not require the owner to reinvent the wheel. The system doesn't need to be refined, tweaked and updated constantly. That system is a franchise. Most, if not all, franchises have proven systems in place. In essence, the system in place at the franchise is a major portion of what you're buying into when you purchase one. So let's take a quick lesson from a franchise giant.

Most of the checks and balances that create the overall success of the franchise system are written out for the owners and their staff to follow. Many franchisors require training for the franchisees and the management team so that they can learn the system and learn it well. In a good franchising system, every method of operation is already laid out for prospective franchisees. Not only are they laid out for management to follow, but a good franchisor sets protocol for all team members at every level of the operation.

It is the franchise management system that determines, for example, when personnel should check bathrooms for cleanliness and how employees are to confirm with management that the bathrooms have been cleaned. It is the franchise system that says when and how team members should suggest meal upgrades to restaurant customers. Even prospective customer interactions have been scripted.

"Would you like to 'go large' for another 69 cents, ma'am?" Scripted.

"Would you like fries and a drink with that?" Scripted.

"Would you like to sign up for our burger club to get coupons and offers to your email?" Scripted.

Everyone is trained to operate in a similar manner. Even the temperature of a cup of coffee at a franchise is pre-determined. In less than 50 years, McDonald's became one of the most successful franchises of all-time. With more than 30,000 restaurants around the world, 80% of them being franchised, McDonald's has demonstrated that franchise systems work. McDonald's Corporation has a training program, being run from their Hamburger University, that teaches franchise owners how to manage the restaurant. The franchise manual actually teaches owners the method to use when laying hamburger patties on the grill. The manual says when burgers are to be flipped, and even when to throw old burgers away. It's a closed system and it's an easy system to learn, implement and follow. That's the key. The McDonald's system is so thorough and so complete that many McDonald's restaurants can be run by teenagers with no previous restaurant experience.

Now when it comes to franchise systems, much of the work associated with running a business – coming up with procedures, designing and testing products, building a customer base – is already done. For the privilege of using that proven franchise system, the franchisee is required to pay a franchisee fee, usually around 4 to 7% of the establishment's gross sales, plus an additional 2-3% to cover the cost of advertising. Many franchisors do advertise for their franchisees.

Sounds great, right? Well it is when it works correctly. But stellar systems aren't just limited to multi-billion dollar corporations. In fact, the stellar system is what got McDonald's to multi-billion dollar status in the first place. Having a good system in place for your micro-business can afford you the time to do other things like...be lazy. Remember, being lazy is not a bad thing. Just like working all day is not a bad thing. The option to be lazy is what you, as a successful businessperson, should be striving to attain. You see, having the option to be both successful in your business and discriminating in where you invest your energy is a good idea. When you have a system in place that is efficient and productive, it frees you from having to deal with day-to-day operations and allows you time to come up with more ideas and other ways to make money.

Let's examine April Quinn, who is running a freelance research firm, called Quinntessential Findings, that specializes in creating white papers for the green energy sector. In creating her brand and building a reputation for her product, she did so through good work, great customer relationships, plenty of long hours, and a lot of writing. However, she's still in a position where she's trading her precious time – a nonrenewable resource – for money. She knows the work, she understands her clientele, and she knows the method. She also knows what talents and skills are needed to complete the research and deliver top-quality content to her clients. In order to get April out of the money-for-time lifestyle, let's see if we can etch out a system that makes sense.

The average job usually takes her between 3 and 5 weeks to complete, depending on the scope of the work. If she hires personnel, she already knows that it's going to cut into her profits. Feasibly, she could outsource the projects to a small research team in the Philippines. The research team is paid a flat rate to deliver specific content in a specific format within 2 days of receiving the assignment. Each member of the research team is responsible for a specific area of the research. When completed, the research itself then goes to April's project manager, an hourly contractor, who reviews the research to make sure that it meets Quinnessential's criteria for white papers. Afterward, the project manager distributes the research to April's domestic writing team, most of them college students and recent graduates, who also work for a flat rate per white paper they write. The writers get 1 day to review the research and another 3 days to write the white paper. Each writer is responsible for generating a specific section of content and nothing more. That content is written according to a pre-determined template that serves as a sort of map to guide writers on where each bit of research goes in the white paper. This method ensures all research is utilized and the white paper is thorough and complete. The completed document is sent to April's project manager, who edits the paper and submits it to the client for review and payment. At the end of the week, the project manager emails April a report of the work that's been done. April pays her team, the client pays her. A process that previously took a month to complete is now completed in a week and April's only time investment is reading her email and scheduling payments to her vendors using her Google checkout account.

Now, let's look at the financial side. April's profit margin was decreased when she hired the two teams to create the white papers along with the project manager to oversee the process. The good thing though is that it will only take her team a quarter of the time it took her to do the same job. (That's often the case when you let go of the reins. You soon find out that the world doesn't stop revolving; things still get done, and, sometimes, they are done better and faster than if you did them yourself.) So the time April saves not writing is time she can spend marketing to get more clientele, creating other products to sell, building new teams that specialize in creating white papers for other trending topics or just being...you guessed it...lazy.

You can only be both lazy and successful if you have developed a solid business design. All checks and balances must be in place. When it comes to your business design, no stone can be left unturned. Every possible issue must be well-thought-out. What that means is when you first start your business, you'll be working hard – very, very hard. You'll need to deal with product issues, find your suppliers, engage your market, push your business and establish a good reputation, all while coming up with a iron clad system of operations that is airtight, efficient and productive. This is nothing out of the ordinary. Businesses prosper when they exist in an environment that allows for them to effectively operate. It's not an easy process, but it's an important one. Your goal, though, should always be to create an enterprise that is self-sufficient. You want to build something that can run just fine with or without you. So if you're able to be lazy and still have a thriving business, you probably have a solid working system. That's why I like micro-businesses. Micro-businesses are much easier than full-service businesses like McDonald's when it comes to creating solid, self-supporting working systems. Most micro-business have fewer moving parts. There's less to manage and less to control.

Now, back to our friend the grasshopper. Let's say that, when spring first kicked in, he got an idea to pull down small leaves for the ants so that they could load their food on the leaf and pull more food in fewer trips. In exchange, they would allow him a small portion of the food on each small leaf. This way, he can still sing songs. His only time investment is pulling down leaves when the ants have worn out the previous leaf. When winter returns, hopefully, he'll have plenty of food to eat.

Chapter 17

Passion and Fear

"There are a lot of things that go into creating success. I don't like to do just the things I like to do. I like to do things that cause the company to succeed. I don't spend a lot of time doing my favorite activities."

- Michael Dell, Founder and Chairman of Dell, Inc.

"Do what you love, but be damned sure it's profitable."

- Steve Pavlina, Blogger

Myth: Find Your Passion

If I were to ask you to name the opposite of "fear," most of you would probably say "strength" or "faith." The true opposite of fear, however, is passion. When one is passionate about an issue or idea, feelings of fear are minimal, if not nonexistent.. The opposite is true as well: when we fear a particular thing, we are not passionate about pursuing it, confronting it, or embracing it; we would just as soon stay away from it altogether.

Both passion and fear can be good motivating emotions that cause either change or inertia. When starting a business, however, you should not allow either emotion to drive you too strongly. Why? Because you want to be as objective as possible – intellectual and smart in how you approach the process. You want to focus on the facts and realities as you research and develop a plan for success.

Do not be swayed by the common allegory that urges you to "find your passion," or "find something you love" when it comes to selecting a product or service that you want to develop as your business. Why do I say this? Because passion is an emotion that can lead you into the wrong direction. Passion can blind you to a number of red flags and indicators that you tell you that you are embarking upon an improper field of endeavor. Passion can cause you to stay committed to a project or business that is failing or unproductive, unwilling to let go before it has you in financial and emotional ruins. Fear, on the other hand, is an emotion that can keep you stuck in cement, unable to make decisions. Fear can immobilize you completely to the point that, days, months and years go by without you having taken any steps toward bringing your ideas to fruition.

While I believe that passion is important, I think it is often misplaced. You don't have to be passionate about your particular ideas, your particular products, or your particular businesses. What you do need to be passionate about, instead, is the opportunity for your idea or business to be successful. I say this to you because, if you're anything like me, above and beyond all else, what matters most is success. I want to win. That's it! I am in business to make money - first and foremost. If you are the type of person who needs to "feel good," "love what you do" all day, or, otherwise, experience puppies and rainbows in your day-to-day business life, this concept will not be easy to stomach. Quite frankly, this approach may be totally contrary to everything you stand for in your life and with regard to your life's purpose. For those of us, like me, who get into business for the purpose of making money, embracing the idea that passion for a particular idea is not necessary can be very liberating.

Listen: you don't have to love it in the beginning. I guarantee you that if you are successful, you will learn to love it in one form or another. Amy Chua, the author of The Tiger Mom, explains how passion develops. Chua points out that many children don't like a given task when they initially engage (or are forced to engage) in it. Learning how to play a piano, for example, is rarely the preferred activity for a kid, when compared to an activity like bicycle riding or playing on a

Nintendo Wii. After long, continuous practice, and once a certain level of success is attained and recognized by the public, most children are delighted with the activity that has brought them achievement and acclaim.

The same holds true in a business context. Passion for the business grows as the business sees more success and public acceptance. This feeling may not be present in the initial stages of business development. Often, it is developed over a period of time.

The father of a close friend of mine owns Earth's Beauty Supply, a successful beauty supply store in St. Paul, Minnesota, that has been in business for over 33 years. This is a guy who had zero previous hair styling or hair supply experience. He had never been in the beauty business and never had an interest in it. Do you think that, at any point in time, during his 33 year career in the beauty supply industry, that he was passionate about hair extensions and flatirons? Let me assure you: he was not. Ever! And he still isn't. What he is very passionate about, though, is that his business has afforded him the opportunity to work for himself for decades, to serve the community needs, and provide for his family. That's something about which to be fired up, no?

Passion must never to mistaken for productivity. Contrary to common self-help rhetoric, the two can be mutually exclusive. How many awesome, but broke, visual artists do you know? What about extraordinarily gifted singers, promoters, dancers, or other entertainers? What about brilliant and talented writers and actors? You know them. Perhaps, one is living rent free in your basement right now. Perhaps I'm talking about... you.

As blogger, Steve Pavlina, says, "If you can't do what you love and make it profitable, you've either got a hobby or a headache, not a sustainable business." That said, it is very possible for you to be on fire for something, but not be particularly good at or productive in it. The latter, a lack of productivity is, of course, unacceptable.

A college friend of mine, Dexter, was never proud about flipping burgers when we was in school. He, actually, hated every minute of it. Some nights, when our friends went out to party, Dexter had to work all night and we would razz him about how he so often missed out on our crew's festivities. One thing he had that we did not see at the time (as immature as we were) was dedication and commitment. He never called in sick, or failed to show up for an appointed shift. He was never late. Dexter worked hard at his crappy job, and insisted that he had a bigger plan.

Through his hard work over the years, he was consistently promoted through the company's ranks to a position in upper management. Eventually, he applied his years of experience and dollars he saved throughout his career to open his own fast food franchise. Now, of course, he has a different perspective on flipping burgers. He is glad to stand in front of the grill and flip, flip away. In fact, me and my crew can't shut him up about the art of flipping burgers. He can fully explain the biophysics of the burger turn. And, this passion is all due to the success he achieved over the years developing a big game plan to own a restaurant. He did not like working at the restaurant in the beginning, but he had a plan. Just like most children don't like piano lessons until they attain a certain level of success, he focused on the opportunity to do well, not on the love of the job. While we were laughing at him years ago, he knew he'd later be laughing all the way to the bank. And he is. When you are researching potential business ideas, do not be concerned if your heart doesn't race when you consider an idea, product or service. Don't focus on how you feel; focus on and access the potential for success. Fall in love with the potential, not the product. No successful junkman was ever born loving junk. Crunch the numbers, research the need, examine the market trends, and assess your ability to make this a viable and profitable idea. Fall in love with that. Potential can trump passion – and that's okay

Overcoming Fear

The polar opposite of passion is fear. Fear is one of the most difficult and important emotions to manage. When you are starting a new micro-business, or any type of business, it is easy to get paralyzed with questions like, "What if I don't do this right?" Or, the big one that is in the back of most people's minds, "What if I end up living in my van, under a bridge?" (I've actually heard people say this. The fear of losing everything is very common, and reasonable, when starting a business.)

These questions are completely normal, and so is fear. Everybody faces fear at one time or another in their business venture; it is common to feel fear when launching, when expanding, when taking on a new product or expanding on a product or service. Fear may also crop up when making plans for your future, and you wonder if you have taken the proper precautions. The bottom line is that when you are putting it all on the line in pursuit of your dreams, things can get a little bit scary. Everyone I know who is successful in business deals with these kind of fears. The difference between those who succeed and those who don't is the ability to deal with the fear in a positive way, so it does not stop them from taking action.

Take a cue from a business owner, Martin. He started his (now) very successful micro-business after moving his family to a new state, where he had no support system. He had prepared to open up a traditional accounting business when he got there, but circumstances caused it to fail before he even started. At this point, Martin could have given up. He could have easily succumbed to the fear and moved his family back, or simply returned to corporate America. But he chose to not do that. He did abandon his original idea of a traditional business in favor of a web-based micro-business. Hubbard Accounting was born. He determined that launching this type of web- based business came with an amount of risk that he could accept and afford. The new business required very little capital investment, and the only thing that was really required to make it work was work ethic. Martin had plenty of that.

If he had let fear overtake him when his first brick and mortar business failed, Martin would have never started his successful micro–business. He would not have the kind of freedom and income-producing product that he now has. The bottom line is this: you should not let fear immobilize you, nor should you allow it to discourage you from continuing efforts until you succeed.

Fear is Important

What I suggest is that you use fear as a motivator. Even though it is uncomfortable, fear serves an important purpose. Fear's main job is to operate as an internal trigger that tells us when we might be doing something wrong. It keeps us from putting our hands on a hot stove or jumping off the proverbial cliff. Without fear, we would run headlong into dangerous situations. For that reason, we should be thankful for this very natural emotion. As important as fear is, if left unchecked, it can seriously get in our way. Since you're reading this book, you probably own a business or have, at least, thought about owning a business that could succeed and make you a profit. The reason that your fear kicks up is because what you want to do is different from what you are doing right now. It is common for your brain to get comfortable with the status quo (even if it is making you miserable) and be resistant to change. The great comedian, Bill Cosby, once said, "In order to succeed in life, your desire for success should be greater than your fear of failure." So even if you hate the job you are in and desperately dream of leaving it, the fear of losing everything and fear of failing can keep you tied to your desk and never ever taking action. It doesn't have to be that way. There are strategies that you can use to help you look your fear in the face and get on with building a business and a life that you want to live. These strategies include learning how to use a micro-business structure to limit risk, and obtaining the information you need to move past your fear.

But What If I Fail?

One of the biggest fears that people have about taking control of their own destiny and becoming an entrepreneur is the fear of failure. They worry not only about failing in business, but also about losing everything else for which they've worked for over the years. They worry that it isn't "the right time." They fear that they won't be able to balance the demands of their new business and the obligations associated with their existing job or career. Believe me, I have been in that position and I know exactly how it feels; these fears are all completely understandable. When I walked away from a very safe career as an educator to start a business in real estate, I was terrified. I did not allow the uncertainty and all of the "what if" questions I had running through my mind stop me from moving forward. I continued to do the necessary due diligence to prepare myself to succeed in business. I researched and studied the path on which I was embarking. As I gathered more information, I became more and more confident. Before I went into business, I never felt 100% certain about my success, as I am smart enough to know that there are no guarantees. But, with more information and insight, I felt better and better about taking the risk of entrepreneurship. This is why I so strongly advocate micro-businesses. This type of business structure greatly increases one's likelihood of success. With a micro-business, the idea is to start small and with little capital investment. You can grow at your own pace. As compared to a full-service business, a micro-business structure allows you to eliminate many of your fears (particularly those related to finances) right off the bat. To start gaining momentum and overcoming your fears, ask yourself these questions:

What is the worst case scenario – what is the worst that could happen if this idea doesn't work?

What am I risking by getting involved in this endeavor?

If I fail, who will be impacted and how?

What do I stand to gain if I can make this work?

Who will be impacted, and what will the nature of the impact be, if I am successful?

Over the years, I have been quite surprised by how many people are so afraid to confront their fears that they will not even bother to take the time to answer these questions. Remember, there is no harm in going through the exercise of determining what the consequences – good and bad- would be if you move forward in business. Putting your head in the sand, so to speak, and avoiding this process will likely immobilize you. If you take the time to think through these questions, and provide honest answers, you may be surprised at what you come up with.

For me, and for most other successful entrepreneurs that I know, the answer to these questions is simple. The worst case scenario in failing with a micro-business (and we will discuss what failure actually means a bit later) is that you end up almost exactly where you are at now. If you've maintained your job throughout the process, you have continued to produce income and have, thus, continued to be able to pay your bills. The biggest new aspect of your life will be that you have more information. You will have learned a lot about yourself, your business style, what you did well, what you did not do well, and more about the industry in which you chose to enter. Furthermore, you will no longer be that guy who sits at work wondering what could be or what could have been, while nervously tapping his pen at his desk. I can almost guarantee that, even in a worst case scenario of failure, you will be happier than you are right now.

Now let's take a look at what might happen if you do nothing about your dreams and continue to work at a job that may be okay, but that doesn't excite you like starting your own business. If you choose to stay where you are, it is very likely that you will still be exactly where you are right now. Of course, you could get promoted to a higher level position, or...you could not. You could get an increase in your salary or... you could not. Each of these possibilities are, mind you, out of your control and based on someone else deciding what they believe it is that you deserve. If what you're doing right now is not even okay and has you, in fact, quite miserable, if you choose to stay where you are it is unlikely that you will even get a promotion or substantial increase, since most miserable employees are not good performers. If you do nothing to change your circumstances, you will be just as miserable one day, one month, and one year from now. If that's not failure, I don't know what is. Not succeeding in a business does not make you, yourself, a failure. Not having the courage to pursue those of your dreams that are realistic and attainable, however, may make you a failure. So, ask yourself: is risking a "fail" in business the true failure or is it staying where you are and not trying something new?

Another way to get over the fear of failure is to redefine what it means to you. There are several ways to do this effectively. I used all of these at one time or another. Use the scientific method to redefine failure: I find that applying the methods that lead to great discovery in science, also work for producing great results in business. I subscribe to the scientific theory that says that you observe, analyze, build a hypothesis, test your hypothesis, get feedback and repeat. In business, this is what it looks like: observe the market, decide what will sell well, test your hypothesis with marketing, get feedback, and repeat and refine.

The great thing about using this process is that it doesn't view failing as failure. It simply views it as part of the learning curve. What if you never failed, but only learned from your results? If you can take this approach in your business, you will find that you start looking at setbacks as learning opportunities instead of as failures. It is a very powerful concept. Redefining failure as part of the natural learning curve (just like scientists do) is a great way to overcome the fear of failure.

So decide what failure actually means to you. Many people don't start businesses because they are afraid that other people will view them as failures if they start a business that doesn't succeed. I would question this thought process. In my mind, allowing yourself to be miserable all the time and not trying is failing. Trying – even if you don't become successful – is success. Think about how much you will learn from your experience, and think about what the worst case scenario will be. Usually, if the business venture doesn't work out, the worst thing that will happen is that you realize that your job wasn't so bad, and you will go get another one. Other people may not understand you or where you are coming from, but you will have the satisfaction of taking action on your dreams, which is the ultimate form of success.

Don't sit at a job that you hate, dreaming of becoming an entrepreneur and being miserable. Decide on the life you want to live and make it happen. Start a micro-business in your spare time and work your butt off in the evenings to get to an income level you want and then quit your job. It is the most amazing feeling in the world.

Overcoming Other Fears

While the general fear of failure is often one's biggest fear when it comes to starting a business, it is by no means the only one. There are numerous other questions and concerns that run through the minds of many would-be entrepreneurs. Again, as with the fear of failing in business, if you take the time to confront many of these issues, you are likely to find that these concerns can be properly addressed through solid planning and research. So it is important that you take an objective look at some of the concerns that may be immobilizing you and ask yourself whether or not these are true issues, or ones that you have created in your mind. By facing your fears, instead of ignoring them, you can move past them more easily.

Let's examine some of the "what ifs" that may be going through your mind.

Economic Downturns. What if the economy crashes again or recovers at too slow a pace? The economy is completely out of your control (mine too... unfortunately). The only thing you can control is how you respond to whatever the current economic crisis is. Please be mindful that many fortunes have been made in difficult economic times by people who saw opportunities among the chaos, rather than obstacles. It is no secret to the wealthy that more wealth is made in bad economic times as compared to boom times. The reasons are numerous: lower wages are acceptable, larger talent pools are available, equipment costs are cheap, those with cash on hand have better bargaining position, etc. I believe the economic crisis of the early portion of the 2010 decade was largely sustained by a massive shift in the way business was, traditionally, being done. Many small and micro-businesses began to reduce their overhead costs by cutting out middlemen or offering products for free that were once for pay. Think: long distance service. Think: Google Docs. Think: anti-virus software. My point here is that fear of an economic downturn should not be given credence because you can succeed whether or not the economy is up or down. If you position yourself with a solution-based business, you stand to profit handsomely as the economy shifts. So, instead of asking yourself what would happen to your business if the economy were to tank, you should ask yourself, "Would I prefer to create my own future or would I rather be at the mercy of an employer that may or may not continue to exist?" Personally, I would put my bets on myself and I hope you would too.

Bad Timing. What if my timing is wrong? I've met lots of would-be entrepreneurs who have put off starting a business because they wanted to be more seasoned. I have also come across would-be entrepreneurs who did not want to start a business because they felt like they were too old. Waiting for the perfect time is a terrible excuse for not following your dreams. Why? In business, the timing is rarely, if ever, perfect. There will always be things in your life that will hold you back if you let them. Something unexpected will happen. Someone will do or respond in a manner in which you did not anticipate. Life is never perfect. Never. Don't let this issue stop you. If you are young, what do you stand to gain by waiting? If you are older, you may want to look at your circumstances as "now or never."

It is true that good timing can help a business succeed. The absence of good timing, however, should not keep one from entering into business. Do you think that when Steve Jobs, the founder of Apple dreamed of making computers accessible to everyone that he thought to wait until the time was right? When would the time be "right" for such a novel product? Obviously, fear was not his barrier. He may have felt his share of fear, but it, certainly, did not keep him from pursuing his dream. In his later years, he made it clear that fear was not a deterrent for him. He was quoted as saying at the 2005 Stanford University graduation commencement address, "Almost everything - all external expectations, all pride, all fear of embarrassment or failure - these things just fall away in the face of death, leaving only what is truly important. Remembering that you are going to die is the best way I know to avoid the trap of thinking you have something to lose.

You are already naked. There is no reason not to follow your heart."

Just think: when he first began to develop Apple, the whole idea of personal computers was revolutionary. In fact, it took Jobs many years to make those accessible computers happen, and many thought he was kind of crazy. After seeing some initial success with the Apple II and the Macintosh, he was forced out of his own company for a decade. Instead of giving up, he worked with Pixar and also founded NeXT computers. It was a twist of fate when Apple bought out NeXT; by doing so, they also brought back Steve. In turn, he led Apple to becoming one of the most profitable companies in the world. This is the kind of confidence it takes to make a company work. If you have it – and believe in yourself - then the time is right - even if all conditions are not perfect. It's not the timing that will make your business work, it is you.

Finding Good Help. Getting good help should not at all be a concern as you plan your business. As the economic climate in the United States has shifted and the market has become more global, identifying and securing people who can help you with your projects is now easier than it ever has been. With the global human resource market at your disposal, you can find contractors to work with you at great rates. You then can train them to operate according to your needs. If I haven't made it clear that outsourcing is a business model that you should embrace, please hear me clearly now. Change your mindset from being locally-oriented to being globally-oriented. Also, modify your thinking from an employer/employee model to one that contemplates temporary and contract-based workers and teams. The people who work with you do not have to be in the United States, and whoever you hire – wherever they are located – only needs to be hired on an as-needed basis. If you need someone to help you with search engine optimization for your website, for example, you can do not need to hire them to be your all-around information technology guru. You can hire them for the sole purpose of addressing that one particular need in your business, for a very specific period of time, as designated by you. If you need a programmer, there are thousands of freelancers from all over the world who are willing to take on a job for you. Be creative, hire the people that you need for just when you need them; you will be amazed by how much you can get done and how affordable it is.

By employing this approach in your micro-business operation, you will increase efficiency and reduce headache. You will not need to pay benefits, nor will you have massive employee salary overhead.

What If I Lose Money? You will lose money – at first. You should be prepared to make some investment before you make any profit – then, you should see your investment pay off. But first, you will definitely be in the hole. Unless your new business is a free blog, know that you will spend something to get your business going. Remember, you will be a business owner – not an employee. Most employees get paid regardless of how the company performs; business owners do not. As a business owner, you must accept that the possibility of losing money is part of the equation. Aim to do everything in your power so that it doesn't happen – including having a solid business model, keeping close track of your finances, and limiting risk where at all possible.

One of the best ways to limit that risk is to have a micro-business. I know, I've said it several times, but I have to say it again. This type of business can easily merge the amazing power of talented people, established resources, and, in many cases, the internet to create a workable concept with very low risk. Your financial investment can range from as small as $100 to a couple of thousand dollars in order to get it off the ground. That is a very small investment relative to those associated with most brick and mortar businesses.

What If This Works and I Make A Lot of Money? I, personally, don't have a problem with making a bunch of money. It's a problem that I would be delighted to have. What surprises me is that this is, actually, a concern for some people. This may sound a little strange, since the reason that the majority of people go into business for themselves is to make money. What I've found is that money can make some people uncomfortable. Some people view making "too much money" as some type of evil. Some traditions view sacrifice as being noble and, for people who believe this, earning too much can be glutinous or cause laziness.

These beliefs about money are usually ingrained in our consciousness from a very early age. I think one of the best ways to handle this is to make a plan. Decide, in advance, how much salary you will take based, on your needs and desires. Then, be vigilant about putting the rest of the money back into the business. If earning too much money is inconsistent with your values, you can decide to designate all earned funds, beyond what you need in order to live, to the charitable organization of your choice.

Another way a plan helps is by showing you how much money you need to make in order to grow and pay your bills. By having a plan in place, you will have targets to shoot for as well as plans for the additional funds that you earn. That should alleviate the concerns you may have about earning more money that you believe you need.

The choice is yours. You can learn to work through the uncertainties, take action and realize your dreams…or you can let your questions about what might or could happen keep you from achieving your goals.

Remember that being in business for yourself is far less risky than it used to be. By starting a micro-business and using technology, you can have a thriving business with minimal up-front risk.

The Absolute Best Way to Overcome Fear. The foremost best way to overcome fear can be summarized in one word: preparation. Prepare, prepare, prepare. As motivational speaker, Tony Robbins, has said, "The meeting of preparation with opportunity generates the offspring we call luck." When I first started investing in real estate, the one thing that gave me tremendous confidence and courage in making deals was that I would only pursue deals that I had thoroughly researched. To select just 1 house, I would have done detailed analysis on over 100 properties. I had so much information to support my investment decisions that I had very little fear that the deals I selected would fail. Even though I was a novice, I never flew by the seat of my pants. I was methodical and diligent. As I gathered more and more information, my confidence grew and my fear subsided.

Do yourself a favor and commit to doing the kind of research and preparation that will make you feel comfortable in moving forward on this business. I'm not saying that you should spend years conducting this research before making a move. No, What I am saying is that proper research is a critical element to allaying your fears of failure. You must balance this requirement for proper preparation with the need that you get on with business already. Develop a high level of knowledge or competence in what you intend to do. If you want to open up a bakery, then you need to understand basic business accounting and how to bake (or hire) a great baker. Running a micro-business is no different. If you have an idea for the next great online platform, then you need to know some basics about how that platform should work. You should also know how other existing platforms work for the purpose of comparison. You most definitely don't have to know all the details (and that would take too much time anyway), but you need to know just enough to be able to effectively hire someone who knows the details. Thankfully, learning the basics doesn't have to be too hard if you know where to look. There are three basic ways to gather the preliminary information you need.

Seminars, Classes and Other Formal Education. To learn more about the industry that you want to enter or the service you want to provide, you may need to get some formal education. The same is true if there are some basic business concepts with which you need to become more familiar. For instance, if you need to learn how to handle business finances, you can take an accounting basics course at your local community college. If you want to start an online micro-business, but aren't computer savvy at all, then it is a good idea to take some classes if only to get familiar with the important basic concepts. Getting the education you need can be as simple as going to a site like Lynda.com or KhanAcademy.com and watching the tutorials on how to do almost everything. As mentioned, many colleges also offer continuing education classes; community groups often do as well. Find a class that you think fits your needs and take it. There are many great resources available now that can easily be found through a search engine. Many professional associations also offer educational seminars. This is a great way to learn about or keep abreast of the trends in your industry. Whether you want to learn how to market via social networking, or develop a hot app, you can usually find this information at some sort of seminar. Thanks to modern technology, you can now attend online seminars, also known as webinars, if you cannot attend a seminar in person. Beware of free seminars. I find that many of these are sales pitches. Sometimes they provide good information, but require you to purchase other items or services to get the "rest of the details." I prefer, when I find appropriate ones, to attend paid webinars and seminars. These will often have high quality information that you can implement immediately. Most of the time, online webinars also come with a replay that you can reference at a later date.

If you decide that you want to take an online class, one of the challenges is that, in this age of information, things are changing all the time. There are many quality classes available online, but there are also many scams. One of the ways that you can protect yourself from the scams is to check out the guarantee that the class, course, or ebook offers, and then pay through Paypal or by using your credit card. That way, if what you bought is a total dud, you can get your money back without too much hassle.

Mentorship. Classes and seminars are great, but they will never replace the value of having a mentor. A mentor can be someone who is only slightly ahead of you in what you want to achieve, or someone who is at the pinnacle of a career in your chosen area. They don't have to be a guru or someone who knows everything – they just have to know more than you. The best way to find a mentor is by networking with other people in your industry. Find someone who has achieved what you are looking to achieve and ask if they will help you get to where they are. Provided that you are not attempting to directly compete with them, many people will gladly share their insight with you. Your potential mentors do not have to be people you already know. T hey can be someone you read about in a news article, or even someone you've seen on television. Do not be afraid to reach out and ask them to speak with you. The worst they can do is ignore your request or simply say "No."

I have had both types of mentors - the ones that I have paid and ones that have not. Depending on who you are trying to obtain mentorship from, paying for their time and advice may be worth every penny. Both methods can work equally well.

Mastermind Group. Another form of mentorship is a mastermind group. This concept is explained in-depth in Napoleon Hill's book, Think and Grow Rich. This is a group of individuals with the experience, skills, background, and/or experience that can help propel you in your chosen venture. They are people who will help you with your plans; likewise, you are to help them with theirs. It is a forum in which you will bounce ideas off of each other. If you have chosen to operate a micro-business that offers auto repair advice, for example, your mastermind group might include someone who has operated a retail auto repair shop, someone who is a skilled business writer, someone who is adept at managing start-up financial matters, and someone who knows how to market services and products on line. You would meet regularly with your mastermind group and gather from them advice, tips, ideas, and constructive criticism on how to move forward.

You can select your mastermind group from among people you know, or you can seek out the people you would like to have in your group. I find that Meetup.com is a good way to find people in your area with specified interests. On this site, you can find thousands of groups that reflect a range of interests. Need to join a group and talk to someone about government contracting with your small business in Tacoma, Washington? There's probably a group for that. If one does not already exist, Meetup.com will allow you to set up the group yourself. Once you get into a good group, the ideas and insights you gain may be priceless.

A great nontraditional way of learning skills that you will need is by joining forums on the particular topic. Forums are online gathering places where other people can answer questions that you post. I also use forums to promote my apps. This can be very valuable, especially in dynamic industries that are in a constant state of change. There are two types of forums - relaxed and professional. Relaxed forums can be good, but beware of the "negative Nelly's" and "newbie bashers" that are more common in free forums. People can be very mean when hiding behind the cloak of anonymity. If you come across someone who is making fun of you for not knowing the ropes, don't take it personally. It happens. Just focus on the people who are positive and helpful; ignore the others. Professional forums are usually well-moderated, so you may experience fewer issues with negative and nasty people – as these types tend to get drummed out of paid forums pretty quickly.

If you know the question you need to ask, then you can often find the answer by simply looking it up on YouTube. I, personally, like to ask a search engine like Google a question and then I look for the video results. You can get all video results by selecting that option in the top menu bar. I'm addicted to YouTube. This is my self-proclaimed classroom. It is amazing how many times someone will have made a short video that explains what I need to know. If you decide to use search engines, remember to engage your brain. Not everything written on the internet is true. Some of it is completely made up. There is, however, also a lot of great, high- quality information at your disposal. Just be sure to look at it with a critical eye and consider the source.

Using Failure as a Learning Tool. While both planning and research are essential to your success in business, no level of planning or researching will prevent the inevitable failures and mistakes that you will make. Everyone makes mistakes in business – there are no exceptions. None. The key is to learn as much as possible, but know that things will still go wrong along the way. The good news is that failures don't have to be the end of your business. If you control your risks and take the time to learn from failures, you can emerge stronger and better than ever. Here are a series of questions for you to ask when failures occur that will help to keep you from making the same error(s) again.

How did I make this mistake? There are many reasons for making business mistakes. They can include: a lack of understanding of your audience, not having enough knowledge of the product or service, accounting errors, and changing market conditions. There are numerous other reasons, of course, but these are, by far, the most common. To reduce the possibility of recurring problems, you must formulate an effective plan that will get you the kind of results that you want. If your advertising, for instance, did not get the kind of response you had hoped for, what can you do to change that? Maybe try dual analysis testing to see what actually works the best. Or, if you had trouble with an employee or contractor, then you should take a look at your hiring and managing practices to spot areas where you can improve. I find that keeping a journal of good and bad results along with questions like, "What did I learn from this?" helps to keep me from making the same mistake over and over again.

Who is responsible for this mistake? If you are the owner of your company, then the buck stops with you. If an error was made, even if it was not, personally, made by you, accept it as your own mistake. Perhaps it was a mistake in hiring the individual who made the error. Perhaps it was a failure to provide proper instruction to the person who made the error. Any way you frame it, it is your responsibility to take ownership of any mistakes made by you or your team members. It is also your responsibility to find a way to fix them. In reference to a security failure in Benghazi, Libya in 2012, and in response to a statement by then Secretary of State, Hillary Clinton, that she took responsibility for the security in Benghazi, United States President Barack Obama insisted that he was responsible. He said, "Secretary Clinton has done an extraordinary job...but she works for me. I'm the President and I am always responsible." This is the type of attitude that you must be prepared to embrace when you own a business. You run the show; you are always responsible. If you are going to be a successful business owner, then you have to realize that mistakes come with the territory and you must be willing to assess what you are doing, tweak your processes, and try again. This process of continual refinement helps to make a successful business.

Am I cut out to be an entrepreneur? Sometimes we think we want something.. until we actually get it. Once we get what we want, and realize what is involved with maintaining it, we have second thoughts. Once you get on the road of entrepreneurship, you may find that it is not what you expected it to be. You will have to assess whether or not you have what it takes to be an entrepreneur. When mistakes occur, do you take responsibility, fix the issues, and try again? Or, do you just throw up your hands in defeat? A true entrepreneur is a person who will persevere through failure. If you want to start a business, then I would challenge you to start. Follow the example of the many, many people before you who are building successful large, small and micro-businesses and living lives that were once only a dream.

Decide to Fail Forward. Since we have established that mistakes are inevitable in business, I suggest you employ the fail forward approach. Simply stated: you're not going to win 'em all. You'll win some and you'll lose some. But don't let the fact that you will lose some keep you from taking action. Take action expecting to be successful some of the time. Learn from the failures, modify your approach, and continue to move forward.

Micro-business owner, Jason, embraces failure as a part of his business model. He is a brilliant online marketer who earns an income of about $400,000 per year from his online businesses. In the initial phases of his business, 6 out of 10 advertising campaigns he set up lost money; even after years of being in business, he deems only 40% of his campaigns to be successful. He, therefore, expects to fail 60 percent of the time, but knows that he will get great results the other 40% of the time. Accepting, at the front end, that you may have more failures than successes is important. Notice that Jason does not refrain from running his advertising campaigns so that he can modify, tweak and refine the process to increase his success rate. The prospect of failure does not keep him for moving forward. He still runs the campaigns and, while he's doing so, he gathers information that, over time, has allowed him to increase his success rate.

Be careful: make sure that you don't fall into the trap of wanting to know everything before you get started. Sometimes it can far better to learn as you go than to just learn. You may be concerned that you will make errors - and you will - however, so will everybody else. If you continue to work, and are moving forward, then you will be way ahead of the people who are waiting until all conditions are "perfect" before taking action.

The important thing here is that you learn how to control or limit your failures, learn from them, and fail forward as quickly as possible. In doing so, you can then rack up more and more successes while you continue to learn through the process. By failing forward quickly, you also rapidly gather information that moves you closer to success. Realizing that failure is a big part of the process of winning will help give you a stronger stomach for it. Once you adopt this perspective on failure, you can more easily get on with the task of building your business. That being said, make sure that as you are failing forward, you are doing everything in your power to minimize casualties and maximize your successes.

Still don't believe that the road to success is paved with failure? Take a look at some of the most famous people in history who have overcome tremendous odds to become successful entrepreneurs and business people.

Always remember that if you do experience business failure, then you are in very good company. Bill Gates of Microsoft, Walt Disney of Disney, and Lewis Tappan, the inventor of credit reporting, all had first ventures that tanked. It is not at all unusual for entrepreneurs to experience one (and often several) failures before they hit the jackpot, so to speak.

Even Oprah Winfrey has a list of failures to her name, including being fired from her job as a news anchor. She was asked many, many times to change the way she looked and to be less emotional. Can you imagine Oprah as less emotional? Her empathy is one of the biggest reasons she rose to eminence. She says this about setbacks and failures:

> *We all stumble. We all have setbacks. If things go wrong, you hit a dead end – as you will – it's just life's way of saying time to change course... If you really get the lesson, you pass and you don't have to repeat the class. If you don't get the lesson, it shows up wearing another pair of pants – or skirt – to give you some remedial work."*

This is good advice, and Oprah, obviously, follows it. She is one of the most influential and richest entrepreneurs in the world.

Award-winning director and actor, Woody Allen, was thrown out of New York University, where he majored in acting. Allen has, himself, classified a good bit of his work to be failures. We all know, however, that he has also had highly acclaimed successes.

These are just a few of the people who have accomplished great things after experiencing massive failure. It is an extremely common occurrence. If it happens to you, know that you are not alone. The good news is that by pursuing a micro-business, you can get to your jackpot a bit quicker. It takes far less effort to get a micro-business off the ground than a traditional business, which means you know if you are winning (or losing) much more quickly.

I would challenge you to ask around. Get to know some of the business people you admire and ask them to tell you their stories. You will hear tales of them ambitiously setting out to accomplish a thing, failing, picking themselves up and trying again. It is only after the initial fall that they began to win. Why? Because, after they fell, they had more information. They knew more about what not to do. This, my friends, is how it usually goes.

Contrary to popular belief, passion should not be your driving force. Fear should not be a debilitating factor either. Your focus, instead, should be on the possibility of being successful in your chosen business. Can I make money doing this? Will this business make a difference? Will people by this product? Ask yourself, "What does it matter if I like this field?" Let me assure you: you will like being successful. With regard to fear, you can allay many of your fears by doing the proper research. Not so much research that you never get on with the endeavor, but enough research to give you the confidence to know that the likely hood that you will fail is slim. Trust that, with more information, you will gain more confidence.

Chapter 18

Bet on You

"If you don't believe in yourself, then who will believe in you? The next man's way of getting there may not necessarily work for me, so I have to create my own ways of getting there."

- Michael Korda, Former Editor-In-Chief of Simon and Schuster

More than anything, what I want you to take away from this book is that there are more opportunities within your reach than you may realize. When you rid yourself of defeating beliefs and fears that you cannot do something or that something is out of your reach because you lack certain experience, education, or background, a whole world of possibilities opens up to you. As Robert Ringer says in his book *Looking Out For #1*, "A lack of formal education or experience shouldn't hold you back any more than the possession of them can guarantee your success. Not having proper credentials in the form of experience is an excuse which won't stand up when it comes face to face with an individual who has already made up his mind that he's going to do it."

As I've discussed, I am an app developer. I am not an app coder, but I am an app developer. I don't have the skills, knowledge or experience to actually write the app or do whatever it is that coders do to make it function properly. What I do know, however, is how the app *should* function, how it *should* look, and how it *should* bring value to those who use it. Beyond that, I do not know, and do not care to know more.

The good news for me and folks like me is that we don't have to know how to perform the technical functions of the development process.

I'm definitely not a computer geek. I'm not a software or technical geek, either. What I do well is conceptualize, execute and manage. The bottom line is this: I am an ideas man. I have ideas… and I implement them. That's it! If there is one foundational element that is most necessary for success in business, it is that – the implementation of an idea. It's about getting something done. D.O.N.E, done! I am a "done" geek – nothing more, nothing less. An idea is useless if it never gets off of the ground. In order to bring it to life, one has to go through various stages – the conceptualization of it, the execution of it and the continued management of it. It is the exercise of these abilities – not specialized knowledge – that have gotten me to where I am now.

Understand: my goal in business has never been to conquer a particular sphere of knowledge. Remember, I don't want or care to know it all. I just need to know enough because, first and foremost, I am an entrepreneur. I am not an app entrepreneur, a construction entrepreneur, a government contracting entrepreneur or even a micro-business entrepreneur. No. I am a guy whose means of creating income is through systems – effective systems – that are consistently profitable. Richard Branson is a great example of what I mean. He has had his hands in a wide range of different types of ventures – ranging from recording companies to an outer space travel company. Do you think that Richard Branson became an expert on outer space travel? Do you think he has the same level of knowledge as an astronaut – one who has dedicated their career to studying space? I strongly doubt it.

Like Branson, my goal is to be the best entrepreneur I can be. That's it! I want to do my best to create terrific businesses, based on sound business models. I want to be sure that I continue to refine what I do and recognize viable opportunities. That's among the list of skills about which I care the most – recognizing opportunities. Lacking specialized knowledge or skill is not my concern, nor is it a hindrance for me. If I determine that a business is worth pursuing, the next step is figuring out how to go about doing it. Because I do not solely rely on my own knowledge and background to get things done, I am not deterred by knowing that, in whatever endeavor I choose, I am likely to need to pull together a team of some sort in order to make it work. I am not discouraged or intimidated by the fact that I will probably have to depend on someone else's technical skill, educational background or other area of expertise. For me, these folks are relatively easy to get and are replaceable. Easily. If a developer I'm using decides to provide poor quality work, miss deadlines or, otherwise, become an unreliable team member, I will simply find another one. Coding is not an unusual talent. There are plenty of people who know how to do it, who like doing it, and would be happy to have me pay them to do it for me. This rule applies to most any kind of service I need.

Just think, Richard Branson and Elon Musk the founder of SpaceX, both were able to find astronauts for their start up space travel companies. So do you think it will be hard to find a good coder or web developer? I believe, with no uncertainty, that I will always be able to find someone who can help me do what I endeavor to do. Therefore, that usually plays a very small part in my decision on whether to pursue the opportunity or not. I suggest you consider the same approach.

I bet on me. Not my developers, not my graphic designers, not my web administrators. Me! The skills I possess are not technical, but they are skills necessary for the success of any business endeavor. Learn to bet on you, as well. Learn to rely on your judgment, your decision-making, and your ability to build and an operation. Be patient with yourself, as it is a process that takes time. Know that, more than anything else, this is what you need to make your business ideas work. Become a person who knows how to manage people and projects not just manage "things." Become a person that even you, yourself, believe in.

I won't pretend that the process is easy. In fact, running a successful business - even a micro-business - is work and, at times, can be very difficult. Throughout my entrepreneurship career, I have experienced a range of emotions from sheer and utter joy, to doubt, uncertainty, and downright fear. There have been times that I've wondered how much longer I could continue to do what I was doing. There were times when I just wanted to take off for a month and disappear. It's hard. Yes it is. But, it's not as hard as you may think. If you have a genuine desire to be an entrepreneur, I want to encourage you. When business design is done properly, the positives, by far, outweigh the negatives. By far. So, if this is something you really want to do for yourself, trust me when I say that it's not as hard as you may think, I'm telling the truth. Often the hardest part will be getting past your own self-sabotaging thoughts and crippling habits.

To help keep you moving forward, you will find it helpful to identify your motivation. It is during the rough times, that you will need to call on that motivation and remember why you embarked upon this entrepreneurship journey in the first place. It is during those rough times that your motivation will help propel you forward, or, at least, keep you from giving up. Why do you want to be in business? In what ways do you believe it would change your life – for better, or for worse? For some of you, the motivation may be the prospect of being able to get out of your 9-to-5, and regaining control of your time and income. For others, it may be the fact that you are otherwise having a difficult time earning income; creating your own business is really your only remaining option.

I, myself, am motivated by two things - fear and success. I know it probably seems that these two motivations are opposite – with one being a negative motivation and one being a positive motivation. As I said in Chapter 17, regarding passion and fear, fear can be good motivating emotion that can cause one to make some changes. The key is ensuring that your fear does not render you immobilized.

For me, fear and success are two sides of the same coin and they work very well hand-in-hand. The fear portion keeps me from being reckless and irresponsible. The success portion, on the other hand, pushes and drives me to do better. So, the fear portion keeps me from being stupid, while the success portion encourages me to be smart, to take risks and continue to grow.

I'll be honest, I'm afraid of a lot stuff. I, Greg Shealey, am afraid of being like my father. I'm afraid of being locked into one thing – one goal, one idea, one business, one source of income. I'm afraid of being unfulfilled and bored. I'm afraid of being in the same position next year as I am today. So when I say that fear motivates me, know that the "fear" of which I speak is not one-dimensional. It is an overall, all-encompassing concern that any number of things will go wrong or be wrong in my life. That's not to say that I don't know and understand rough times. I come from rough times. I know what it's like to not have electricity in my home and to use the kitchen oven as a method by which to heat the house. I know bad times. I don't expect perfection in life, but I sure as hell don't want to go back to what I came from. I don't ever want that for myself or for my family.

On those days that I'm struggling to stay productive, I remember what I don't want. I remember how I don't want to be. I don't want to be a bad businessman like my father. I don't want to be the example of a person who repeatedly fumbles important decisions. I, certainly, don't want any of my children writing a book saying that I was a terrible provider.

On these rough days, I also reflect on my experience as an educator. While I was not miserable as a teacher, I was not nearly as fulfilled as I am working for myself. I have so much control over what I do and how it's done that it is now very difficult for me to imagine going back to being in a position where someone else dictates not only how I spend my time (that is, where I have to be and when), but also how much I can earn. If you really think about it, having someone else determine what you earn – regardless of whether or not such figure is based on your merit and hard work – is a very crippling position in which to be. And to know that, on any given day, that person can decide that they are no longer willing to pay you, is even more crippling. To know that you can, in a matter of minutes, have your income stream cut to zero, based on the whims of someone else is not only scary, but risky. When you're in business for yourself, provided you have more than one client or customer, if you're fired, you don't lose your entire business. You only lose that portion of your income. But guess what? The same way you were able to get that customer, you can get another one. While you're replacing that customer, however, your revenue is not at zero, as it would be if you were fired from a job that was your only source of income.

I say all this to say that I'm afraid of ever being someone's worker bee again. If I don't remain successful in business, I could very likely land in that position. Well, either in the rat race or starving under a bridge. Since both options are unacceptable to me, I keep moving forward in business, even when I'm tired and frustrated.

As Timothy Ferriss said in *The Four-Hour Workweek*, the opposite of happiness is not sadness – it's boredom. I know that this is true. Boredom can be numbing and, over time, depressing and unhealthy. That's why I am afraid of it. I don't want to live life having nothing to look forward to – being content with doing the same things over and over. Doing this not only kills one's professional advancement, but it also kills one's spirit. I've seen it with some of the people who are close to me. I've witnessed friends who are intellectually brilliant, who were miserable in their work, become cynical, negative and complacent because the work they did sucked the life out of them. I don't come from the "do what you love and the money will follow" school of thought, but I, certainly, don't subscribe to the "stay miserable for decades" approach, either. I do not take for granted the toll that stagnation can take on one's self-esteem and outlook on life. It can be damaging. Because I'm well aware of that, I remind myself that complacency is simply not an option.

One last fear that I have is, simply put, being a loser. I don't ever want to look back on my life and realize that I was inadequate. I don't want to feel that I "punked out" on life and didn't have the courage to pursue my dreams and happiness. I don't want to look back and feel like one epic failure.

On the flip side, I am motivated by success. That probably sounds vague, but that's what it boils down to – success breeds success. When you experience the excitement of doing well in one endeavor, you want to experience that feeling even more. So, you pursue it more.

Remember Amy Chua, the self-proclaimed Tiger Mom? In her popular *Wall Street Journal* article, "Why Chinese Mothers Are Superior" she states, "Once a child starts to excel at something—whether it's math, piano, pitching or ballet — he or she gets praise, admiration and satisfaction. This builds confidence and makes the once not-fun activity fun."

I think this idea can apply to adults as well. I totally subscribe to this because it's part of what keeps me motivated. Getting one project off the ground makes me want to get another off the ground. And another. And another. Making money in one endeavor, keeps me eager to learn how I can make money in other endeavors. I love finding opportunities that I can make work. I love feeling that I worked hard toward a goal and actually accomplished it.

Over the years, creating productive businesses has, naturally, increased my self-confidence. I know I can be successful. Why? Because I've done it before. You can take away all of what I have, but I assure you that, in fairly short order, I will be back on my feet. Not because I'm special (remember, I'm just "some guy"), but because I'm confident that I know what I'm doing. Plus, I know how to pick businesses that I am likely to be able to make profitable. I'm not wedded to any particular type of business. My criterion is simply this: can I make this business work? I'm not even wedded to a mobile app business, despite me being the author of this book. If ever there comes a time when running an app development business no longer makes sense for me, I will stop doing it. When it stops being successful, I will stop doing it and go on to something else. I view business trends in the same manner in which I view clothing trends – if it doesn't look good on me, then I'm not buying it, no matter how many other people look nice in it. Not everything will work for everyone.

I was fortunate that my decision to get into real estate investing was fruitful. It was very popular at the time and "everyone" was doing it, but I, Greg Shealey, didn't go into it until I had thoroughly evaluated it for me. I evaluated whether I thought I could make it work as a business. It was of no consequence to me that other people were doing it and making it work. I had to determine whether it was something that I believed I could execute successfully. Of course, I could not be totally sure, but I had done the due diligence needed and felt very comfortable pursuing it.

Speaking of business trends, I think it is very, very important to not get wrapped up in what other people are doing. The key is whether or not you can make that thing work for you. Think about how many people you know who went into real estate during the boom, and are no longer in business. Think about how many people you know who got into this or that multi-level marketing program, only to quit after the first few weeks of trying. I'm not saying that people shouldn't try different things to see what works. I'm just want to stress how important it is that you evaluate who you are and what your needs are so that you can pick a business in which you can find your own success.

I only choose what I think I can make viable. And, having been in business for many years now, I am getting better and better at identifying those opportunities that are a good fit for me. I wasn't always good at this (remember my first business that failed?), but I've gotten better and better over time. With each success, my confidence increased. Now, I will bet on me. I do not invest in the stock market, bonds or Forex. I don't have a 401k account. Because I believe in me, I invest in me. I know what I'm capable of, I know my work ethic, I know my motivations and I know that I will do everything in my power to not let myself down. I always, always, bet on me. I've learned to become my own best cheerleader. I've learned that to seek validation from others is a kiss of death. That doesn't mean that I don't care at all about what others think. It means that I care way more about what I think. Like Henry Ford once said, if he always listened to what other people wanted he would have invented a better horse.

When it comes to ideas, I have plenty of them. I have ideas that I have come up with myself, as well as ideas that I've developed, based on other products or services that already exist. As I have refined my entrepreneurial skills over time, I have become better and better at recognizing opportunities. I can now evaluate an idea and quickly determine the likelihood of its success. Every successful entrepreneur I know has said something similar: when you've been in business long enough, you can see a good idea from a mile away. The same holds true for a bad idea. Not one successful business person has told me otherwise. Because I own several businesses, I'm exposed to a never-ending succession of great business opportunities and am constantly evaluating business models to determine the likelihood of success.

My friends, family and associates know my background and what I do for a living, so I often get invited to lunch or coffee, where a friend or associate wants to know what I think about the newest idea they have. You learn what works. I use my own experiences plus concepts and strategies I pick up in my personal studies, which includes reading numerous books and articles, talking with business mentors, as well as attending conferences for personal and professional development. I work at it. I'm always looking for ways to be sharper, quicker, better and more effective. Obviously, that doesn't mean that every idea is going to be extraordinarily profitable or become the next Microsoft. The point is that, as with anything, you get better and better at sifting the good from the bad.

I wasn't born with this ability. I learned it. I learned from my experiences. I also learned from my own failures and successes. I've invested in attending numerous conferences and seminars. I've also been committed to the learning process. I am an avid reader – of source materials such as magazine articles and business blogs – and I am constantly in search for new ways to be better. I'm in search of how I can be both a better person as well as a better businessperson. I am in search of ways to improve my mindset, so that the things I do and say are consistent with the goals I have. Because my personal development and growth is so important to me, I invest in it. I spend time and money acquiring materials that I believe will be of value. What's more is that I actually spend time engaging with them and implementing what I learned. At this stage of my career, I have heard most of the common business principles. I am familiar with all of the classic business and wealth-related books (e.g., *The Millionaire Next*

Door, *Think and Grow Rich*, *Good to Great*, *Rich Dad, Poor Dad*, *The Lean Startup*, *How to Win Friends and Influence People*, and *Seven Habits of Highly Successful People*, just to name a few). Having a fundamental understanding of many basic business principles, what I look for now is just one new idea from anything I read. I'm looking for one thing I can apply to my existing systems. That one idea can make a huge difference in my business. For example, I recently read the book *Delivering Happiness* by Tony Hsieh, the Chief Executive Officer of Zappos.com. The primary insight I took away from the book is the value of having a clearly-defined set of company values and operating the company from top to bottom, based on those stated values. Even though Zappos.com is a large company, and my focus is micro-businesses, this is one idea that I can take away that I can apply to the models that I have.

Because of this self-education, I've been able to hone my management skills behind the scenes much like a songwriter or performer does. A great artist often can make delivering the most complex piece of work look effortless. Does Luciano Pavarotti ever look like he is struggling on stage? I think not. That's because all the heavy lifting – the years of study and hours of practice - is done behind the scenes. Becoming a great entrepreneur is no different. It may not be easy at first, but you'll get better at it as time goes on. It's like anything else; you learn from your mistakes and you learn from your successes. As you navigate your way through the business world, you also meet others who have been down the path that you're taking. Many of them will eagerly offer you advice and insights, based on what they've learned. Remember that one good business idea often leads to another, particularly when it comes to micro-businesses. You work at one, succeed in it, then you move on to the next. The more you work at it and the more new things you try, the better you'll get at running your businesses. To others who see your accomplishments, it will appear as if you had it easy. Some may even have the audacity to say something to that effect of, "Awww, you've got it easy, man. You're livin' the good life." Yes, you will be living the "good life," ... as a result of your good efforts. Others may not give you credit for it, but it will be the truth.

* * *

After over a decade in various businesses, having seen what I have seen, I've become a big supporter of micro-businesses. I strongly believe that a micro-business is a great way for would-be entrepreneurs to get started, without risking everything they've earned up to that point. It is often the case that if you run one micro-business, you'll decide to run another because you can actually run several of these businesses at once.

My company, NPI, is a full-service construction company, while my app business, iQuick Tools, is one of several micro-businesses that I also run. Micro-businesses offer a lot of flexibility. They have low start up costs, low overhead, and require relatively little by way of investment in terms of time and resources. Although my full-service business has always been successful, to be totally honest, I like running the micro-businesses better. I believe that a micro-business is the best way to create for yourself a nice stream of sleep money that can free you from the restraints of working a 9 to 5 job. For business owners, and employees, too, "apping your business" may be the best way to start a micro-business without having to worry about threatening your existing business or leaving your day job. Remember the story of my friend who created ThePerfectContract.com? That was done while she was working full time. And its foundation was the work she was already doing on a day-to-day basis. She knows how to write contracts and other documents that are valuable to people in business. So, instead of simply supplying documents on an individual basis to individual clients, she figured out a way to provide that same value to multiple people, around the world. She took her regular line of business and extended it. She did exactly what I did when I used my construction experience to create construction apps that get downloaded around the globe. You can do that, too. Change the way you think about business. Do away with traditional concepts of big, corporate entities as being the only real measure of entrepreneurial success. Thinking small is the new "think big."

So do that. *Think small.* Think in terms of businesses that are but a blip on the radar. Keep your business small. *Micro.* Just as I did, you can start with an industry or line of work with which you are familiar. Then, you can find ways to address the needs of individuals and businesses in that industry. That is how my business has developed. I now have apps that are not related to the construction industry, but construction was my niche. I know it well, so I could easily create products that bring value to those who work in that industry. Consider doing the same to develop a niche for yourself. To what groups can you relate? What voids are specific to that market? If you're a new mother, for example, can you think of an app that would make your life more convenient? If you work in the fitness arena, think in terms of products that are already in the app market that you may use and that could stand to be improved upon. Think about the areas of life with which you are familiar. These do not have to be areas of your business life; they can be areas of your personal life, as well.

Think portable. The beauty of the micro-business concept is that it usually does not have to be operated from one location. If it is your desire to be able to work from anywhere, be sure that your ideas revolve around businesses that do not have to be conducted in any particular place. Think about something that you can take or do anywhere, both for the sake of your business and for the sake of your customer. The point of a micro-business is to have an income source that does not require you to be chained to your desk or stuck in the office all the time. Rumor has it that when Instagram first launched and was experiencing substantial growth, Kevin Systrom and Mike Krieger were known to cart their laptops around to guard against the server crashing, whether they were sitting down to dinner or at their desks. You want that kind of portability - something that you can quickly manage from anywhere if you have to manage it at all.

Think flexible. You want a business that can be easily adapted to change. These could be changes in the business climate or changes in your life. A cumbersome traditional business usually cannot be so adaptable. If I were to become disabled tomorrow, for example, NPI would have a difficult time continuing to function exactly as it does. iQuick Tools, on the other hand, would hardly be impacted. I could opt to not develop another app for a year, and the current income produced by iQuick Tools would be virtually unchanged. Consider a business and business model that would not fall apart if something dramatic were to happen. Know that you, too, will need to be flexible. If your initial plan or idea does not work as you expected, do not immediately give up on it. The idea may still be sound; it may need some tweaking. Or, your execution may be the faulty part of the plan. So, keep flexibility in mind when you choose a business, and also be flexible in your execution of that business.

Chapter 19

Paying It Forward

"Service to others is the rent you pay for your room here on earth."

- Muhammad Ali, Boxer, Former Heavyweight Champion

"We make a living by what we get, but we make a life by what we give."

- Winston Churchill, Former British Politician

To whom much is given, much is expected. As cliché as that statement has now become, it is, nevertheless, true. To those of us who care to make contributions to the world (I hope that includes you), using and sharing our skills and knowledge for the benefit of others is an important and easy way to improve the lives of those around us. You may not realize the value that what you know can bring to others. But you have or know something that can make someone else's life easier. Even if you think you have made all of the wrong decisions in life, you are well-positioned to tell others what not to do. There's tremendous value in that. No one grabs success on his own. After you've conceptualized a great idea, started a business, and implemented your process, commit to sharing the lessons you've learned with other would-be entrepreneurs. The advice you received on your journey is valuable. The team that supported you is valuable. The people who paved the way before you are valuable. So look forward to being a source of support for someone else. Information in, information out - that's the lifeline of responsible business.

At this point, I'm happy with what I've become. As I said, I was raised poor - one of eight children. Now, most would consider me to be a successful businessman. Beyond the value that my businesses bring to their users, I am dedicated to sharing information with others. I do not hoard what I know out of fear that someone will compete with me or undermine what I'm doing. I subscribe fully to the idea that there is an abundance of opportunity available and that no one can take away from me what is rightfully mine. Should someone succeed in doing that, I, thankfully, have the knowledge and wisdom to pursue other endeavors.

I have had countless meetings with people who want to learn how to become an app developer. I openly share what knowledge that I have. And, to the extent that they have an idea that could, effectively, compete with what I'm doing, I do not discourage them. In fact, I do the opposite – I encourage everyone I can to use what I've learned (through both good and bad experiences) to improve their lives.

Getting into business, literally, changed my life. I will shout it from any rooftop. It has changed my life so much for the better that I'm willing to help others who want to change their lives in the same regard. Being the owner of micro-businesses has changed my life even further. This aspect of my portfolio has added a level of flexibility and security that I could not have even imagined. I encourage you to do the same. Share what you know and share what you've learned – even before you consider yourself "successful." Send it out into the world – for someone will benefit from it – and see it return to you tenfold.

I wish you the very best.

Notes:

Made in the USA
Middletown, DE
22 November 2015